PENGUIN  CLASS

DE ANIMA

ADVISORY EDITOR: BETTY RADICE

ARISTOTLE was born at Stageira, in the dominion of the kings of Macedonia, in 384 B.C. For twenty years he studied at Athens in the Academy of Plato, on whose death in 347 he left, and some time later became tutor of the young Alexander the Great. When Alexander succeeded to the throne of Macedonia in 336, Aristotle returned to Athens and established his own school and research institute, the Lyceum, to which his great erudition attracted a large number of scholars. After Alexander's death in 323, anti-Macedonian feelings drove Aristotle out of Athens, and he fled to Chalcis in Euboea, where he died in 322. His writings, which were of extraordinary range, profoundly affected the whole course of ancient and medieval philosophy, and they are still eagerly studied and debated by philosophers today. Very many of them have survived, and among the most famous are the *Ethics* and the *Politics*.

HUGH LAWSON-TANCRED was born in 1955 and educated at Eton and Balliol College, Oxford. After a *stage* with the European Commission in Brussels and a subsidiary of the Dresdner Bank in Hamburg, he joined the Investment Department of the London merchant bank Singer and Friedlander. He is now Head of the Classics Department at Mander, Portman, Woodward and is reading for a Ph.D in the Philosophy of Mind at Birbeck College in the University of London, where his supervisor is Roger Scruton.

ARISTOTLE

DE ANIMA
(ON THE SOUL)

TRANSLATED,
WITH AN INTRODUCTION AND NOTES,
BY HUGH LAWSON-TANCRED

PENGUIN BOOKS

Penguin Books Ltd, Harmondsworth, Middlesex, England
Viking Penguin Inc., 40 West 23rd Street, New York, New York 10010, U.S.A.
Penguin Books Australia Ltd, Ringwood, Victoria, Australia
Penguin Books Canada Limited, 2801 John Street, Markham, Ontario, Canada L3R 1B4
Penguin Books (N.Z.) Ltd, 182–190 Wairau Road, Auckland 10, New Zealand

First published 1986
Translation, Introduction and Notes copyright © Hugh Lawson-Tancred, 1986
All rights reserved

Made and printed in Great Britain by
Richard Clay (The Chaucer Press) Ltd,
Bungay, Suffolk
Filmset in Monophoto Baskerville

22
Oct
89

THE GETHY with
Chip and David
on a Wonderful
Rainy Day in Malibu.
CMB
*

(And) of the soul the body form doth take;
For soul is form, and doth the body make

CONTENTS

ON THE SOUL

CONTENTS

FOREWORD

In this rendering of Aristotle's *De Anima*, I have tried to produce a version at once accessible to the layman and tolerable to the initiate. However, even if I had discharged this task with unexampled felicity, readers unfamiliar with Aristotle's thought would, if confronted with an unsupported text, have at times been left wondering what was going on. For these readers I have provided a fairly long Introduction, in which I have tried to offer a conspectus of recent discussion of the work. I hope its central themes will have been thrown into perspective, although it goes without saying that I offer the serious student no more than a starting-point to further inquiry.

My debt to many writers will be abundantly clear and I have mentioned in the Bibliography some of the works that I have found most useful. I must, however, single out Professor Hamlyn's stimulating notes in the Clarendon edition for especial acknowledgement. I am no less indebted to Professor Hamlyn's kindness in reading through my typescript and suggesting a large number of improvements at which I would scarcely have arrived without his assistance, but this expression of gratitude should not be taken as an attempt in any way to bring this still very imperfect work under the shadow of his authority. A debt of a different order I owe to Roger Scruton. He has encouraged me to what reflections I have reached in connection with the subject of this work and has saved both Translation and Introduction from some conspicuous blunders. I must, however, firmly exclude him from any responsibility for the many that remain. Two friends, Edward Jenkyns and Andrew Radice, also read the Translation in draft, and their comments on its readability were valuable and engagingly discreet. Finally, I would like

to thank Miranda Dear for a contribution that has evolved
from being of clerical to being of editorial scope.

Hugh Lawson-Tancred
Holland Park
London

INTRODUCTION

I. Entelechism

It was the opinion of Hegel, not a philosopher conspicuous for his sympathy of outlook with Aristotle, that the present work was the only text earlier than his own writings worth serious attention on the subject of the soul.[1] This judgement, strikingly original in its day, would have been almost a commonplace in thirteenth-century Paris or ninth-century Baghdad. Today mental philosophy bears a very different cast from that which it bore for the Schoolmen, and Hegel's verdict has a paradoxical air. The air of paradox will be increased, not diminished, for many readers by confrontation with the text. There will be some who will be at a loss to see the connection between the subject-matter of this treatise and its title. For the English word 'soul' is, in the title of this translation, being made, in deference to convention, to stand proxy for the Greek term *psyche*. This word had a wide variety of meanings for various Ancient Greeks at various times, but most of them were remote from the usual associations in English of the word 'soul'. This is certainly the case with Aristotle's use of the term, and, inevitably, the difference in meaning between the English word 'soul' and the Greek word *psyche* is responsible for the difference between the subject-matter of the present work and that which might be expected from a tract with the English title 'On the Soul'; but it can plausibly be argued that it is in many ways a more worthy subject of philosophical reflection and that the value of Aristotle's remarks during the course of the work for contemporary mental philosophy is not diminished by their being primarily intended as contributions to an account of an entity of which we have no habitual cognizance.

What, then, is the exact meaning for Aristotle of the Greek word *psyche*? What precisely is the subject of this work? The answer to this question is in fact simple. The psyche, for Aristotle, is that in virtue of which something is alive. The most accurate translation of the term into English would be 'principle of life' or 'principle of animation'. Stylistic reasons, however, clearly render this unacceptable in practice. Now, it should be clear after only brief reflection that 'psyche' so defined is a much wider concept than the English terms 'soul', 'mind' or 'consciousness' denote. This being so, the study of psyche will correspondingly be wider than that of these concepts, and since it is they that form the principle subject-matter of modern philosophy of mind and psychology (along with such terms as 'self', 'personality' and so on which are dependent on them), it is clear that Aristotle is addressing himself in this work to a broader topic than is usually discussed by modern philosophers. Since the time of Descartes, the central problem of human nature has seemed to be the subjectivity with which each individual is aware of the world. If, with Descartes, we take this subjective viewpoint as our starting-point, so that I, for instance, will be concerned to show how my view of the world is itself to be found a place within my general theory of the world, we soon arrive at the intractable difficulties of Dualism, at the need to coordinate the content of our consciousness with our objective conception of the world itself. Now, even if Descartes' starting-point is not in fact a legitimate one, it at least seems reasonable and it requires a philosophical argument to show that it is not. In our century such arguments have been produced, and it would not be wrong to say that contemporary philosophy of mind centres on the question of whether or not they are successful. Thus our debate distracts us from the subject-matter of Aristotle's inquiry. For we are interested in a problem which only fully arises in the case of human beings, Aristotle in a feature of all animate creatures. The Cartesian controversy is a controversy about that vague entity, the mind. It is an assumption of that controversy that the peculiar features of mental life are more philosophically important than the general features of all life. Aristotle, however, reverses this order of relative importance. He certainly considers those features of human life that might come under the Cartesian heading of 'Mental Properties', but he considers them strictly within the context of a general survey of all the features of any form of life, and it is clear that it is the general concept of life that he hopes to clarify by producing his account of psyche. Thus, one of the rewards this work offers its students is the illustration of what perhaps familiar terrain can look like from a quite new perspective.

Aristotle looks on life as a biologist, while Descartes looks on his experience as its subject. A convenient way of expressing this difference is to say that Aristotle's position is *third-personal*, in that his own enunciation of his theories is irrelevant to their content, while Descartes' position is *first-personal*, in that he is concerned to explain experiences that seem to be privately available to him alone. Those philosophers who have tried to repudiate Descartes' starting-point in the philosophy of mind have often sought to use linguistic considerations to discredit the priority that he must claim for the first-personal over the third-personal perspective. For them the third-personal perspective is the correct starting-point for investigation of mental phenomena. In this opinion they agree with Aristotle, but we must be very clear about the difference, which is fundamental, between such modern anti-Cartesians as Ryle and Wittgenstein and their followers and Aristotle. For the modern thinkers the right to look on mental items from the third-personal perspective had to be fought for by subtle and difficult arguments, whose success is indeed still controversial, whereas Aristotle, who gives no evidence of feeling any need to defend his own third-personal stance, gives nothing remotely comparable to such arguments either in this work or anywhere else. If we had to answer the question whether Aristotle would, had he lived in our time, have favoured Wittgenstein or Descartes, it seems that the answer must be the Austrian, but the weight of his support is greatly diminished by his complete indifference to the problem of consciousness in connection with which that support would be most conspicuously required.

Aristotle cannot be pressed into service in the modern debate about the mind, because he does not directly consider the problem that is the centre of that debate – the problem of consciousness – but his theory does offer a model of how we might arrange our theory of the general features of living things, if we can conclude that the ghost of Descartes has been finally laid. What is this model?

One of the most striking features of Aristotle's philosophy is that, while Plato seems for most of his life to have been persuaded that that which changes is ultimately unreal, the founder of the Lyceum conceived the explanation of change as being the prime task of the science of nature. It was primarily to perform this task that Aristotle introduced his celebrated dichotomy of Form and Matter. Unfortunately, Aristotle's presentation of this dichotomy is never wholly explicit, and this has rendered it susceptible of a wide variety of interpretations, some at least much cruder than Aristotle seems chiefly to have had in mind. It can usefully be said in general, perhaps, that to grasp the Aristotelian conception of Form, one must realize that it presupposes a close correspondence between the arrangement and the functioning of any item. Thus, if we were to ask in the case of a motor car what its form was, it would be in a way right to answer with its shape and in a way right to answer with its characteristic activity, travelling on roads or perhaps the disposition to do so. The crucial point is that Aristotle feels that if either of these two answers were investigated sufficiently it would turn out to be the same as the other. In Aristotle's general metaphysics the notions of Form and of function are closely connected.

Now, Aristotle's Form–Matter dichotomy is a part of his general conceptual scheme for the explanation of nature. What relevance can it have to the question with which we began, the question what model Aristotle is offering us of a theory of life? The answer, unsurprisingly, is that Aristotle's theory of animation amounts to the claim that particular living things, like all particular items, can, to put it an un-Aristotelian way, be analysed into their Form and their Matter, but that in the exceptional case of living things their Form can be identified with the traditional concept of their soul. To put this more concisely, we might use his own words, that the soul is the form of a living body. This formulation is certainly a simplification, but the first thing to be grasped is the boldness of Aristotle's approach. As he makes clear in Book I of this work, the soul had mostly been identified by his predecessors as some kind of material substance. Aristotle has answered the traditional question as to the soul's nature with a different type of answer. In this a great deal of the originality of his treatment resides. One of the most important questions to determine in connection with the *De Anima*, as this work is conventionally known in Latin, is just how different it is to say that the soul is Form and to say, for instance, with Heraclitus, that it is fire. However, on any account it represents a great step forward in sophistication.

The doctrine that the soul is the Form of a living body is the core of Aristotle's mature psychological view, presented in this work. As we have seen, the concepts of Form and function are closely connected for Aristotle. As it is in virtue of a thing's Form that it can perform its functions, so to know its functions is to know its Form. Furthermore, any functional entity can be at any time either in the exercise of any given function or not, if only logically, but, as it will not change its nature between periods of exercise of any or all of its functions, the Form denotes that feature in virtue of which it is able to retain the capacity to function without actually doing so. Aristotle captures this by refining his notion that the soul is the Form of the living body to the view that it is the first Actuality of the living body, the second Actuality being that in virtue of which the body actually is in the exercise of its functions. Since the word that I here, and in the text, translate as Actuality is *entelecheia*, and since, as we have seen, this view is the core of the whole theory, that theory has reasonably, if by no means universally, been dubbed Entelechism. The label seems as satisfactory as any other in bringing out the special features of this theory.

I have tried to suggest in very sketchy outline the central insight of the theory developed in this work. It would in itself be enough to make the work startlingly original. However, it might well be objected that it is not clear how the mere act of legislation that the Forms of living things be called 'souls' suffices to explain what is peculiar to those things. The fact is, of course, that it does not. The great merit of this approach to the soul is not that it reveals in itself what is unique about living things, but that it provides a conceptual framework within which the peculiarity can be brought out. For from the central conception of soul as Form, as from the trunk of a tree, there grow the branches representing the different explications of the central concept to account for the different manifestations of life that are to be explained by a general biological theory. It is this fact that gives the work its architectural neatness and impact. However, Aristotle approaches the task of explaining each area of animal functioning flexibly enough to permit his account to adjust as far as necessary away from the central framework and this is what gives the work its fecundity in the examination of such areas as sense-perception and imagination.

Thus Aristotle's approach to psychology is in essence very simple and is exactly mirrored in the structure of this work. After the first Book has exposed the shortcomings of previous theories, the central conception of the soul is immediately presented and developed and then shown to apply in the areas traditionally to be explained by a theory of the soul. However, while the strategy is clear, the tactics often involve the crossing of extremely treacherous terrain and the work constantly provokes further questions than it answers. For this reason, I have tried in this Introduction to set the work in its complicated context and at the same time to suggest how some of the points that Aristotle is making might be most clearly connected with modern discussions. I have tried as little as possible to presuppose either philosophical expertise or Classical knowledge, and those with either or both may well find my remarks only of cursory interest. For those readers, however, who, relatively fresh to this subject, are my principal audience, I offer a selective introductory survey of the work and of its contemporary relevance, preceded by a brief account of its author's life.

II. The Life of Aristotle

Aristotle was born in 384 B.C. in Stageira, a small town in Chalcidice, the three-fingered peninsula that stretches into the Northern Aegean. His father, Nicomachus, was a doctor who, some time in Aristotle's minority, became the court physician of Amyntas II of the neighbouring and at this time turbulent state of Macedon. It is very likely and has often been suggested that Aristotle's subsequent interest in biology stems ultimately from an introduction at a tender age to the rudiments of the medical science of his time. In any case the connection of Aristotle's family with the Macedonian royal house was fraught with consequence for his subsequent career, as philosophy was no apolitical vocation in the fourth century. After the death of his father (*c.* 374 B.C.), Aristotle passed into the guardianship of a relative, Proxenus of Atarneus, who secured for him a sound, fashionably Hellenizing secondary education. These few facts are more or less all that can be established with certainty about the childhood of Aristotle.

The first major turning-point in what was to be an eventful life came in 367 B.C., when he had reached the age of seventeen. In that year, perhaps because of renewed political disturbances in Macedonia, Aristotle travelled south to Athens, to enroll in the Academy of Plato, itself only a few years older than he was. The arrival of an obscure doctor's son from the semi-civilized north would no doubt have seemed to contemporary Academicians an event of little note, when set, for instance, beside the departure of Plato himself in the same year on the first of his two fruitless attempts to intervene in the development of the Syracusan tyranny. However, over the course of the next twenty years, until the death of Plato in 347 B.C., a period interrupted only by the second Syracusan trip in 361 B.C., there can be little doubt that Aristotle established himself as the most brilliant Platonist of his generation. Biographers of Aristotle usually divide his life into three phases. The first phase is usually known as the first Athenian period, the period when Aristotle was a member of the Academy, presumably engaged in extensive philosophical discussion with the ageing, but very far from sterile, Master. The second phase lasts from Plato's death in 347 B.C. to Aristotle's return to Athens in 335 B.C., and is sometimes rather picturesquely known as the period of the wanderings; and the last phase, the second Athenian period, lasts from Aristotle's return to Athens in 335 B.C. to his death in Euboea in 322 B.C.

It is a matter of some dispute just how loyal Aristotle was in the first Athenian period to the central tenets of Platonism. The dispute is complicated by Plato's own remarkable late development away from some of the characteristic positions of his middle years. What is clear is that the Academy, in the years of Aristotle's membership, was no mere museum for the Theory of Forms and the associated dogmata of the middle Platonic dialogues. Rather, these views seem to have been the subject of constant 'dialectical' criticism and to have accordingly undergone an evolution to which, insofar as we can trace it, we are tempted to give a mixture of applause and censure. While many of his colleagues seemed to have moved towards such areas as number mysticism, the Pythagorean conception that all the mysteries of nature could be explained by meditation on the even more inscrutable mysteries of mathematics, Plato's own philosophy shows a marked critical development towards the pursuit of logical rigour. At the same time the septuagenarian giant seems to have broadened the range of his interests to include in the *Timaeus* an admittedly rather idiosyncratic foray into the area of physical science that had hitherto been as completely neglected by himself as by his hallowed master, and betrayed mentor, Socrates. For how much of this development the credit must be given to Aristotle's forceful and presumably decreasingly deferential objections we can only guess. As to Aristotle's own position at this time, if this can be reconstructed at all, then it can only be from such fragments as have survived of his published works.

In antiquity Aristotle was equally famous for literary–philosophical dialogues in the Platonic manner as for the very unliterary treatises that we have. These dialogues, for consumption by a wider public than the specialist audience of the treatises, and thus conventionally labelled 'exoteric', appear to have put forward views much closer to those of Plato than the positions to be found in the extant treatises. It was this circumstance that prompted Werner Jaeger to advance his epoch-making suggestion in 1922 that from the fragments and treatises we can reconstruct the growth of Aristotle's thought away from an earlier Platonizing period towards the very different stance of the latest treatises. This proposal is still very widely accepted, but predictably less unanimity has characterized the detailed arrangement of the treatises into chronological order. Apart from Jaeger's own arrangement, one of the most ambitious and comprehensive attempts to establish the chronology of Aristotle's works has been made by the Belgian scholar Nuyens. Since his criterion of dating is the relation of the works to his reconstruction of the Psychological view, I have dealt with it at greater length elsewhere. I have also mentioned in the Bibliography various works that offer an entrée into this enormously debated but still fascinating question. At the moment it seems safe to conclude that by the death of Plato in 347 B.C., Aristotle had yet to evolve a really distinctive position of his own, and that it took him most of the next twelve years to rid himself, insofar as he ever did, of Platonism.

On Plato's death, Aristotle abruptly left Athens. This is usually and plausibly ascribed to pique at his non-election to the Scholarchy in succession to Plato, compounded in whatever degree by alarm at the anti-Macedonian, and thus for him personally threatening, mood of Athens in the wake of the aggression of Amyntas' successor on the Macedonian throne, the unlovely figure of Philip the Great who, in 348 B.C., had brilliantly outmanoeuvred the strategically somnolent Athenians to seize the key city of Olynthus in Aristotle's native Chalcidice. In any case, Aristotle now settled at Atarneus in northern Asia Minor, where he married Pythias, the daughter of the local tyrant Hermias. It is now seldom disputed that it was at Atarneus that Aristotle began his extensive researches into animal life, which are preserved for us in the *Historia Animalium*, a huge notebook of observational evidence. It is highly likely that the teleological outlook so characteristic of his general philosophy first began to develop amidst these empirical biological researches. Hermias himself was an old friend of the Academy and seems to have offered every encouragement to its disgruntled epigone. This happy arrangement was modified perforce in about 344 B.C. by the fall of Hermias and Aristotle's perhaps consequent removal to the nearby island of Lesbos. Here the natural investigations seem to have proceeded relentlessly, possibly now with the assistance of Theophrastus, a native of the island and Aristotle's eventual successor as head of the Lyceum. This work, together with the 'dialectical' training of the Academy and Aristotle's existing Macedonian connection, were enough to qualify him to be summoned by the devious and ruthless monarch of the expanding northern state to supervise the education of the next generation of rulers, whose responsibilities were bidding fair to be extensive, and especially of their prince, the young Alexander. It is unlikely that Aristotle felt much impeded by the republicanism of his probably contemporary work the *Politics* from obliging the autocrat.

In a very readable survey of Aristotle's life, Grayeff has advanced the view that Philip's real purpose in recalling Aristotle to Macedonia at this time was to breed him as a friendly head of the politically significant Academy. When Speusippus died in 339 B.C. and was succeeded by the colourless if sagacious Xenocrates, butt of Aristotelian castigation in the first Book of the *De Anima*, Philip, if Grayeff is right, passed Aristotle over. He was then taken up by Philip's marshal Antipater and so moved into the circle of Olympias and Alexander, who in 336 B.C. almost certainly compassed the death of Philip, welcomely brief master of Hellas. After the murder, Alexander stepped rapidly into his father's shoes and inherited his aim of securing a favourable influence among the philosophers of Athens. It was then, in 335 B.C., that Aristotle was dispatched to the school of Greece, not indeed to become head of the Academy, but to found a new and competitive institution in the grove of Apollo Lyceus. For this he was given every cooperation by a compliant Athenian government. He remained, until his departure from Athens in 323 B.C., a loyal servant of Alexander.

There certainly are difficulties in Grayeff's view, but it is not by any means wholly rebarbative to the facts, and it seems very probable that, even if the Lyceum was not founded at Alexander's instigation, it yet enjoyed his blessing, so that ancient stories of the provision by the great soldier of specimens of rare biological species for his old tutor need not be mere fantasy or embroidery.

Certain it is, in any case, that the Lyceum was founded in 335 B.C. and developed rapidly into a major centre for research and the dissemination of its results. It seems likely that at least the majority of the works that traditionally stand to Aristotle's name either are, or are directly descended from, either Aristotle's own notes for lectures given in these years or the notes of attentive pupils. This fact evidently leaves the possibility open either that some elements in the treatises, including perhaps important doctrines, are later interpolations, or that the views expressed in these works, though all authentically Aristotelian, yet developed at widely different times in his career. Without wishing to enter into this controversy, which shows every sign of the vigour of youth, it would, I think, be fair to ascribe to at least a substantial section of informed opinion the view that the *De Anima* constitutes the first part of a course of lectures that would also have comprised at least the *Parva Naturalia*, the *De Partibus*, the *De Motu* and the *De Generatione*, and which would have thus amounted to a general introductory course on the science of Biology. If this is so, then it is reasonable to suppose that these texts contain nothing substantial that would have been objectionable to Aristotle in the last phase of his career.

It is probably right to call the Lyceum rather than the Academy the first true University. The former, but not the latter, had all the paraphernalia of a major centre not just for abstract inquiry but for the collection and systematic preservation of detailed empirical evidence, and seems to have taken the practice of academic specialization to something like its modern lengths. It is interesting that we have at least one more or less complete text by a minor member of the Lyceum, the *Athenian Constitution*, produced as one of the one hundred and fifty similar studies of individual city constitutions commissioned by Aristotle to form the empirical background to the *Politics*. The *Athenian Constitution* is certainly no masterpiece either of history or political science, still less of literature, but its value for the study of classical Athenian society is not easily exaggerated.

Aristotle, however, was not destined to end his days in the hive of scientific activity that he had himself set up. The sudden death of Alexander in 323 B.C. has often been considered one of the most momentous contingencies in human history. It certainly had immediate adverse consequences for Aristotle. The hawkish politician Demosthenes, returning triumphantly from exile, fanned the flames of an always latent resentment against the deplorable half-Greeks who had reduced the city of Pericles to the political status of a village. Aristotle was charged, in the traditional way, with impiety, and left Athens for his mother's estate on Euboea, lest, as he modestly put it (referring to the execution of Socrates in 399), the Athenians should sin twice against philosophy. He died there in the subsequent year and there is some anecdotal attraction, if no historical probability, in the story that he met death while attempting to measure the tide in the notoriously temperamental Euripus, the narrow straits between Euboea and mainland Greece.

If Aristotle wrote only most of the works attributed to him, then he cannot be denied to have been one of the greatest thinkers, and surely one of the widest ranging inquirers, who has ever lived. The style, however, of the extant works, is with the exception of one or two justly famous passages, of a severity and impersonality with few parallels. Given this fact and the extreme paucity of reliable biographical details, it is idle to pretend that acquaintance with the man is now possible even to the most agile historical imagination. I have no insights to offer on this subject and eschew gossip. It is enough perhaps to support Barnes'[2] suspicion that he was more admirable than amiable by citing the fragment of his lost Statesman that justifies rage as being noble, just, useful and sweet.[3]

III. The Philosophical Background

Presocratic Philosophy of Mind

Aristotle could not be said to be being unfair to the previous
Greek philosophical tradition on the problems of life and
mind if he summed up its two main areas of interest as being
the explanation of the capacity for self-movement displayed
by living things and their no less remarkable capacity for
various kinds of cognition. Nor indeed could the Greek
tradition in taking these problems as its main concerns in
this area of philosophy be judged to be preoccupied with
difficulties radically different from those that confront contemporary philosophers. What is, however, strikingly different about these early thinkers is the range of answers that
they contrived to produce, only some of which seem even to
have a *prima facie* claim on modern attention. There are
many ways in which theories about the soul can be categ-
orized, but the one which has perhaps the most general
application is into those theories that can be called substantial and those that can be called insubstantial; between those,
that is, that see the term 'soul' as naming some kind of thing
and those who see it not as naming a thing but rather as a
term of more or less dubious internal coherence that is pressed
into service to allow a compendious or otherwise convenient
treatment of certain aspects of the world that present peculiar
problems. In the general course of Western thought, the
former group of theories have had a much better innings
than the latter and so it was also with the Greeks, although
as we shall see there is reason to feel that the latter group was
not altogether unrepresented in Antiquity. It can, however,
be said that all Presocratic theories of the soul, with one
important exception, were firmly substantialist. The substantialist category of psychological theories, however, is by
no means without its own sub-divisions. Evidently, if the
soul is to be taken as some kind of substance, the question
arises as to what further individuating characteristics can be
offered to identify it. Furthermore, if, as is usually the case,
the world is also taken to be composed of some kind of

substance, a similar question arises in this case. And thus, evidently, the further question looms of whether the substance we have identified as being that of the soul is the same as or different from that of the world. This question does not indeed look a particularly clear one, and on closer inspection the determination of distinctive features of substances has turned out to be no less elusive than it appears. However, there are some labels that have traditionally been applied in this area, and which continue to have, or seem to have, some intelligibility in current usage. Of these the most comprehensive and important for the present investigation are those of 'physical' and 'spiritual'. If, for the moment we admit some rough and ready understanding of these terms, we are presented with a quadripartite scheme of possibilities. Either both body and soul can be spiritual, or body can be spiritual and soul physical, or body can be physical and soul spiritual, or both body and soul can be physical. Of these possibilities, the first is the classical position of Idealism, which, in some ways, is anticipated in antiquity by Plato, the second is a possiblity that is both rather odd in itself and has the rare feature of having never been espoused by any philosophical school, the third is paradigmatically the position of the modern Cartesian Dualist, and the fourth is a position without prominent exponents in the modern period but extremely common, indeed the standard view, in Presocratic philosophy. It is clear that the conception of the soul as a physical substance is both one for which Aristotle has a more or less untempered scorn and one that hardly looks likely to be the beneficiary of a modern revival. Nevertheless, it is worth at least a passing glance, because it defines the category into which most of the views discussed by Aristotle in Book I fall, and thus significantly provides the background against which Aristotle develops his own view.

What, then, was it that induced the early Greek philosophers to argue that the soul was some kind of physical substance? The short answer is, of course, that they knew no better, that the problems incident upon the explanatory poverty of this account were not yet apparent. But latently, perhaps, one might identify as the root of the idea the problem which has in modern times been labelled 'psychic emergence'.[4] If, with the universal agreement of the Presocratics, we hold that the world is physical and substantial, then we evidently confine ourselves either to the view that in the midst of this physically substantial world are to be found spiritually substantial entities, or that there are no such entities and all items are alike physically substantial. Of these two positions, the first is notoriously that of the Cartesian Dualist and presents only too familiar problems. A dim precognition of these problems, combined with a naive reluctance to suppose a real object of reference for all nouns, perhaps induced the Presocratic thinkers to look favourably on the idea that even the soul, obviously the most impressive candidate for spiritual status in the universe, might yet be composed of the same physical substance, which we might call matter, as the rest of the world, only organized in some more complex way or existing in some more rarefied or attenuated form. If this view seems to us a non-starter, we could profitably reflect on the range of knowledge that has had to become available to us for us to be able to consider it risible. There are two main sources of such knowledge. On the one hand, there is our growing awareness of the internal structure of those organs in which the material soul might be held to reside. This awareness eventually made it obvious, at an early point in the modern era, that there is simply no available space, no room, for a material soul to fit into the material of the body. On the other hand, we have come to have a far closer feel for the structure of that matter of which we suppose the world to be composed, and all our theories of it, all our prognostications about it, seem to indicate in it a structure that is not illuminatively paralleled with any structure of psychic material that we might be tempted to posit if we favoured a materialist substantialist theory of the soul. It is the sophistication, then, of our conception of matter that entitles us to patronizing amusement at the role assigned by the Presocratics to this concept. And the Presocratic conception of matter is strikingly naive. Modern historians contemplating the emergence of the Milesian cosmogonical systems from the earlier and contemporary creation stories of both Greek and Middle Eastern poetry and myth, are usually most impressed by the rationality of what they see,[5] and indeed are often tempted to confuse the rationality that is genuinely there with a sophistication that is not. The fact is that these thinkers were able to ascribe to their chosen substances so wide a cosmological role precisely because they saw in the substances themselves properties that we would be strongly tempted to call magical. It is not, surely, that great a step from saying that all things are made from fire or from water to saying that it is in virtue of a part of our own bodies that is made of a special kind, say, of fire that we have perception or that we have locomotion. It is of course in this light that we should see Thales' celebrated remark about the magnet's having a soul if it is capable of moving iron.[6] There is an element of inconsistency in an attitude to this philosophy that admires the rationality of their single-substance cosmologies while scoffing at their materialist–substantialist psychologies.

We should perhaps note one other feature of these theories. This is that their very bizarreness is in a way a tribute to the tenacity of the hold enjoyed by substantialism over early Greek thought. The difficulties of substantialism, of any form, are very great, perhaps insuperable, but it has been the consistent modern feeling that they are increased not diminished by the substantialists' thesis being of the materialist variety. Yet it is an unargued premise, so far as we can tell, of all these thinkers that the soul will be a substance of some kind. Indeed, it may well be supposed that when the doctrine of the soul's being a spiritual substance first received technical philosophical articulation in Greece, many will have turned to it in relief, assuming that this alteration in substantialism would save the overall theory at the expense of a relatively minor feature. We have considerable evidence of a materialist–dualist controversy in the fourth and fifth centuries but relatively little of a substantialist–non-substantialist one. Thus, with an important exception which remains to be considered, the theories of the soul current in Greece before the composition of the *De Anima* would seem universally to have been not just substantialist but un-

reflectingly substantialist and indeed to have been deterred
from involvement in the obvious difficulties of such positions
not even by quite full realization of those difficulties. It is
thus at least reasonable to suppose that if a Greek thinker
had clearly arrived at the idea that the soul need not be
substance after all, or, as it might perhaps better be put, that
there is no substance to which the label soul can usefully be
applied, then he could be expected to show some recognition
of his own originality. Neither of the views, however, for
which this claim might reasonably be entered, make any
such pretensions. Of the two possible views, one, the
Harmony Theory, perhaps to be assigned in origin to Philolaus of Croton, is too little documented for us to be sure
that it was not claimed by its author to be, what it certainly
seems to us to be reasonable to call it, in essence a non-
substantialist theory, and the other, the Formal conception
of the soul presented in the *De Anima* itself, is explicitly said
by its author to be the account of a substance, albeit a
substance of a technically given and perhaps irretrievably
opaque kind.

I propose to review the materialist psychological theses
that are mentioned in the first Book of the *De Anima*, and
then pass to the spiritualist accounts of soul associated with
the Pythagoreans, before considering finally the Harmony
Theory, which must be taken seriously as a possible candidate for non-substantialism, and which, even if not to be
ascribed to Philolaus, seems very likely to have been a product of some form of heterodox Pythagoreanism.

Let us remember that, according to Aristotle, an account
of the soul had for the speculators of the fifth and fourth
centuries, as for their modern successors, to meet two requirements: it had (i) to explain how the bodies of two kinds
of existing thing, plants and animals including man, come to
be able to originate physical processes, which in some cases
subsequently produce movement or alteration of some kind
in other items, and which very broadly we might say amount
in combination to what is popularly, and precisely, known
as spontaneous movement; and it had (ii) to account for the
fact that some of these existing things were further, and in a

way whose association with the former capacity was already perceived to be obscure, capable of having something that can loosely be labelled cognition of the surrounding world. Sufficiently broadly defined, this can in turn be taken as a requirement that the theory be explicative of what may be called mentality, the possession of mind. With these constraints on a good theory of the soul few would wish to disagree, but there is a further constraint that is unmistakably a feature of the modern debate, but for whose formal enunciation we may also give Aristotle the credit of priority. This is that the theory must ensure that there is some degree of unity, at least some principle of unity, between these two, such that it can broadly be said to be in virtue of a single factor that an animal is capable of both the feats to be explained. Aristotle clearly enunciates this requirement in Book I and suggests that all his predecessors have failed to meet it. In this claim he may be considered to have some grounds if we survey the evidence available, much of it through him. As to whether his own theory is any more successful in meeting the unity requirement we may perhaps attempt to decide later.

In turning to the materialist psychologists themselves, we can introduce a further categorization. We can discern three groups. First there are those who hold what we might label single-stuff theories. These views are evidently of great structural simplicity. The soul is just supposed to be a single type of substance, in effect one of the four elements, and psychic peculiarities in nature are ascribed to special features of the element in question. If, as is usually the case, the element continues to play a role in the functioning of the non-souled world, the question of what is special about the element when it forms a soul but not at other times is dealt with in a rhetorical or perhaps poetic way. The popular Greek opinion of this sort of view is given by the scene in Aristophanes' *Clouds* where Socrates is made to claim that suspension in the air helps him to think better as his mind is then immersed in its congener stuff.[7] A second broad type of materialist psychologist is the man who holds that the soul is composed of some plurality of stuffs. Him we might label the many-stuff theorist. Of his group the clearest example is Empedocles, if he believed that the soul, like everything else, was composed from the four elements. The third group can be more sharply distinguished from the other two. A psychologist of either of the first two groups could share with one of the other a general metaphysical scheme. Both would agree that the world was made up of elemental stuffs. They would disagree only as to the allocation of those stuffs to the particular items called souls. The third group, however, is drawn from thinkers who would not in general accept that the material world was made from elemental stuffs. These are of course the Atomists, whose composition of the soul squared with their general atomist materialist metaphysic. The relation of their psychological theories to their general systems was the same as in the case of the single- or plural-stuff theorists, and the kinds of consideration that they thought lent credibility to their view of the soul were wholly similar, as Aristotle brings out, to those of the other theorists, or indeed, we might be tempted to think, to those of anyone who seeks to explain the soul as a material substance. It goes without saying that between these groups there was controversy in every way as fierce as that between the proponents of materialist theses and proponents of spiritualist or even, perhaps, non-substantialist theories of the soul.

Most of the single-stuff theorists are discussed by Aristotle in the unfortunately rather confused survey of his predecessors that constitutes the second chapter of Book I of the *De Anima*. Heraclitus of Ephesus (*c.* 540–*c.* 480 B.C.) held that the soul, like everything else, was made of fire. Diogenes of Apollonia (*fl.* 440–430 B.C.), reverting to the earlier theory of Anaximenes of Miletus (*fl.* 540 B.C.), saw air as the underlying material substance, and this he further identified with soul. Critias of Athens (460–403 B.C.) held the soul to be blood, whereas Hippon of Samos (*fl.* 425 B.C.), thought that it was seed. Aristotle treats these two last views as subdivisions of the view that the soul is made from water, and concludes his survey of the single substance theorists by remarking that none has yet sought to explain the soul as being composed only of earth, which may be of some consolation to those disconcerted by the extreme naivety of these views.

The single substance theorists may indeed seem too naive to have much call on our attention. Yet they are worth some thought both because Aristotle rather confusingly assimilates to them other Presocratic views which seem in fact to have been of greater subtlety, and also because he seeks, reasonably enough, to use them as an effective background to his own vastly more sophisticated conception. Before, then, we look at the objections that Aristotle presents in Book I against these theorists, we should consider the way in which other more or less materialist conceptions of the soul have been assimilated to them. The most glaring case of unwarranted assimilation is the treatment of the great atomist thinker Democritus of Abdera (*fl.* 420 B.C.), who is effectively classed by Aristotle as holding the view that the soul is made of fire. In fact his doctrine is the more subtle one that the soul is made of the smallest and most mobile of the atoms and thus has many of the properties of the similarly constituted fire. However, to Aristotle's credit this difference does eventually emerge and indeed it is largely against Democritean atomism, his most worthy opponent, that his criticism of the materialist conception of the soul is directed. A similar difficulty arises over Aristotle's treatment of Empedocles of Acragas, to whom he ascribes a many-stuff theory of the soul as well as a much more subtle and promising account of soul as *logos*, or proportion. It seems clear that the ascription of the multi-substantial composition account of the soul to Empedocles is an injustice, and that it was not the soul that was for this thinker composed of many substances but the ensouled body, while the soul was rather the ratio of the mixture whereby such bodies are capable of performing their characteristic functions. This consideration shows that Aristotle was right to associate Empedocles with his attack on the Harmony Theory, but wrong in directing against him the arguments he uses to confound the many substance account of sensation. Empedocles was probably not committed to the mistake of which Aristotle accuses him, of thinking that to perceive something is to perceive only its substance.

Before considering the full brunt of Aristotle's objections to psychological materialism, we should first look at two thinkers who only partly seem to fit into his categorization. First there is Alcmaeon of Croton who held that the soul must be a god because of the resemblance its always being in motion gives it to the heavenly bodies. This view has a fair amount in common with Platonic–Pythagorean ideas of the soul as a self-mover, as well of course as their official doctrine that the soul is a god incarcerated in the body. Alcmaeon's view would not seem to have any special interest but for the fact that Aristotle includes it along with the view of Thales, to which we are not in a position to give any very specific characterization, among what seems to be a survey of single substance views. This perhaps may be taken to show how comparatively unimportant for Aristotle was the distinction between material and spiritual substantialism.

The treatment of Anaxagoras also raises some difficulties. He is a notoriously difficult thinker for us to pin down, and the central difficulty of his system is that which is most relevant to the immediate range of problems, namely his celebrated doctrine of *nous*, or mind. This central idea of Anaxagoras seems to be trying to bridge the gap which otherwise very noticeably appears between the materialism of the Ionian tradition in fifth-century thought, of which Anaxagoras is the last great representative, and the subjective stance of the Sophists, Socrates and Plato. His *nous* is, as Aristotle points out, at once both a cosmic motive force and a principle of order or rationality. Yet it is not clear at all how something is to combine these two roles. In any case we have eloquent testimony in the words put into Socrates' mouth in a famous passage of the *Phaedo*[8] that he at least found the conjunction unsatisfying. The same dissatisfaction is shared both by Plato himself and by Aristotle and leads to the demiurge of the *Timaeus*[9] and the Primum Mobile of the *Metaphysics*,[10] the realization in the characteristic vein of each philosopher of the promise latent but unfulfilled in the Anaxagorean *nous*. In any case, the obscurity of our grasp of Anaxagoras' own position and perhaps its intrinsically underdeveloped state prevent us from attempting to assess what influence it may have exercised, however indirectly, on Platonic cosmology or on Aristotelian psychology.

The real thrust, then, of Aristotle's objections to the materialist philosophers of the Presocratic era amounts to the rejection of the Democritean account of psychic motion and the rejection of what he takes as the Empedoclean account of cognition. These two refutations are crucial for the contrast that Aristotle is seeking to establish between his psychology and that of his materialist predecessors, for whom of course he has strikingly more sympathy than did Plato or the early Academy. It is extremely important to grasp the character of these refutations, which is essentially the same in the two cases, because it is highly eloquent of Aristotle's entire approach to the problem of the soul. The essence, then, of the Aristotelian rejection of both Democritus and Empedocles is that in seeking to explain psychic functions the way they do, they are giving *the wrong kind of account*. A recent scholar has usefully labelled the purely materialist accounts of Democritus and Empedocles as being 'low-level'.[11] This expression describes the attempt to account for a phenomenon in terms only of the Matter that is involved in it. The accounts of Democritus and Empedocles are reductivist in this way, seeking to show how everything that happens in nature can be reduced to the play of fundamental material particles. Against this reductivism the face of Aristotle is firmly set.

Now this disagreement between Aristotle and Democritus is no mere parochial squabble of a long outmoded set of explanatory theories; rather it lies at the heart of a central current debate in the philosophy of science. Very roughly put, this is the debate as to whether our account of nature, and specifically of animate nature, can or ought to be framed in those purely reductivist terms which modern post-Newtonian Physics shares with the uncompromising materialism of Democritus. This amounts to the question whether the science of Biology can be reduced via Chemistry to Physics, and whether even if this can be achieved any advantage to scientific understanding is to be derived. This modern debate, framed as it is in the much more sophisticated conceptual apparatus of modern scientific jargon, is in essence only a repetition of the issue here contested between Aristotle and Democritus. In the scientific era in which Newtonian mechanics reigned supreme and all sciences aspired to render themselves compatible with atomist physics, the names of Democritus, Leucippus, Epicurus and Lucretius were held in high regard, not without reason, and that of Aristotle was frequently castigated and reviled. The Stagirite was held to have fathered on the world a bogusly teleological account of nature which, because of its unfortunate subsequent canonization, set back the advance of science for the entire medieval epoch. The notion of a comprehensively teleological account of the world remains anathema to the modern scientific outlook, but Aristotle's stock as a philosopher of science has very sharply risen over the last fifty years for two reasons. First, painstaking scholarship has exposed as fallacious the attribution to him of a comprehensive teleology. This is a large question with which we cannot deal totally here; but an impressive array of modern interpreters have seen in Aristotle's work not a comprehensive teleology, such as delighted the minds of the medieval theistic exponents of 'Aristotlianism', but a limited and moderate view especially of one area of scientific inquiry, the study of life. This view is usually labelled Functionalism. It is perhaps best to specify it further as Biological Functionalism in distinction from the rather different and wholly philosophical theory that is advanced under the same name and whose connection with Aristotle will be investigated later.[12] The essence of the Functionalist thesis now ascribed to Aristotle in the life sciences is that we need not strive, and perhaps cannot even expect, to account for all the features of the activity of living organisms entirely in terms of their material constitution; rather we should respect the fact that integral to this activity is the principle of arrangement of this material and that this principle of arrangement can only be intelligibly specified by reference to the function that it is intended to fulfil. We will hopefully see later why this is a position that might plausibly be ascribed to Aristotle. In any case, the second factor that has led to a rise in Aristotle's philosophical stock in recent times has been just that this Functionalist approach to

Biology has been steadily gaining in influence at the expense of the comprehensive Positivism of the last century. Indeed it would not seem an exaggeration to say that it now seems to some as arbitrary to seek to account for all natural phenomena as being without some *intrinsic* end as it seemed to the contemporaries and successors of Bacon to be unscientific to account for everything as subservient to some *higher* end.

If we turn to consider in detail the actual arguments that Aristotle deploys against Democritus and 'Empedocles', we see, I hope, that the large claims made above for Aristotle's conception of scientific method in Biology are not entirely unjustified. Two arguments of his in particular might be considered. He compares Democritus' theory of animal movement with the idea of the comic poet Philippus that Daedalus might render mobile the wooden statue of the Goddess Athena by pouring into it molten silver,[13] and he shows 'Empedocles'' theory of real cognition to have the absurd requirement that composite particulars must be supposed somehow to exist in the soul. In both cases Aristotle is directly attacking a 'low-level' account and pointing out the need for something much more like a Functionalist explanation. In the first case, Aristotle complains that the way that the soul produces motion in the animal body cannot possibly be by any kind of communication of similar motion. Such a supposition would not account for obvious and important features of animal movement, such as conspicuously its alternation with periods of rest, but above all would not answer our fundamental intuition in this area that psychic motivation does involve a degree of thought and choice. Nevertheless, psychic motivation also involves a physiological mechanism – the body that is by whatever means moved is after all a physical thing – and Aristotle in due course, though not in the *De Anima*, presents a theory, that of the connate *pneuma*, that covers this area of psycho-physical integration. No doubt it would not be unreasonable to point out that there are greater affinities than Aristotle anywhere allows on a purely physiological level between his and Democritus' accounts. After all, both of them make use of the central idea of heat, though in different ways, the difference perhaps reflecting in modern eyes rather to the credit of Democritus. But what Aristotle is concerned here to establish is the conceptual inadequacy of the Democritean account – whatever theory we are eventually going to offer of the physiology of animal motivation we must also take into account other features, those which we label 'intentional'. Otherwise we lose sight of just what it is that we have to explain. It may or may not, of course, be the case that these intentional features can eventually be eliminated, but this is very much to be shown. The enormous advance that the Aristotelian account achieves over the Democritean is that it very clearly focuses on the true explanandum in this area. Whether or not the explanation that Aristotle eventually offers is adequate to the problem, what is indisputable is his entitlement to great credit as the first thinker clearly to state that in this area both aspects of the phenomenon of animal motivation, the mechanical and the intentional, must be captured by the explanation. This is in effect to say that our account of this matter must be Functionalist until the case for reductivism has been established, which is at the moment a long way from being the situation, as far perhaps as it was in Aristotle's time.

The treatment of 'Empedocles' is essentially similar, except insofar as the ascription of the view in question to Empedocles is historically suspect. (It seems best to suspend judgement on the legitimacy of the ascription to Empedocles of a naive like by like account of cognition, and concentrate on Aristotle's objection to the theory itself. Here we see clearly the same Functionalist tendency at work.) Aristotle considers a theory in which the soul of the animal effects the cognition of the real objects of its environment by the similarity between the elements of those objects and its own material constitution. Now evidently such a view is open to the objection that the similarity criterion is both inherently vague and unsupported by any rational considerations, and indeed in his detailed treatment of sensation Aristotle will deal at least with the vagueness of the like by like criterion. But immediately his attack takes a different line. The central idea is that any such theory must involve the reduction of the sense-perception of an external entity to the perception of its material constituents. Aristotle concentrates on the case of perception and here the theory under attack might be thought to have at least superficial plausibility – it is not hard to see the difficulty that a more general theory of cognition might have in the area of numerical and other abstract knowledge. But even for perception he counters that such a reduction is wholly inappropriate. The observation of a physical object involves indeed the observation of the matter of which it is composed, but it also involves observation of the arrangement of that matter in virtue of which it is what it is. How is the perception of this arrangement to be captured by the materialist psychologist? The answer must evidently be that the material constituents of the percipient which are engaged in perception must somehow come to be arranged into the same pattern as that which is perceived. But how is this to come about? Once again, as with the refutation of Democritean theories of animal motivation, this is not a question to which the eventual Aristotelian answer – or for that matter any subsequent answer – is uncontroversial, but once again that is not the point; rather we should notice that here too Aristotle is demanding that there must be in the percipient something to account for its coming to be arranged at least in some way in the same pattern as that which is perceived, and that this cannot merely be one of the things of which the object is composed and which happens also to be found in the percipient. Once again Aristotle's point reaches right into the modern debate. Nowhere do we see more clearly than in these two arguments a fact that is perhaps obvious but must always be borne in mind in the assessment of Aristotle's work in psychology, and indeed far beyond. This is that the progress of Physiology is of supreme irrelevance to the central problems of the philosophy of animation. No light whatever is shed on the conceptual difficulties that confront any explanation of either motivation or cognition by the substitution for the perhaps charming, perhaps vexing, naiveties of Democritean and 'Empedoclean' physiology of the latest and most sophisticated products of modern neurology.

Aristotle's refutation of the naive materialism of the majority of his predecessors would perhaps in itself earn him the title of Father of Psychology. Instead of the explanation of biological activity in terms of the chance presence of essentially foreign matter within the physical constitution of the animal's body, Aristotle insists that there must be a necessary structural Parallelism between soul and body. Any activity of a living body will be explicable in one way in terms of the matter that composes the body itself and in another way in terms of the soul, but it will be the same activity that is explained on both occasions.

Now here philosophically aware readers will sit up straight. If this is what Aristotle is saying, is he not directly anticipating the Physicalist theories so dominant in contemporary philosophy of psychology? The essential hallmark of all those theories that merit the label 'Physicalist' is that they account for those features of animal and especially human activity that might be ascribed to the operation within the animal of a non-material soul in terms only of the bodily animal itself, but usually with the acknowledgement that these features, even though they are features of the body, cannot be directly reduced to the features more directly pertaining to the body as a physical object. Another way, perhaps, of putting this is to say that a Physicalist must hold an Attribute Theory of the soul, that he must say that insofar as we can intelligibly answer the question 'What is the soul?' we can do so only with the reply 'It is a set of attributes of the corresponding body.' Many animal activities will be explicable only by the employment of some of these attributes but this in no way licenses the admission of any entities beyond the body itself, however much we should have to respect the problematic, indeed irreducible, character of the 'psychic' attributes.

Evidently this view has strong affinities with the Aristotelian position. Can we hail the Stagirite as the Father, not indeed of psychology, but of Physicalism, and as the founder of the Attribute Theory? This is the central question in the interpretation of the *De Anima* and must therefore be postponed for later consideration.[14] We must, however, consider the case of one of the pre-Aristotelian theories to be considered as the first Attribute View. In surveying Aristotle's predecessors, I have so far concentrated, as he does himself, on those that offered what must be called materialist accounts of the soul and its works. Not only, however, was this out and out materialism at odds with the assumptions of Greek religion and various therefrom emanating forms of mysticism, but it was confronted from, at the latest, the end of the sixth century by an organized philosophical school firmly advocating the contrary doctrine, that the soul is a substance of quite a different kind from those that compose the world, to whit an immortal god trapped in a succession of animate and even inanimate bodies. This school is of course that associated with Pythagoras. The characterization just given of their psychological view is conventional but not uncontroversial. However, for the present purposes it matters little whether Pythagoras and his mystical, vegetarian mathematicians held a view anticipating the problems of Cartesian Dualism, without having, it seems, any inkling of those problems, or believed in the more subtle doctrines that have been found to be logically compatible with the fragments we have of their teachings.[15] It is obviously the case that a spiritual-substantialist view of the kind outlined is to be found full grown in the works of Plato (and we shall shortly be considering the connection of his thought and that of his great pupil) and, furthermore, Aristotle neither shows any awareness of the subtle interpretation of orthodox Pythagoreanism nor would need any further illustration beyond that provided by his master, and, as we shall see, at one time embraced by himself, of the attractions and difficulties of treating the soul as a non-physical substance. Orthodox Pythagoreanism belongs firmly in the philosophical museum. It is heterodox Pythagoreanism that seems to have produced a theory that might reasonably be hailed as the first Attribute Account of the soul. Once again I beg intriguing historical questions, but once again no matter.

The first version of the Attribute Theory said the following: 'The soul is nothing but the harmony of the various parts of the body.' This is the account of the soul attacked by Plato's

Socrates in the famous passage of the *Phaedo*. It was also, it seems, attacked in an early work of Aristotle, his dialogue the *Eudemus*. It is certainly possible that the view stems from the rather shadowy heterodox Pythagorean Philolaus. The reason for thinking this is that he is known to have been the master of Simmias, the proponent of the theory in Plato's dialogue, and also that the idea of Harmonia seems to have been an important general feature of his account of the world. More significantly, the closely similar theory that the soul is the ratio of the mixing of the bodily elements, which Aristotle ascribes to Empedocles in the course of attacking both these views, is perhaps the true Empedoclean view, a circumstance that would, as we have seen, invalidate Aristotle's later remarks on the materialist theory of cognition as criticisms of Empedocles. In any case, what is most important is to see that both these views really do amount to Attribute Theories. It is not in fact clear how they differ at all, if it is allowed that ratio in the latter theory can be taken broadly to mean either conglomerate of ratios or even perhaps ratio of ratios. Both theories define the soul as something that is not really a thing. Barnes[16] is quite right to say that 'I have a soul' is under these theories logically similar not to 'I have a raincoat' but to 'I have a temper' – 'has a soul' is a monadic not a dyadic predicate. Whether or not, if we then ask what is the criterion for the 'possession' of soul, the answer is to be found in some feature of the animal's behaviour that might properly be called 'functional' is rather less clear, but, if this is a historical question, answers must evidently be speculative, and if it is philosophical, its interest in the immediate context is diminished by an important fact. This fact is that Aristotle explicitly rejects the 'Harmony' and 'Ratio' theories for the same reasons.

Now this is an important fact, because there is an influential school of thought that sees Aristotle's own psychological theory as being nothing but a sophisticated refinement of the Harmony Theory.[17] Such an interpretation evidently confronts some serious difficulties. First, Aristotle sets out the Harmony Theory, considers it, and specifically rejects it. Moreover, he rejects it not because, despite being an Attribute Theory and thus having a *prima facie* case for consideration, it then turns out to be the wrong sort of Attribute Theory, but on grounds that seemed at least to two of the ancient commentators [18] to rule out the acceptability of anything that might count as an Attribute Theory, and what is more, on grounds that seem actually to embody a valid objection to any Attribute Theory no matter how much more sophisticated than those of Philolaus and Empedocles. It is not wholly clear what are the grounds for overlooking so clear and trenchant a *prise de position* by Aristotle. However, I suppose that it is not outrageous to believe even Aristotle capable of the meanest kind of philosophical vanity, although, given his avowed intention of taking from his predecessors whatever they may have produced of value, this would seem here to be supplemented by improbably transparent hypocrisy. Yet the alternative to the vanity explanation of Aristotle's eminently unambiguous position seems to be the supposition in him of a failure to perceive the affinities of the Harmony view with his own. This too seems improbable. Such then is the first difficulty in saying that Aristotle is no more than a Harmony theorist *de luxe.*

The other major difficulty seems on the surface no less considerable. At the beginning of Book I, Aristotle reminds us that he is himself the inventor of the conceptual framework whereby we distinguish between things that are and their properties, and explicitly asks to which of these two groups the soul is to be assigned. No answer is given until the start of Book II, where Aristotle, with no mention of the various types of attribute which the soul might be thought to be, refreshes our memory of his views about substance, *ousia.* This, he tells us, divides into three kinds: Form, Matter and the composite. He then proceeds to show how the soul fits into one of these kinds, namely of course the first, Form. By Aristotelian logic, if soul is Form and Form is substance, then soul is substance. A second embarrassment for the attribute-interpreters.

Now, it is not my intention to imply that those who hold Aristotle to be advancing an Attribute Theory have simply overlooked the remarks as to Form's being a substance at the beginning of Book II, nor indeed that they are unfamiliar with the extensive treatment of this topic in the *Metaphysics*. Their position, rather, is that this merely illustrates the great difference between the Aristotelian concept of *ousia* and the modern concept of substance. So great is this difference that when Aristotle tells us that soul is substance as Form, we can smile indulgently and explain that he is only harmlessly, and indeed with extraordinary foresight, saying what has become in our time a commonplace, namely that the soul only 'is' a set of attributes, that the term 'soul' denotes no entity. However, this approach only dubiously meets the second objection. I shall discuss later what we have a warrant to take Aristotle to be meaning when he tells us that soul is Form, and I shall hope to show that this amounts to more than the claim that the sense of the word 'soul' can be given by some disjunction of animal properties. But in any case if the Attribute construal of the Form's substantiality is right, does not Aristotle's own theory confront the very objections that he raises against the Harmony view in Book I? I shall claim that one of those arguments would be fatal to it in Aristotle's thinking.

Aristotle begins by identifying the Harmony and Ratio Theories, which, as suggested above, seems not unreasonable; he then explicitly says that soul 'cannot be either of these'. Unfortunately, he does not say why this is so, but both the commentator Philoponus and the paraphrast Themistius explain that this is because the soul is an *ousia*. This in itself only begs the question, but the real argument is still to come. Aristotle produces several arguments against the Harmony view, some familiar from his earlier Platonizing dialogue, the *Eudemus*, and indeed from Plato's *Phaedo* itself. Most of these, it is true, count specifically against the Harmony view and not in general against any Attribute Theory, but there is one, the briefest and the first, which would seem to have a much wider application. For Aristotle objects that 'Moving could not be a feature of a Harmony, and it is that above all that all ascribe to the soul'. Now the latter part of the claim is incontrovertible and important; not only did all previous thinkers agree that this was that feature of animal activity, its spontaneity, that above all had to be explained by a theory of the soul, but also this is evidently central to Aristotle's conception of the scientific task. But it is the first part that is crucial. It is hard to see how the objection could fail to establish the specific point that Aristotle hopes to make by it. A 'Harmony', whatever else it may be, is not surely a thing that could set in motion a physical object – it must be an effect not a cause thereof. Even the 'Harmony' of the lyre, which is perhaps not the paradigm of the idea, in no sense sets the lyre in motion, thus producing the sound. But the real question is what mere set of attributes ever could be the origin of motion in the way required. What is needed as the first element of any chain of movement of physical objects is some *cause* for their movement. Now evidently we can talk sensibly about causal attributes, causal dispositions and so forth, and we can delimit the causal properties of an entity, as Aristotle in effect does with the soul in the *De Anima*. But unless we can elucidate just what it is for one thing to cause another, we have a flaw in any comprehensive scientific account of reality. Now it may indeed be the case that the notion of cause is inescapably problematic, that we can give no simple account of real or objective causation, but it seems as clear as anything in the history of philosophy that Aristotle thought that the notion of real causation was coherent. In reflecting on the soul he rejected his own early idea that it could be something quite different from the body. He came to think that in a certain way it was the same thing as the body. But he did not reach the fully modern position that it was merely a set of attributes of the body. He did not take this step, not because it did not occur to him – on the contrary, he was familiar with a view of this kind – but because if the soul were reduced to being no more than a set of the properties of the merely material body, he could not see how animate matter came to have the property that for a realist it so conspicuously does have of spontaneous causal origination. How, indeed, this feature is to be explained was perhaps for Aristotle one of the most difficult questions in the philosophy of science. The answer could only be provided by a whole metaphysical system, and in Aristotle's system the core was, of course, the analysis of composite particulars into Form and Matter, both of which would have an equal claim to substantiality. Whatever we are to make of this metaphysic, it is clear that it is in the area of the soul that Aristotle considers it to have its most direct and salient application.

Plato and the Academy

By the middle of the fifth century B.C., the Sophists, those freely operating intellectual entrepreneurs, had pioneered the study of successful human life, especially political success. This practical study had already begun to rival in maturity the longer established physical philosophy of Ionia and western Greece, when it underwent a revolution. Socrates of Athens (469–399 B.C.) seems certainly to have placed at the centre of the investigation of success the study of two central concepts, justice and virtue. Thus was moral philosophy born. Moral philosophy is an empty study for those whose wills are bound, and it was the need for there to be free moral agents that drove, if not Socrates himself, certainly at least his greatest disciple to that system of thought in contemporary Greece that most clearly affirmed the insistence on human freedom. Plato became a Pythagorean in his psychology. Like most features of Plato's thought his view of the human soul went through several important changes, but elements certainly remained constant. He was throughout loyal to the idea that the human soul or at least the most important part of it, far from being closely tied to the body by its nature, was in fact a stranger to it, incarcerated at a stage in an immensely long cycle of reincarnation, and in all his disquisitions on the soul it is apparent that he, in sharp contrast to the Aristotle of the *De Anima*, is chiefly interested in the soul as it occurs in men. Plato never compromised or qualified his central psychological message, that the soul is a non-physical, a spiritual, substance. As such it was inherently free from the causal *nexus*, and restricted only by its penitentiary entrammelment in a mortal body. Such a view

would seem eminently liable to the dangers of modern
Dualism – how is the non-physical and perhaps non-spatial
soul to engage in intercourse with the physically extended
body? But of the escape routes from the Dualist's dilemma,
Bishop Berkeley's is the neatest, and this was in effect the
route that Plato took. To retain the immateriality of the
soul, he was prepared at least to compromise the reality of
the empirically perceived world. The Platonic view is thus
loftily detached from the scientific psychologist's task,
which it holds to be unreal. But, irrelevant as this may
render Plato to the modern conception of the soul–body
problem, it can hardly be denied that Plato's contribution
to the study of subjective psychology has been profoundly
influential, no less so than his contribution to the closely
related study of moral philosophy. Plato's lack of sympathy, however, for the psycho-physiological standpoint
that we see so fully developed in Aristotle did not wholly
preclude his advancing an elaborate theory of the divisions
of the soul. This, like everything else in Plato's philosophy,
went through various mutations during the course of his
creative life, but is to be found at its most systematically
complete in the dialogues of the middle period, especially
the *Republic* and the *Phaedrus*. These seem to be in agreement as to the following broad outline of the soul's constitution. There are within the soul three great faculties or
principles, each responsible for its proper area of human
activity. These are the rational faculty, the status-seeking
faculty and the appetitive faculty. Their objective and operations are by no means naturally co-incident and there
inevitably ensues strife between them. In this strife, there
is, fortunately, a pre-disposition for the status-seeking
faculty to ally itself to the rational faculty, and together
these are pitted against the appetitive forces, which represent those elements in the soul that are most directed
towards its incarnate existence. Good men can be distinguished from bad men in that in the former the alliance of
reason and self-respect triumphs over appetite while in the
latter the reverse is the case. The most memorable and
poetic depiction of this struggle is the justly famous myth

of reason as the charioteer of the soul, with two horses one cooperative the other not, which crowns the psychological section of the *Phaedrus*.

From the point of view of Aristotle's mature conception of the soul, Plato is relevant for two reasons. The first reason is simply that there can be no denying that there was a period in Aristotle's life when he adhered closely to all the major features of Plato's mature view, including the view of the soul. I shall discuss this at slightly greater length in the next section, but it is hardly necessary to point out that the whole system of Aristotle developed originally in criticism of Plato and that this must be no less borne in mind in considering Aristotelian psychology than in considering any other area. The second reason is rather more specific. It is that the final stage that Plato reached in the evolution of his conception of the soul was that of the *Timaeus*.[19] This work has a very good claim to be the single most extraordinary relic of Antiquity, and does not easily lend itself to a balanced judgement. It begins as a dialogue, and indeed is connected into a tetralogy that was in fact to remain incomplete, but after only a few pages it has become a monologue. Timaeus, a distinguished visitor to Athens from southern Italy, has been asked to give an account of the origin and structure of the world. The account that he proceeds to give represents both Plato's only systematic treatment of the subject of natural philosophy and, unless the traditional dating to the end of his life is in fact wrong, the last stage of development of his psychological theory. The theory propounded could well be used as an acid test for the presence of the scientific spirit in the young. Uncompromisingly teleological in approach and openly theodical in purpose, it yet exceeds in grandeur of conception and expression all the other many masterpieces of Classical Greek prose. These merits, however, are not conducive to clarity, and the doctrine of the soul that is here advanced is baffling in many respects. The first difficulty is that Plato, in the spirit of Anaxagoras and others of the early natural philosophers, notably Xenophanes, takes the wide concept of soul to cover both the World Soul that animates the entire created cosmos and the human soul that dwells in

45

man. Indeed, just as in the political vision of the *Republic* the structure of the human individual soul echoes that of the state, so in the *Timaeus* there is a symmetry between the soul of the individual and that of the world. (And here no doubt it is right to see a final mark of Plato's Pythagoreanism.) The *Timaeus* vouchsafes details on the creation of the World Soul and on its functioning, especially its production of movement in the Cosmos, and these are subjected to criticism by Aristotle in the first Book of the *De Anima*. As Plato's World Soul is hardly a scientific or philosophical going concern, I have tried in a note to explain the controversy as clearly as possible, but will not touch on it here. What more immediately calls for comment is the important circumstance, not mentioned in the *De Anima*, that in the *Timaeus* the human soul is expressly divided into an immortal and superior and a mortal and inferior part. This double conception of soul is indeed present in a rather less elaborate way in Homer [20] and, although there is little affinity of detail, it is important to remember the structural precedent of the *Timaeus* in assessing the notorious Aristotelian two-tier conception of the intellect that is presented in Book III of the *De Anima*.

But the division of the soul in the *Timaeus* into an immortal and a mortal part is the end point of a long Platonic journey in search of the most suitable way of dividing up the soul. And this concept of the faculty division of the soul is also an example of Platonic influence on the mature Aristotelian view. It is important to give Plato the credit he deserves for introducing the principle of the faculty division of the soul, for although it is seldom in his hands scientific and has come under fire in this century for offering a misleading schema, yet it is the ancestor of all attempts usefully to categorize different mental states, and this obviously has had an enormous influence both on psychological reflection and on moral thought. In any case the idea of the faculty division of the soul has, as we have said, an obvious structural influence on the view put forward in the *De Anima*, though, as Aristotle makes clear, the faculty divisions in his theory are as much a reaction against, as a continuation of, those in Platonic texts.

The Platonic conception of psychic divisions is also extremely important for another requirement that Aristotle makes of an adequate explanation of the soul, namely that its principle of unity should be apparent. Aristotle does not specifically press this point against Plato but he would no doubt have felt that it had a certain force against, for instance, the famous image of the soul as a chariot in the *Phaedrus*. However, in general, it is reasonable to say that, apart from the critique of the *Timaeus* account of psychic motion in Book I, and allusions in the discussion on the division of the soul in Book III, Chapter Nine, the influence of Plato on Aristotle's mature psychological theory is indirect, even subliminal. As such, however, its scope is not easy to calculate.

There is, however, one further important legacy of Platonism which impinges, if only marginally, on the view of the *De Anima*. This is the number mysticism that is apparent to some extent in the later works of Plato himself, especially the *Timaeus*, and seems to have been taken very much further by some at least of his successors. It is often suggested that it was not least the trend towards number mysticism, which must at all stages have been profoundly suspect to one of Aristotle's temperament, that helped to speed his departure from Athens after the death of Plato in 347 B.C. However that may be, we can be certain that the second of Plato's successors as head of the Academy, the uninspiring figure of Xenocrates, was an enthusiastic advocate of various number theories. One of these, his account of the soul as being a self-moving number, is directly attacked in the first Book of the *De Anima*. Few who have considered Xenocrates' theory have come to a judgement very different from Aristotle's trenchant rejection, and the theory does not merit independent assessment here. It is, however, worth remembering that Xenocrates has conflated two Academic views with which Aristotle is at issue, both, that is, that the soul is a self-mover, and that it is the number of the body. No doubt the Stagirite's polemical tone reflects to some extent his personal disappointment at not becoming himself third Scholarch of the Academy, but the most important point is that the fact that Aristotle felt obliged to argue against this view is an indication of the sort of accounts of the soul available in the philosophical market at the time when the *De Anima* was composed, somewhere around 330 B.C.

Aristotle's mature theory of soul is conservative, indeed in Academic terms almost reactionary, in that it addresses itself to the same problem as had confronted the last and greatest of the fifth-century natural philosophers. It represents the fruit of a gradual progression away from Platonism, and bears at points the stamp of hostility to the contemporary Academy. It sets its face against the most interesting approach to the problem of the soul that emerged from the Presocratic period, that of the Harmony Theory and the Ratio Theory, but retains important affinities with them. The question why Aristotle did not himself favour an Attribute Theory, such as we have seen the Harmony and Ratio Theories to be, but arrived eventually at a view which although structurally similar is metaphysically quite different, has already been touched on briefly. We must now try to answer it in full by a consideration of the whole story of his growth as a psychologist and the whole scope of his mature view.

IV. The Development and Scope of Entelechism

The theory of the soul advanced by Aristotle in the *De Anima* is an exercise in what might be called Meta-biology. That is to say, it seeks to give a coherent conceptual framework within which the phenomena of life can be most comprehensively, economically and adequately explained. Not all those who have written treatises on 'the soul' have had this objective and it is of the last importance to bear this in mind when Aristotle's theory is compared with that of other thinkers. This special character of Aristotle's viewpoint in considering the soul has also made the account he has given peculiarly open to misunderstanding and even misrepresentation. Aristotle's extremely valuable remarks on what he is trying to talk about have often been ignored in favour of the attempt to extract from his words some answer to questions arising out of quite different debates to which his line of inquiry is in fact only tangentially relevant. The two most important examples of this misuse of Aristotle have been his introduction into the debate about the immortality of the soul – on which his position in this work is that of aporetic agnosticism – and into that about the ontology of consciousness as it has presented itself to the central post-Cartesian tradition of modern philosophy. I shall try to show that Aristotle's text, and indeed the psychological remarks elsewhere in the corpus, throw no light on these problems, and that for anyone for whom these questions are what the problem of the soul 'is about', the *De Anima* will seem very much Hamlet without the Prince. Any diminution of interest this may bring in Aristotle as a psychologist or philosopher of mind is, however, aptly compensated for by the richness of the *De Anima* as a demonstration of the fecundity of the Functional approach in the life sciences and as an exercise in conceptual analysis, in an area where precisely those philosophical interests to which Aristotle is immune have tended to have a distorting effect.[21] However, before we see more clearly what Aristotle is not doing in this work, we must try to understand what exactly the theory in the *De Anima* is seeking to explain, how these problems came to seem important to Aristotle, what the essence of his explanation is, and how it works out in practice in the different areas of animal functioning that he considers, above all in the area of perception.

The task of the *De Anima* is clearly stated at the opening of the work. It is to explain the principle of animal, and, though Aristotle omits to mention it, also plant life. Living beings are all characterized by the capacity to take note of their environment and, in some cases, to be spontaneous sources of motion and change. Since the beginning of natural philosophy, if not long before, men had been puzzled by these facts, and had sought to explain them. Their explanations had been given in the form of the identification of that which in the living thing constituted its *psyche* or soul. As we have seen, Aristotle is aware of this long pre-history to his inquiry

49

and has looked at those features of it that he finds most interesting in Book I. It is not at all clear how fair Aristotle is being to the greatest of his predecessors in this field, either as thinkers in their own right or as influences on his own theory, but it is at least clear, implicitly at the beginning of Book I, and explicitly at the beginning of Book II, that he thinks that he has a quite new theory, not significantly anticipated by any previous researcher, which will succeed because of its greater conceptual richness in dealing with the problems that both Aristotle and his predecessors find central but which they in his opinion have failed to resolve. The crucial conceptual innovation is of course going to be the dichotomy of Form and Matter, forged indeed in another area of inquiry but in Aristotle's opinion eminently applicable to this one.

As we have said, however, the expression *psyche* is hardly less vague in Greek than the expression 'soul' in English, and it would by no means be obvious to a thinking Greek of Aristotle's time that the discussion of what the soul is belongs quite so firmly in the area of the foundations of Biology. This fact would not in itself distract us for long from the investigation of Aristotle's ideas were it not the case that Aristotle seems himself at one stage in his life to have held a distinctly non-biological view of the soul. It is even possible that his views went through several different stages of development, of which the present text may represent the last, or be some transitional view, or even offer a cross section of his views. This is a matter of intense scholarly debate, to which I will hope to provide here an introduction rather than a contribution.

In 367 B.C., the seventeen-year-old Aristotle entered the hardly older Academy of the sixty-year-old Plato. As suggested in the *Life of Aristotle*, it seems reasonable to assume that these two Olympians engaged in constant philosophical exchange, interrupted only by Plato's second period of misguided absence in Syracuse, until, on the co-incidence of Plato's death with the election of Speusippus in 347 B.C. and in the wake of Macedonian aggression at Olynthus in 348 B.C., Aristotle left Athens for the coast of northern Asia Minor. The mature philosophies of Plato and Aristotle have always seemed to show that difference so sublimely evoked in Raphael's Vatican fresco, Aristotelian concentration on the fascination of the given contrasting with the soaring aspiration of Platonic metaphysics. Closer inspection than the Renaissance master may have thought appropriate to his theme no doubt considerably diminishes the clarity of this contrast. The system of neither philosopher, if indeed we can use the word 'system' of their thinking at all, is wholly consistent either in detail or in orientation. This complexity characterizes not least their views about our immediate topic, the soul. Plato's psychological view, as mentioned earlier, evolved throughout his life, though remaining loyal to its central insight of psychic divinity. Aristotle's view also seems certainly to have gone through at least one change, and this greater than any in Plato's thinking. It was, however, from Plato that Aristotle started, and from the earliest stage of Plato's development. In the *Phaedo*, Plato put into the mouth of the condemned Socrates the supremely eloquent defence of a remarkably simple theory of the soul. Here the soul is the incarcerated Pythagorean god, for whom there is no greater good than eventual complete release from the cycle of regeneration. In this conception not only is the soul immortal, but its connection with any given body is purely contingent and quite irrelevant to the investigation of its nature and it is not characterized by any divisions within itself. With this picture Plato later came to be dissatisfied, and in the *Phaedrus* and the *Republic* he has already moved towards that more complex picture of the soul's constitution that is given its final presentation in the *Timaeus*. The impact of the *Phaedo* must, however, have been very great on Plato's first audience, and it seems clear that it was this work that most fascinated Aristotle as a young entrant into the Academy. It was, in any case, the *Phaedo* that provided the direct model for the first theory that we know Aristotle to have propagated on the subject of the soul.

Eudemus of Cyprus was a personal friend of the young Aristotle, and when he was killed fighting in Sicily the Macedonian wrote a dialogue, called after him, whose function was essentially consolatory, and of which we have rather meagre evidence, including some fragments. This fugitive testimony has been enough to fuel a scholarly controversy on the connection between the ideas expressed in this work by Aristotle and those of the Platonic Socrates of the *Phaedo*. It can safely be said that this has yet to be wholly resolved, but at least some clearly Platonizing tendencies cannot be denied. The consensus of the fragments firmly suggests that the idea of the soul here adopted by Aristotle was such that it could be represented as both surviving this incarnation and even in the Platonic manner having experiences in its disembodied state which it is only prevented from recollecting in this world by its 'diseased' condition of embodiment. There is some reason, indeed, to think that in later Antiquity this view was sometimes held to be as much Aristotelian as Platonic. It is of course possible that Aristotle's thinking is coloured by his literary purpose or indeed even by his state of mind at the recent loss of a close friend. But that the dialogue presents a picture of an immortal soul, not of its nature having any business with a mortal body, caught in such a body through misfortune and perhaps punishment, this much cannot be doubted. Such a view would seem on the surface to be as far removed as possible from the subtle and intrinsically psychosomatic conception of the mature 'entelechism' of the *De Anima*. Indeed, those who subscribe to the theory that the entelechist account is an Attribute Theory will presumably claim that the history of Aristotle's development as a psychologist is that of a move, perhaps with intermediary resting points, from one end of the available spectrum to the other, from a wholehearted Cartesianism, in modern terms, to a thoroughgoing Physicalism. Such a story is by no means improbable – it could easily be paralleled by no less impressive *volte faces* on central topics by many other philosophers. However, as we have seen, there are grounds for rejecting the attribute interpretation of the entelechist thesis, and for replacing it with something that contrasts less dramatically with the view that seems to be on offer in the *Eudemus*. Moreover, on the less dramatic interpretation we are able to deal with one piece of evidence about the *Eudemus* which is otherwise rather hard to handle.

Simplicius, in his commentary on the *De Anima*,[22] tells us that in the *Eudemus*, no less than in the mature work, Aristotle asserted that the soul was a form and expressed admiration for those who said that the noetic soul was receptive of forms. This, given the general theory that seems to be being put forward in the *Eudemus*, is certainly surprising. How could Aristotle possibly have wanted to label the conception of the soul that he there presents as a Form? Now, Simplicius' remark occurs in the course of a discussion of the senses of the word *eidos*, Form, in the two philosophers, and it is certainly plausible to suggest that Simplicius mistook Aristotle's uncharacteristically Platonizing use of this term for the mature use of *Metaphysics* Zeta and of the *De Anima*. However, as Lloyd[23] has pointed out, this hardly helps matters, as the remark that the soul is a Form, no matter how Platonically the word 'Form' is to be construed, could not possibly be taken as any Platonic psychological theory. The soul is indeed receptive of the Forms for Plato as for his pupil even in the mature period, but that is quite another thing from the soul's being a Form. Nothing very much is therefore to be gained from taking Aristotle's use of the term Form here in the *Eudemus* to mean something radically different from what it means in the mature theory. But then there certainly is a difficulty for those who wish to say that in that theory the expression *eidos* or its effective synonym *entelechy* mean no more than 'set of attributes', have no more substantiality than implied by that phrase. If, however, we insist that an entelechy is, as Aristotle puts it, in a way a substance, and leave aside for the moment the problem of whether anything can be achieved, as is not obvious, by talk of things being 'in a way substance', then the problem presented here by Simplicius, without indeed entirely evaporating, certainly becomes manageable. We are left with a concept that has made only the rather short passage from being a purely spiritual substance, captured in a body that is alien to it, to being a spiritual substance that finds its necessary location in the realization that it constitutes a certain matter. To call such a transition 'rather short' may seem odd. It is so of course only by comparison with that required by the supposition of a one hundred and eighty degree turn in Aristotle's psychological theory. On that view we are required to suppose a sharp and progressive reaction on Aristotle's part from a Platonism to which he was once himself amenable. This is possible, and in accordance with the picture that Jaeger gives of Aristotle's development.[24] However, no less attractive, surely, is the view that Aristotle never seriously questioned the assumption, which is implicit in the theories of all philosophers except the Harmony theorists and perhaps Empedocles, that the soul is a substance, but came gradually to see that the Platonic interpretation of that substance was inadequate to its playing its appropriate part in the emerging science of Biology, and, without wanting to embrace the full-blown materialism of Democritus and others, developed his own subtle and Functionalist conception of that substance.

The *Eudemus* is probably to be assigned to the 350s, the *De Anima* probably to the early 320s. This leaves a good quarter century in which Aristotle's thoughts can mature and evolve. Is it possible to trace this evolution and even perhaps to detect some of the influences on it? Current discussion of this important question centres on the thesis of a Belgian scholar called François Nuyens. In his important book *L'Evolution de la psychologie d'Aristote* (Louvain, 1948),[25] Nuyens attempted to adapt the genetic approach to the interpretation of the Aristotelian corpus that had been initiated by Jaeger to the specifically psychological writings, in the belief that in the remarks about the soul scattered through the corpus there could be found evidence of a linear development, that this development could be gradated and correlated with known facts about Aristotle's career, and that thus psychological asides could be used to date even those of the works that were not primarily of psychological purport, rather in the way that carbon deposits can be used to date archaeological strata. This was a bold and ingenious approach and Nuyens argued with some skill. His precise conclusion was that Aristotle's psychological development falls into three main stages. The first is the Platonizing stage that is represented for us by the *Eudemus* and to a lesser extent by some other fragments of the early dialogues; the last is the Entelechism to be found in the *De Anima*. The claims neither for Platonism nor for Entelechism were new. Aristotle certainly held views that can properly be so labelled at the beginning and the end of his career as a psychological thinker. What was much more open to criticism in Nuyens' account was the intermediate stage that he postulated. This stage he labelled Instrumentism, though, for reasons that will become clear, it is perhaps easier to follow a recent scholar in calling it the Heart view. The content of this theory, according to Nuyens, was that the soul was still spiritual substance not inherently connected with the body to which it was attached, but that whereas in the previous High Platonic phase the soul had been, as in the *Phaedo*, an unwilling prisoner in the body, in the new theory it was the natural and appropriate controller of the body and indeed used the body to carry out its various activities. The body was now the instrument, not the prison, of the soul, and in the light of this fact it was possible, indeed it became necessary, to locate the soul rather more specifically than had previously been done within the body, and, in a break with the Platonic precedent that was variously unfortunate, the heart was chosen as its seat. It is not hard to see how Nuyens thought the Instrumentist or Heart theory was the perfect resting point for Aristotle on his way from the Platonism of the *Eudemus* to the Entelechism of the *De Anima*. It had in common with the former view the conception of the soul as a spiritual substance not, as it were, structurally determined by the body, and with the latter the strong feeling of close cooperation, for mutual advantage, of body and soul.

Nuyens' view, however, has come under attack, and indeed is not now tenable in the form originally advanced. It has been revealed to have two great weaknesses. The first is that, although the course of development sketched is certainly one that Aristotle might have taken, the evidence that he did take it, with the in many ways startling consequences for the chronology of many works, was at best highly ambiguous. The observation, now a commonplace of Aristotelian scholarship, that so much can be said of almost any particular 'genetic' hypothesis, cannot excuse Nuyens' view from its underdetermination by the facts. The second weakness of Nuyens' view is, however, in many ways the more interesting. The scholars who have argued against Nuyens have been unable to deny that there are indeed many passages which have the Instrumentist ring that he seeks to ascribe to them. They, however, have taken the view that, *pace* Nuyens, this does not afford evidence for the priority of these passages to the *De Anima*. In one case indeed the order has been reversed, and talk of the soul's being connected with the heart has been taken as evidence of later composition than the *De Anima*, on the grounds that it embodies further development in the physiological view. Other scholars have argued, however, that the two views outlined by Nuyens and claimed by him to be mutually incompatible are in fact wholly consistent.[26] Aristotle's mature psychological theory, it has been claimed,[27] treats the soul as being something like the light in an illuminated light bulb. The light emanates from the central filament but it permeates the entire bulb; so is it with the soul. It emanates from the heart but it pervades the entire body. Its residence especially in the heart in no way excludes it from its role as the Form of the body. This picture is perhaps only in need of one modification to be quite correct. This is that in the case of the bulb the light does indeed permeate from the filament through the whole, and this is paralleled by the permeation of the whole body by the soul, but it also spreads beyond for an indefinite distance, and with this feature there is no analogy in the case of the soul. Nevertheless, the simile gives, I think, a good picture of the theory advanced in the *De Anima*. Careful reading of the text reveals many passages that are certainly most intelligible from an Instrumentist position, and this we should take as showing that Aristotle does not consider such ways of thinking essentially at odds with the central theory. There are only two other possible explanations of these Instrumentist passages in the work, neither of which is very attractive. The first is that Aristotle, or conceivably his pupil, was wholly indifferent to the need to evolve a single clear theory in the work at all. The other is that the work as we have it is a patchwork of passages from different periods in Aristotle's development and has been rather hastily and unsatisfactorily cobbled together. Neither of these views survives an attentive reading through of the work as a whole.

But the fact that Entelechism in this way embraces Instrumentism is in itself important for what it tells us about Entelechism. For if the entelechy is something that could be thought of as using the body as an instrument, this is surely an indication of its having some kind of substantiality. It will be countered that Aristotle says similar things about the ability of skills to use material objects, but as a soul is on any account rather a different thing from a skill it is not clear how valid an objection this is. In any case, if even a skill is the sort of thing that can be thought to use material objects, then we are surely right to take a broad view of the Aristotelian concept of substantiality.

The picture, then, that emerges from as it were the reformed Nuyens is that of a simple development of Aristotle away from the Platonism of his early maturity towards the view of the *De Anima* and the corpus in general. This view centres on the account given of the soul in *De Anima* Book II, Chapters One–Three, and is thus best labelled Entelechism, but it is amenable to remarks found elsewhere in the *De Anima* and beyond which in themselves are more deserving of some such label as Instrumentism or 'Heart' Theory. This 'reformation' of Nuyens evidently deprives his account of any relevance it might have pretended to have to the difficult question of the chronology of the corpus. This question, however, except insofar as it bears on the relevant dating of the *De Anima* and the *Parva Naturalia*, has little significance for the understanding of the *De Anima* itself, and I do not intend to embroil the reader in it. Even so, on the simplified version of Nuyens here presented, it would be of great interest to identify the influences that led to so marked a change of emphasis in the Aristotelian psychology.

This brings us to a central issue in the current interpretation of Aristotle's thought: the importance for the corpus as a whole of the teleological approach characteristic of the Biological works. Ever since a celebrated observation of D'Arcy Thompson[28] that most of the place names in the *Historia Animalium* are from the area of the north-eastern Aegean where Aristotle spent the years 347–340 B.C., and that many species are also peculiar to this area, it has been a plausible suggestion that the intensive particularist empirical researches of these years had a profound influence on Aristotle's whole outlook, converting the Platonic axiomatizer of the *Posterior Analytics* into the aporetic questioner whose presence in the bulk of the corpus had always been found embarrassing, even disturbing. As to the validity of such larger claims, which have been expertly discussed,[29] we need not here be concerned, but it would seem of importance to recognize the phase of practical biological investigation as of salient influence on the psychological theory. It was surely during these years that he came to be dissatisfied with an inquiry into the soul conceived in terms of what it was that might survive the bodily death of a Socrates or a Eudemus and began to look on this subject rather as the investigation of what it was, in addition to their detachable parts, about living creatures in virtue of which they performed their characteristic functions. Further, it seems a no less reasonable conjecture that at this time too the answer occurred to him that just as all particular objects must be constituted by Matter and Form, so would it also be with living things, and that in their case it would be just this Form that would provide the key to their successful and consistent functioning.

There thus arose the possibility of a complete presentation of the science of Biology, complete not of course in the sense that it would be immune from subsequent emendation or expansion in the light of new facts, but in the sense that a comprehensive foundation would have been laid for all the major areas of the subject. These major areas would be that of the Form of living creatures, that of their Matter, and that of their functions as composites of the two. The account of the Matter of living things is given in the *De Partibus Animalium*, that of the functions in the *Parva Naturalia*, the *De Generatione Animalium* and the *De Motu Animalium*. It falls to the *De Anima*, having first cleared away the detritus of early confusing talk about the soul, to reveal that expression's true

use to indicate the general Form of living things. It is highly
probable that these works, as we now have them, constituted
a complete lecture course on Biology, and almost certain, in
that case, that the *De Anima* formed the first section of that
course.

The presentation of the soul, then, as the general Form of
living things, the Entelechist thesis, plays a crucial part in
Aristotle's whole exposition of Biology, central to which is
the application of the Form–Matter distinction to living
things. Nothing is more important than a clear appreciation
of this fact for the avoidance of the imputation into the text
of suggestions quite foreign to its purpose and import, as I
shall hope to show. However, it is time to turn directly to the
entelechist thesis itself and ask what exactly Aristotle meant
in saying that the soul was 'the first entelechy of a natural
body endowed with organs'.

In making the claim that the soul is the Form of the body,
Aristotle challenges his interpreter to plunge into one of the
densest thickets in the entire corpus, the general metaphysical
dichotomy of Form and Matter and their obscure connection
with the central notion of *ousia*, substance. On the surface
the distinction between Form and Matter might seem
commonsensical and straightforward, and it evidently lends
itself to some very simple applications. But no application is
more indicative of the intrinsic subtlety of this dichotomy
than that under immediate study in the *De Anima*. To try to
bring out this subtlety, I shall seek to show how one very
natural way of taking the claim that the soul is the Form of
the body turns out to be unsatisfactory. The natural way,
then, of construing the remark is that the body, the
underlying Matter, is what Aristotle holds that there is, while
the Form, which is of course the soul, is an abstract noun
serving compendiously to denote the congeries of properties
or attributes of the body, in virtue of which it is alive. We
may leave aside the question of what, if any, properties a
living body has which are not constitutive of its being alive
and how these are to be conceptually or practically distinguished from those that come, as it were, under the psychic
umbrella. This attribute interpretation of the presentation

of soul as Form is certainly intelligible, and, though its explicative force is hardly beyond question, it is closely analogous to many very similar views popular among contemporary philosophers. Furthermore, this view has found favour with a number of commentators on the *De Anima*. One of its clearest advocates is Barnes.[30] He offers the following account of the argument to establish the general definition of soul at the beginning of Book II:

Its conclusion is this: 'if, then, we must say something common for every soul, it will be the first actuality of an organic natural body' (412b4–6). I take this to amount to: (D1) x has a soul $= df x$ is a living organic natural body.

After some discussion, the next chapter opens with a caution that 'the definitory formula must not only show the fact . . . but the explanation too must inhere in it and shine through' (413a13–16). A second argument then leads to a second general account: 'the soul is a principle of the aforesaid things, i.e., it is defined by these – nutritive, perceptive, intellectual, motion' (413b11–13). I take this to amount to: (D2) x has a soul $= df x$ can nourish itself OR x can perceive OR x can think OR x can move itself.

Since the features disjoined on the right of this equation are precisely those in virtue of which a natural body is called living (413a22–5), (D2) in a sense provides an 'explanation' of the 'fact' laid down in (D1). The crucial characteristic of both these definitions is that they construe the soul not as a substance (like, say, the heart or the brain) but as an attribute (like, say, life or health). Neither (D1) nor (D2) gives or implies any definition of the term 'soul' or the predicate '. . . is a soul': the definiendum is ' . . . has a soul'; and, as each definiens makes clear, this one-place predicate is not analysable into a two-place predicate '. . . has –' and a substance term 'soul', as '. . . has a brain' might be analysed into '. . . has –' and 'brain'. If 'an animal is made from soul and body' (*Politics*, 1227a6), it is not as a motor-car is made from engine and coachwork, but rather as a motor-car with its engine running is 'made from' the running and the works.[31]

This trenchant defence of the attribute construal of Aristotle's thesis is echoed in Barnes' treatment elsewhere of the similarities that he sees, and which we have come to reject, between the Aristotelian view and the Harmony Theory.

Barnes is here presenting an analysis in the familiar tradition of Russell's theory of descriptions. He is arguing that the definition of the soul here given is not really saying what it seems to be saying. His analysis makes implicit use of the contrast between 'surface' and 'depth' grammar. Now, indisputably, the surface grammar of Aristotle's definition connects the subject 'psyche' via the two-place copula 'is' to the defining predicate. However, this in itself obviously shows nothing. No one would want to claim that when I say 'I have a cold' I am asserting my title to the possession of a thing – the expression is only dyadic on the surface and could in the interests of logical purity be replaced either by a single one-place predicate, such as '. . . am *enrheumé*' or whatever disjunction of logically similar predicates might be thought appropriate. Nor is this deceptive feature of language confined to philosophically uninteresting statements of this kind. Although it could certainly be argued that Greek idiom is in this respect much less logically wanton than English, yet the claim that Aristotle's surface grammar is here seriously misleading is not *prima facie* outrageous. But if we ask why it is that we treat 'I have a dog' as dyadic in English and 'I have a cold' as really monadic, the answer is, of course, that a dog is a thing and a cold is not. Therefore, if 'I have a soul' is to be classed logically with 'I have a cold' and not with 'I have a dog', we must hold that souls like colds are not in any real sense things. This, of course, is precisely the view that Barnes is imputing to Aristotle. As remarked earlier, however, Aristotle opens the second Book with the pointed assertion that Forms are substances, and goes on to claim that souls are Forms, thus committing himself to the claim that souls are substances.[32] Thus, it would seem that the only way Barnes can avoid flat contradiction with Aristotle, is by claiming that this remark too is deceptive. He must claim that Forms are not really substances in the proper sense – and this is just what, at a later point, he does claim.

We see clearly then that the issue of the substantiality of Forms is cardinal to the interpretation of the central doctrine of the *De Anima*. Given the completely organic structure of the work, and the consistency with which it seeks to work out the consequences of the central thesis, it is evident that our assessment of the whole work, and with it, because of its compatibility with psychological remarks elsewhere, of Aristotle's final deliberations on the soul, life and the mind, will hinge on our ascription to the soul of a greater or lesser degree of substantiality. The most important single fruit perhaps of an acknowledgement of the substantiality of the soul as Form will be a far smoother transition from those psychic areas where the soul is immersed in the Matter of the body to those where it is held to be capable of separation and immaterial existence.

But how to determine whether Forms are substances? The answer to this question must perforce be that we turn to Book Zeta of the *Metaphysics*. Now the *Metaphysics* has always been considered one of the more opaque masterpieces of philosophical literature. There are many good reasons for this. Not only does the work advance views of very great subtlety and complexity, and in a severely esoteric style seldom relieved by any more than perfunctory exemplification, and complicating the reader's grasp of dubiously consistent jargon with oracular ellipse, but it seems clear that the work is in no sense a single coherent treatise – this had been recognized even before the Jaeger revolution – but a compilation from various sources and perhaps by various hands. All these remarks apply *par excellence* to Book Zeta. This Book has been skilfully analysed by Grayeff[33] as amounting to a somewhat confused and incomplete combination of treatments of Being and Substance from three different standpoints, a critique of previous theories, a logical analysis of the concepts, and an attempted metaphysical characterization of Substance. This last comprises Chapters Seven to Nine of the Book. Given the decidedly confused state of the *Metaphysics* as a whole and this Book in particular, any attempt to argue from its doctrines to conclusions for the *De Anima* is open to the charge of anachronism. Since, however, excessive sensitivity to this forces the interpreter of the *De Anima* to consider the sense of the words *eidos* (Form), and *entelecheia*, as used in the work, to be entirely peculiar to the work, I embark robustly on an exercise to which the alternative would seem to be a counsel of despair.

Throughout Book Zeta, and indeed in the continuation of the discussion in the subsequent Eta, Aristotle is officially discussing four candidates for the status of substantiality in the fullest sense. These are essence, universal, genus and substrate. The competition turns out, however, to be in a way one without losers, as it seems that in some way all these four, with the possible exception only of genus, have a claim to some of the features of substantiality. However, the clear impression from the two books is that Aristotle's real favourite is the *substrate, to hupokeimenon.* If, however, we are prepared to assert, as we have warrant to do, that substance is really *to hupokeimenon,* still we have not resolved the onto-logical riddle of the *De Anima.* For it is just this notion of the substrate that divides in Aristotle's system into the three aspects of Form, Matter and their combination. Thus the real question at the centre of *Metaphysics* Zeta and Eta, just as at the centre of the rather more lucidly arranged and, for the most part, better expressed *De Anima,* is which of these three is really substance. Aristotle's resolution of this point is no more exclusively in favour of any one possibility than was the case with the ascription of relative degrees of sub-stantiality to substrate, essence, genus and universal, but he does give at least clear indication of what the grounds are on which the decision is to be made. For something to be substance in the fullest sense, it must be the possible subject of a definition and thus of fundamental knowledge, and it must thus constitute the *logos* of a particular thing. It is further required that it should be connected with a thing's persisting through change and indeed be the cause of its so doing. Finally, it must represent the fulfilment or realization of the particular thing. None of these requirements is wholly clear in itself, but it does seem that Aristotle's mind is made up that these, vague as they are, will be the features of that which he will be most ready to recognize as deserving to be called Substance, and on these grounds it is clear enough that the most successful candidates will be essence and the closely related notion of form. That Aristotle should come, however, tentatively, to the conclusion that *ousia* in the fullest sense is form or essence may of course induce us to be disposed to reject the translation 'substance' for the term *ousia*, and evidently anyone is at liberty to make the not implausible claim that our ordinary use of the expression 'substance' is incompatible with its being said to be in the truest sense Form. We may even be disposed, in a reductivist spirit, to treat the whole idea of gradations of substance with suspicion. But this does not exempt us from trying to understand what exactly Aristotle did mean by saying that *ousia* is in the truest sense *eidos*, for it is this doctrine that lies behind the assertion of the substantiality of the soul at the beginning of the second Book of the *De Anima*. The proper treatment of this substantiality thesis will be either to accept, at least in some ways, the Aristotelian conception of substance, and construe the substantiality of the soul accordingly, or, if we cannot stomach the broad conception of substance, then provide a basis for the reconstrual into more acceptable guise of those remarks which predicate substantiality of, say, the soul. But surely the discussion in *Metaphysics* Zeta and Eta at least shows that any such reconstrual must leave the soul as being at least something more than a mere disjunction of attributes. In any case, I shall try to show that the use made by Aristotle of the definition of the soul at the start of Book II shows that, far from being unfortunately phrased in tendentious, misleading and now outmoded jargon, it in fact exhibits a subtle and complex conceptual structure that lends itself to remarkably varied exploitation throughout the work, and that the rival attribute construal often leaves Aristotle saying things that would be hard for any philosopher, and above all for him, to swallow.

The application by Aristotle to the analysis of *psyche* of the Form–Matter dichotomy can thus be defended from the charge of otiosity. It has recently been confronted, however, with another allegation hardly less serious. Professor Ackrill[34] has suggested that the entelechy thesis is of dubious logical hygiene. I shall try to set out briefly his objection and say why I think that it is misplaced, and then pass to the consideration of how the central notion of soul as Form is employed through the bulk of the work to give an admirably perspicuous and elegantly economical account of a wide range of psychic phenomena.

Ackrill's attack, then, is not directly on the notion of Form as applied in Aristotelian psychology, but on the complementary treatment of the living body as the corresponding matter to that Form. The Form–Matter dichotomy, he argues, requires that the Matter of any particular composite be capable of existing as Matter, and as the same Matter, when in-formed by another Form. Thus, a bronze sphere, to take his example, is constituted by the Matter bronze arranged by the Form sphericity. Just as the same Form could in-form other Matter, such as wood perhaps, so the same Matter could eminently be in-formed by some other Form, perhaps that of a statue. The point is that either composite contains the same Matter, which was potentially both but not necessarily either. Thus if you tell me that there is a piece of bronze in the next door room I have as yet no knowledge of its Form (though, significantly, the possible range is not unlimited). Thus some useful purpose can be served by your telling me that its Form is in fact sphericity. The contingency of its being spherical is what prevents the application of the Form–Matter dichotomy to it from being otiose – it could have been something else. With this feature, however, argues Ackrill, there is in the case of the soul, as the Form of the body, no analogue. This is so because of what he calls the homonymy principle, which is Aristotle's claim that a body without *psyche* is not a body except in the 'degenerate', homonymous sense. Whereas the bronze persisted as bronze through its various metamorphoses, the body changes as Matter from being homonymously body before the life of the composite animal to being body in the true sense while informed by *psyche* during the animal's life, to being homonymously body again after its demise. Thus it fails to have that persistent character through change that is required of the material side of Aristotle's dichotomy.

Ackrill considers three possible ways out of this difficulty for Aristotle. The first is simply that the homonymy principle be relaxed, as least in this case, so that we can say that a body, which, though clinically dead, yet could be revived, would be a body in the true sense and not merely homonymously. This option, though Ackrill sees it as permissible

for Aristotle, is not really satisfactory, as it fails to do justice
to the functional character of Aristotle's conception of the
role of *psyche* as Form. Aristotle would want to say that the
complexity of the body's arrangement reflected its assistance
of the soul in the performance of the natural functions, and
that it could hardly retain that complexity of structure, to no
end, unsupported by the teleological driving power, so to
speak, of soul. The functioning of the animal and its physical
arrangement are too closely linked by Aristotle for him to
want to say that they could be so separated that the one
would 'go with' the soul, the other with the body. The second
possible escape from Aristotle's difficulty that Ackrill considers is that the Matter of the animal might be thought to
be not so much its body as a whole, but the homoeomerous [35]
parts out of which the body is composed. It is a standard
feature of Aristotelian zoology to distinguish in an animal
between those items such as the limbs, whose whole is not
similar to their parts, and those, such as the flesh and bones
of mammals, which have this similarity. We have seen that
there is a difficulty about the separate existence of bodies as
a whole and, by the same token, of their limbs. Could we not
instead suppose the possible separate existence of flesh and
bones and so forth? This possibility Ackrill rejects. Flesh and
bones are no more capable than the limbs themselves of
separate existence in nature, or participation as such in any
other composites than those in-formed by soul. Indeed, it is
because of the fleshly constitution of a man's arm that it
cannot be severed from him and made part of a statue. The
homoeomerous parts of the animal are more, not less,
involved in the life of the animal then the anhomoeomerous.

The final possibility that Ackrill considers is that we
should think of the Matter of the body, which soul successfully
arranges into the composite of the animal or plant, as being
neither the limbs nor the homoeomerous parts, but the
elements themselves from which the homoeomerous parts
are, like everything else in nature, made up. Now here we
certainly have something that is capable of pre-existing and
surviving the life of the composite in its proper nature. The
carbon that composes the animal, on our theories, or the

four elements on the Peripatetic view, are certainly capable of returning as they were whence they came and subsequently of partaking in a range of composites. If I am told that there is a certain amount of fire, air, water and earth in the next door room, it certainly seems a pertinent question to ask what their form is. However, Ackrill rejects this suggestion too. He does so on the strength of a passage which he quotes from the *Metaphysics*:

> Is earth potentially a man? No – but rather when it has already become seed, and perhaps not even then . . . A thing is potentially all those things which it will be of itself if nothing external hinders it. E.g., the seed is not yet potentially man; for it must be deposited in something other than itself and undergo a change. But once it has through its own motive principle got such and such attributes, then it is potentially a man.[36]

This passage, however, while it would indeed seem to go against the claim that the elements are potentially the body in the direct way in which the bronze is potentially the sphere, would not seem to exclude their being potentially the body in a more remote way. After all, if earth is potentially seed and seed is potentially man, then there is surely a clear sense in which earth is potentially man. The reason why Aristotle frowns on this in the *Metaphysics* passage is that it is obviously a rather strange thing to say, and only dubiously informative. This, however, does not prevent him from responding to Ackrill's pressure to state what it is that is informed by the soul during animal life but that both has pre-existed this and will survive it as itself. Surely it is possible, if somewhat Empedoclean, to look on the ensouled body as a functional arrangement of amounts of the four elements, though this has that air of manoeuvre about it that suggests the response to a merely logical difficulty. If we are prepared to allow the appropriate breadth to the Form–Matter dichotomy, we can see, I think, how Ackrill's difficulty can be overcome, and adopt the attitude to it perhaps that it is just the sort of minor hitch in the psychological Hylomorphism[37] that might have been relatively painlessly removed had Aristotle had the good fortune to have founded a school really capable of continuing the thrust of his research and theory.

The Entelechist thesis presented by Aristotle at the beginning of the second Book of the *De Anima* springs directly from his general metaphysical system, and cannot thus be assimilated to modern reductionist accounts of the soul in terms of mere sets of attributes. It stands in sharp contrast to all previous theories of the soul, including the Harmony Theory, its closest antecedent. It contains no conceptual contradictions and represents a legitimate deployment of its chosen analytical tools. Although it is not directed either at the question of the soul's possibly surviving wholly or in part the death of the body or at the explication of the phenomenon of consciousness and the problems connected with the subjective viewpoint on the world enjoyed by the first person, it nevertheless constitutes a comprehensive and convincing basis for an objective analysis of all the phenomena of vegetable and animal life.

It is to this, last, claim that we must now turn. How is Aristotle able to make his central theory fit the varied facts of the behaviour of natural species, and account for their hierarchy of powers in a systematic and elegant manner?

The Aristotelian world is nothing if it is not hierarchic. A precisely defined ladder of being rises from the most primitive arrangements of inanimate Matter, as little removed as possible from that merely material substrate, the possibility of whose existence is no more than conceptual, by clearly defined degrees to that which is least material of all, the divine self-substantiating thought that is the origin of movement and the 'one king' of the last words of *Metaphysics* Lambda. Yet there are in this seemingly complete world-system enough uncertainties to worry the scholastic 'Aristotelians' and give heart to the vindicators of the aporetic Aristotle who is the hero of much modern criticism. Nevertheless, Aristotle is loyal to his conception of the cosmos in all the areas of science, and the conception pervades the presentation of his biological researches, to which the *De Anima* probably provides the introduction. It is thus no surprise that the hierarchic design finds an echo in the arrangement of this work.

The Aristotelian cosmos is divided into two superficially antagonistic, but in fact subtly interconnected, halves. From the centrally located earth a succession of concentric spheres ascend towards the highest being. Of these the lowest is that of the moon, above which all motion is that of eternally immutable rotation. Below lies that sector whose contents are subject to change, the world of our familiar experience as earth-dwellers. Amongst the furniture of this world are some items which, in virtue of a capacity for a puzzlingly complex response to their environment and, in some cases, the origination of their own movement, are said to be alive, and it is of these that the science of Biology treats. Although it would be going too far to call Aristotle the founder of this science, yet his contribution can be described without hyperbole as epoch-making. Above all, he was the first to attempt to capture in a conceptual framework the notion of life itself as an explanatory idea. He attempted to locate this most baffling feature of the perceptible environment in a conceptual context distinct alike from those of its earlier theological or mechanistic exponents. This involved an exercise which stands in the same relation to the study of living things as Metaphysics is supposed to stand in to that of things in general, and may therefore not fancifully be labelled Meta-biology. Since the concept which for Aristotle, as for his predecessors, was central to the explanation of the notion of life was soul, it is above all in the *De Anima* that the framework of Aristotelian Meta-biology is laid down. If we bear this constantly in mind, we may be able to resist the temptation to take as contributions to the controversies of later philosophical ages remarks which Aristotle could hardly have avoided making but which, while dealing with matters of peripheral importance for him, are pregnant with suggestions on topics that seem of central importance to us.

The task of the *De Anima*, then, is to use the concept of soul to explain the phenomena of life. It is with this ambitious object in mind that Aristotle, having exploded all previous lines of inquiry into the soul, adapts to it the central dichotomy of his general metaphysic. It is the bold presupposition of the work that the concepts of Matter, Form and that which is derived from them as a composite, with which the more general concept of change has already been treated, can be adapted to form the core of a comprehensive explanation of animate activity. For this to achieve the intended clarification, the subtlety of the concept of Form must be exploited to the full. It is standard Aristotelian doctrine that there are gradations in the realization of any potential. He expresses this by saying that a composite particular may have a first and second actualization. It is in virtue of the first of these that its Matter is so arranged as to render it capable of performing its characteristic functions and it is in virtue of the second that it 'actually' performs them. For example, the Matter of a radio is converted by the man who makes it into the exercise of the first actuality of a radio and by the man who switches it on into the second. There is an obvious, but important, point about this example: it illustrates how the idea of the first and second realization, or, as I shall from now on call it, entelechy, of any given potentiality is not at all peculiar to biological explanation. This, indeed, provokes an important objection to the account here offered of the soul. It might be said that the concept of soul is being explicated within a framework not designed to capture the peculiarities that distinguish animate from inanimate activity. How, it is asked, can what is special about life be captured by the mere transfer to living things of a conceptual dichotomy adequate, as it is claimed, to the general explanation of change? This objection seems persuasive, but it misses the point. For it is not that the dichotomy is in itself being offered as an explanation of soul as the source of life, but rather that the dichotomy, familiar from general use, can be in this special area so embedded in a peculiar conceptual framework as to yield a comprehensive account of life. In other words, the double concept of entelechy is introduced not to provide the explicatory illumination appropriate to meta-biology, but, crucially, to provide the other concepts that are to be explanatory with their systematic unity. The Entelechist thesis I take to amount to the claim that if the concept of a second entelechy can be rendered adequate to the explanation of the activity of living things, then that of a first entelechy will of itself be adequate to the explanation of their structure and material arrangement.

It is thus the articulation of concepts around the central dichotomy that is to give this theory of the soul its cutting edge. This articulation will both be comprehensive in its coverage of the ways in which life manifests itself and also render perspicuous the hierarchic interconnection between them. The central conception of soul as first entelechy will be developed into a series of psychic faculties. These faculties of the soul will be denoted in the way that least commits Aristotle to having to give more precise answers than he would like to such irrelevant questions as what the exact analogy is between the relation in which absolute potentiality stands to the first entelechy and that in which this stands to the second. He therefore exploits the capacity of Greek to form, by the *-ikon*[38] ending, nouns which are as clearly connected with the verbs from which they are derived as they are clearly not connected with any other noun to which they might stand as adjectives. The bulk of the *De Anima* consists in an investigation of the operation of these psychic faculties, denoted in this non-committal way.

What are the faculties of the soul for Aristotle, and how do they come to compose a hierarchy? On the surface it is not obvious that the various activities that constitute life can fruitfully be assigned positions on a value scale, though Aristotle is not unique in thinking that this is so. For Aristotle, however, the animate part of nature self-evidently bears the stamp of hierarchy. There are clear gradations between plants at the lowest end, and animals, between animals and men, and between men and whatever beings may be their superiors, gradations that are expressed not only in the wider range of capacities enjoyed by the higher groups but also by the relative superiority of the hallmark of each new grade to the features shared with it and that below. It is the task of the theory of the soul, as we have said, so to explain the life common to all of these grades as to render their hierarchical structure internal to that explanation. For this task the faculty approach is well suited.

It will be on the basis of its range of psychic faculties that a living thing will be assigned its grade within Aristotle's hierarchy. What faculties does Aristotle identify and how do they correlate with the grades of the living? At 413a20, Aristotle, having used the mathematical example of squaring to illustrate what constraints he is putting upon his as yet quite schematic account of soul, announces the real beginning of his inquiry. The hallmark of that which has soul is that it is alive. But there are many ways in which things are said to be alive. The list that he here gives of the ways of being alive will serve, if its order is rearranged, as a list of the faculties of the soul in the order in which they are to be treated. It is in virtue of the most basic faculty of the soul that a living thing has the ability to nourish and to reproduce itself. The faculty next above this is that whereby it perceives, and that above this is the faculty whereby it thinks. If we accept imagination as closely connected with sense-perception, these three faculties comprise all the activities of living things except those of spatial movement and purposive action or its motivation. These two faculties are in fact one and, as Aristotle will later show, this single faculty cannot be neatly fitted into the hierarchic arrangement of the other three. The introduction of these faculties quickly leads to the explanation of the hierarchical order of living things. We are familiar with a three-grade hierarchy rising from plants through animals to men. This is explained for Aristotle by the supposition that plants possess only the most basic faculty of soul, that of nourishment and reproduction, animals possess this and the faculty of perception, or at least sensation, and men possess both these and that of thought. It is by their functional differentiae that the animate grades are distinguished, and these are treated as being inherently hierarchic. Furthermore, while of those grades of life with which we are familiar none has a higher faculty without possession of all below it, this fact is related contingently to their being living things, so that a living thing endowed only with the highest of the faculties that we know can be entertained within this theory as a possibility. Though this possibility is not excluded by the framework of faculties but rather acknowledged now and then by Aristotle, it is one to which he rightly devotes no space in this work. The task of the *De Anima* is to show how nutrition occurs in plants, animals and men, how perception and motivation occur in animals and men but not plants, and how thought occurs in men alone of the species of which we have certain knowledge.

The structure of the work exactly reflects this task. The first Book has upheld the validity of the questions raised by the earlier inquirers into the soul; how, that is, the soul explains the self-movement and the capacity for perception of living things, but has reduced to rubble all their attempts at answers. On the site that has thus been cleared there arise at the start of the second Book the foundations of the Entelechist thesis – the conception of the soul as entelechy is introduced in the most general way. Then, in the second chapter of this Book the range of its application is displayed and, in the third chapter, connected with the natural hierarchy of living things. Now we are ready to pass to the investigation of the various faculties themselves, and it is this that is to occupy all the rest of the work. In Chapter Four of Book II the nutritive faculty is presented, and its operation accounted for according to the central schema of potentiality and realization. Then, at appropriately greater length from Book II, Chapter Five, to Book III, Chapter Two, Aristotle covers the faculty of perception, first in general, in Book II, Chapters Five to Six, and then by a specific investigation of each of the senses in Book II, Chapters Seven to Eleven, then again generally in Book II, Chapter Twelve, to Book III, Chapter Two. It is in the treatment both of the general phenomenon of perception and of the operation of the individual senses that Aristotle's conceptual analysis seems particularly fecund, and retains a permanent philosophical interest, despite its complete eschewal of any investigation of the role of consciousness in perception, and I shall shortly attempt to indicate the course of recent discussion of these two topics. From the analysis of the perceptive faculty, Aristotle passes via that of Imagination in Book III, Chapter Three to that of thought in Book III, Chapters Four to Seven. His remarks on the Imagination have recently been claimed to be more illuminating than they might at first seem, and I shall try to show why this is so. The chapters on thought itself, however, are notoriously opaque. The doctrines they appear to contain, above all that of the Active and Passive Intellects in Chapter Five, are usually now thought to be more or less seriously vitiated by the fact that thinking is the area of psychic activity least amenable to the application of Aristotle's central dichotomy.[39] This, however, in no way reflects the judgement of previous centuries, and I shall attempt by way of a historical sketch of the work's influence to show how Aristotle's few and dark remarks have been the centre of a remarkably long-lived and almost wholly valueless controversy. Chapter Eight of Book III forms a short but interesting appendix to the preceding discussion of perception, imagination and thought, and in Chapters Nine to Eleven, Aristotle moves to the discussion of the motivating capacity of soul. Here the central notion is that of *orexis*, usually translated as desire, and this is interestingly connected by Aristotle throughout the work with the concept of perceptivity. The final two chapters of the work re-affirm its broad teleological thrust, and prepare the way for the transition to the lectures that are to follow the *De Anima* in the general Biology course, and which are known to us under the general label of *Parva Naturalia*. The arrangement of the work is of admirable clarity and lucidity and exactly reflects the intellectual progression, which is that of a systematic explication of the complex notion of soul expounded in Book II, Chapters One and Two.

The *De Anima* cannot be denied the merits of sound architecture, nor those of originality as the first discussion of the conceptual foundations of Biology. I have attempted to outline the central conception of the soul that the work offers, and I shall try later to show how this does and does not connect with modern interests in this area. Historically, the most influential part of the work has undoubtedly been the discussion of thinking, especially in view of the possible connection between the Aristotelian doctrine of the active and passive intellects and belief in the possibility of the survival by the human soul of bodily death. It is a com-

monplace now to remark on the sterility, absurdity or tri-
viality of this discussion, and, acquiescing in this judgement,
I shall seek to point morals for our own attitudes to this
work. But apart from the two areas of the general conception
of the soul and the interpretation of the account of the
Intellect, the *De Anima* offers thoughts on other features of
the soul's activity. Of these, three, the treatment of perception, of imagination and of desire, advance theses of interest
in their own right. I shall now try to indicate the tenor of
recent discussion of the handling of these in the *De Anima*.

V. Perception, Imagination and Desire

The Perceptive Faculty

That psychic faculty to which by far the most attention is
devoted in the *De Anima* is the faculty of perception, which is
also the subject of the first treatise of the *Parva Naturalia*. It
has been convincingly argued that the accounts given of
sensation and perception in these two works are intended to
be continuous, indeed 'ingressive'. Let us attempt to outline
the general theory of sense-perception launched in the *De
Anima* and completed in the *Parva Naturalia*, and then pass
to survey recent modern commentary. A much fuller
treatment than can be offered here can be found in Ross's
admirable accounts of the Aristotelian psychological theory
in his edition of the *De Anima* and his general work on
Aristotle.

What then is Aristotle's general theory of sense-perception
and how are the five senses, the three remote senses of sight,
hearing and smell, and the two contact senses of touch and
taste, related to it? As we have seen, Aristotle devotes
altogether ten chapters of the work to the discussion of the
perceptive faculty of the soul. Of these, five deal each with
one of the individual or, as Aristotle calls them, special,
senses, and the remaining five with the capacity for sensation
and perception in general. These are much freer from
outmoded physiological assumptions than those on the

special senses and have usually been found of greater philosophical interest. However, it is by no means certain that
they offer a doctrine that is entirely clear or entirely consistent.

Professor Hamlyn[40] has interpreted Aristotle's general
doctrine of sense given in the *De Anima* as passing through a
transition between two positions, whose latent mutual in-
compatibility is only perhaps half realized by Aristotle and
never expressly acknowledged by him. Readers of Professor
Hamlyn's writings on this subject will not fail to recognize
my debt to him in what follows. The first chapter, then, to
deal with perception in general, Chapter Five of Book II,
presents an account of the sense faculty that is wholly consistent with the general doctrine of the soul. For sense-
perception is here being presented as an alteration (*alloiosis*)
of the sense faculty such that that which senses becomes like
that which is sensed, having previously been unlike it. Since
the psychic faculty of perception (*aesthesis*) is the Form of the
perceptive body as such, the alteration of the Form must be
correlated with the alteration of the Matter, the body, that
is, as perceptive, and thus an external object of perception is
required to excite the original alteration. It is thus that sense-
perception is necessarily of an external object in the way that
thought is not. Now the alteration that constitutes an act of
sensation can be represented as the transition from a state of
potential similarity with the object to one of actual similarity,
and thus Aristotle can apply to the act of sensation as previously to the process of nutrition the notion of the realization
of potentiality. This realization, the transition from potential
to actual similarity with the sense-object by the sense-organ
and the sense faculty, is one instance of the transition from
the first to the second entelechy of the body which is the
transition from the animal capable of the functions of life to
that actually performing them. This transition is, however,
not merely a simple one from potentiality to realization, but
involves an intervening stage, which Aristotle calls a *hexis*
(from which our 'habit' is derived) and the consequent
complicating of the stages in which animal Matter is brought
to the performance of the life functions requires an extended

digression on the sequence of *dynamis–hexis–energeia*. This ties
the account here given into the general metaphysics but
reinforces our impression that what is peculiar to sense-
perception may not be being caught. In any case Aristotle
clearly intends not only that the alteration account of sense-
perception here being given will sit well with the general
account of the soul, but also that it will provide a very
characteristic solution to one of the traditional problems for
Greek thought in this area, the question whether sense-
perception is of like by like or of unlike by unlike. The
tendency, as we see clearly in Aristotle's criticism of his
predecessors in the first Book, was to assume that like perceives like – but Aristotle prepares the way in Chapter Five
of that Book for his eventual demonstration in Chapter
Twelve of this Book that perception is in one way of like by
like and in another of unlike by unlike, as that which perceives moves from a state of actual dissimilarity from that
which is perceived to a state of actual similarity. This issue
may well seem empty to us as neither of its terms is readily
intelligible within our conception of sense-perception, but
Aristotle, with his usual sensitivity to his own place in the
history of Greek thought, is obviously proud to have reconciled a longstanding dispute. In any case it was no doubt
his concentration on this question that prevented him from
seeing a point, the overlooking of which Hamlyn has shown
seriously to diminish the value of the theory of sense-
perception given in the work as a whole.[41] This point is one
partly obscured for Aristotle by a peculiarity of Greek
language. To arrive at conceptual clarity in connection with
our use of the senses to gain information about the world, it
is important to stress the distinction between an act of sensation and one of perception. The former of these two can no
doubt with some justice be represented as the mere alteration
of a part of the body to bring it in some way into greater
similarity with what is being sensed. But the latter is a more
complex notion and on any account must be acknowledged
to be closer to an act of judgement. Now this contrast is in a
way present in Aristotle's account, as we shall see, in that
while here he concentrates on the treatment of *aesthesis* as an

alteration, he will later concentrate rather on its being a mean, an aspect that is far more redolent of its affinities with judgement. The problem, of course, is that Aristotle fails to realize that these two mutually incompatible accounts of what for him is the single activity of *aesthesis* should in fact be directed at the two distinct activities of sensation and perception. It is the change of interest as between the two sides of this bogusly holistic concept that accounts for what Hamlyn calls the transitional character of the account of *aesthesis* in general. It must also be said that while either of the two concepts in effect here being discussed could be so treated as to connect with the general problem of consciousness, Aristotle shows no explicit awareness of this possibility, though there are indeed occasional remarks which it is tempting to construe in the light of this problem. We must, however, resist the temptation to take these isolated remarks as indications of Aristotelian awareness of the difficulties of consciousness or of the need to give any account of them within the scope of the present work. In a familiar way, the problem is obscured for Aristotle by the fact that the same word *aesthesis*, which as we have seen is capable of bearing the meanings both of sensation and of perception, is also the nearest Aristotelian expression to the post-Cartesian concept of consciousness. I shall, however, say something later about attempts to impute to Aristotle a modern notion of consciousness or something like it.

Having given his first broad sketch of the general notion of *aesthesis*, a sketch which we have seen to suit far better its sense as 'sensation' than as 'perception', Aristotle goes on to draw distinctions of kind within the notion of *aesthesis* which interestingly connect with certain modern distinctions. In the very short sixth chapter, a tripartite division of the objects of sense is introduced. Sense-objects we are told are such either in themselves or incidentally, and of the first group some are directly perceived each by one special sense and some are perceived by at least two. We thus have special sense-objects, such as a sight-object, that are the object of one sense only but are the direct object of that sense, common sense-objects, such as motion and size, that are equally available to several sense-organs but only non-essentially, and incidental sense-objects, such as a white object's being a certain man, which are incidental properties of the special sense-objects. Now in his discussion of the special senses, Aristotle is to tell us that the special sense-object of sight is colour, that of hearing sound, and so it will turn out that Aristotle's class of special sense-objects will more or less corres- pond to Locke's secondary qualities, and his class of common sense-objects more or less to Locke's primary qualities. Aristotle, however, goes beyond Locke in saying that it is of the special sense-objects that the sense is never or very seldom deceived. That Aristotle should have come to this view has recently been explained by Block [42] in terms of his general teleological approach. Block argues that Aristotle would have felt that the perception of the special sense-objects would be least open (for Aristotle) to error, just as in an act of direct sensation of a special sense-object we are exercising an organ in its most natural way, we are performing with it that which is its true function. If it is *for* this that the organ was designed by nature, then how could it be that in the exercise of it, unless in exceptional circumstances, we could be any- thing other than successful perceivers? The comparison that Block draws between this interpretation and the Cartesian notion that the validity of our sense-perception is under- written by the impossibility that God could have allowed our senses to be deliberately misleading, seems quite justified. We must, I think, accept Block's account of the immunity to error of the perception of the special sense-objects, as we must also accept his repudiation of any attempt to construe Aristotle's account of such perception in terms of the incor- rigible perception of immediate sense-data. It is external objects and their properties that are here the objects of sense, whether this is special or common. As to the distinction between things perceived in themselves and things perceived incidentally, it is perhaps right to see here as elsewhere in the account of *aesthesis* a reaching out towards the modern dis- tinction between sensation and perception. What Aristotle classes as incidental sensation it is unlikely, indeed, that we would want to class as mere sensation at all.

79

From these two general introductory chapters on sensation, Aristotle passes to the treatment of each of the five senses in order. Here we see even more clearly than in the general discussion the physiological emphasis of the thinking. Of those remarks that occur in the discussion of sense and that suggest an awareness of the problematic character of consciousness, almost none occur in the treatment of the special senses. Rather we have considerable discussion of such matters as the functioning of air and water as the media for sight and sound, and, broadly speaking, all such investigations have that vulnerability to the progress of physiology in the modern period to which the more strictly conceptual analysis of the bulk of the *De Anima* is immune. I have, however, attempted to draw attention in the notes to points of special interest. Between the discussion of touch, the last of the special senses, and the conclusion of the whole discussion of sense-perception, come three chapters which renew the general treatment of *aesthesis*, with, as we shall see, what appear to be at least changes in emphasis and are perhaps real changes in doctrine. In effect, the whole sense-perception section of the *De Anima* consists of two chapters on sensation in general, followed by five chapters on the particular senses, followed by three chapters on perception. This structure, however, is obscured in the text itself by the ambiguity to which attention has already been drawn in the meaning of the term *aesthesis*. It is certain at least that the last two chapters of this section (Book III, Chapters One and Two), which are surely best seen as a discussion of perception, are where the problem of consciousness looms largest in the entire work. The chapter which precedes them introduces the new idea that perception is the reception of the Form of the percept without its Matter. This idea seems promisingly subtle and is capable of being drawn out in various more or less sophisticated ways. Yet it is not at once obvious how it is to be reconciled with the original presentation of *aesthesis* as an alteration in both organ and sense, nor does Aristotle acknowledge our need for illumination. In one way, this new idea is retrogressive in that it seems less, not more, promising as a way of showing why the effect of a sense-object should be different on a perceptive and on a non-perceptive thing. This is indeed the problem that Aristotle passes to at the end of the chapter, taking the example of smell. Insofar as an answer is provided it is that the distinction between the reaction of the sentient and the non-sentient in their exposure to smell can be marked by the word *aesthesis*. The natural temptation to take that word in this context to mean 'consciousness' has been too strong for many, but in fact to do so is to read into the whole account an underlying supposition which, had it been present at all, could surely not have been left tacit in the way required and then brought in only as a kind of fleeting *deus ex machina* when a puzzle has proved intractable without it. In fact the last sentence of the chapter merely begs the question that it is intended to answer and gives us no grounds for imputing to Aristotle either a full awareness of the question itself or latent sympathy with any of the various ways of dealing with it that have been proposed in modern times.[43]

More important matters are broached in the chapters that, in the traditional arrangement, are the first two of Book III. The first of these begins, indeed, with an extraordinary argument designed to establish the necessity of our having the senses we do and no more. This seems no more than a curiosity and I attempt to deal with it *ad loc*. However, we soon move on to important further details about the perception of the common sense-objects that have been introduced to us in Chapter Six of Book II. The point Aristotle is here making has been much misunderstood and is worth a brief elucidation. We are told first that there can be no special perception of the common sense-objects and a little later that we have *aesthesis koine*, or common awareness, of these. These remarks have been taken to show the presence, otherwise unattestable, in the *De Anima* of the common sense faculty familiar from the *Parva Naturalia*. However, it is an unnecessary and in fact incorrect step to move from the admission by Aristotle of common sense-objects which cannot of course be denied to the supposition that we here allow a common sense faculty whereby we perceive these. Rather the point that Aristotle is making is that the perception of the common sense-objects is necessarily not the business of any one sense, special or not, and must be cast firmly within the framework of the incidental operation of the special senses, by at least two of which any common object must be perceived. Neither here nor in the discussion of the integration of the senses in the next chapter is the subsequently presented, though not therefore necessarily subsequently evolved, doctrine of common sense foreshadowed.

It is, however, to the concluding chapter of the discussion of sense-perception (Book III, Chapter Two) that we must now turn. The structure of this chapter is perversely rambling but it devotes itself to three clear tasks. They are (i) explaining how it is that we see that we see, (ii) showing how in a way it is right and in a way wrong to say that there is no sounding without hearing and so forth, and (iii) showing how it is that we are aware of which sense we are using in any given instance. Of these three problems (ii) is that which Aristotle treats in a way least illuminating for those with modern interests, but here, as with the question of whether perception was of like by like or of unlike by unlike, Aristotle conceived himself as playing a historical role in reconciling a long-standing dispute within the tradition of thought about these matters. Questions (i) and (iii) on the other hand have certainly excited a considerable amount of modern attention and this is hardly surprising. For it is in treating these two puzzles that Aristotle comes nearest of all the places in the *De Anima* to examining something approximating to the traditional problems of philosophy from the first-person perspective such as they have presented themselves in the post-Cartesian era. The most illuminating recent treatment of them is that of Kahn, who seeks to locate them within the course of what he analyses to be a continuous and ingressively developing treatment of the whole area of sensation, perception and awareness that runs through the lecture course partly comprised by the *De Anima* and the *Parva Naturalia*. Kahn concludes that the central notion of *aesthesis* here presented, with its capacity both to perceive perception, as it were, and to discriminate as between senses, is as near as Aristotle comes to the Cartesian concept of consciousness.

But he rightly stresses that Aristotle is still a great way from Descartes. Overwhelmingly the most important feature of the Cartesian treatment of consciousness is the stress laid on subjectivity. It was Descartes' stupendous achievement to have located the first-person perspective on the world as the centre of philosophical interest.[44] The centrality, from our point of view, of the debate thereby excited, which has taken such a fascinating turn in our own century, should not blind us to its complete unimportance for all the predecessors of Descartes except for, and in a rather different way, Plato and his followers.

Certainly Aristotle's flirtation with the problems of subjectivity, the first person, the self, the personality and all the related modern 'conceptual baggage' is hardly more than chilly, and the fact that subjectivity is not introduced here where above all it seems to be required is a sure indication that Aristotle does not consider it to fall within the scope of a theory of the soul. Given this eschewal, what is remarkable is the degree of coherence that he does manage to produce in his answer to these two puzzles, which must inevitably arise and yet are undeniably an embarrassment for one who seeks, like Aristotle, to give a purely physiological account of sense-perception.

Aristotle's treatment of sense-perception in the *De Anima* is an excellent example of the proneness of philosophical fecundity to triumph over system in his work. The price to be paid is an account that is disjointed in itself and moves progressively away from the originally close correlation it had received with the central doctrine of soul. The safest course is to look on it, with Professor Hamlyn, as a theory in transition.

The Imagination in the De Anima

We have seen how Aristotle's discussion of the concept of *aisthesis* is bedevilled, from our point of view, by the Protean character of that concept. Some of Aristotle's remarks seem to fit our notion of sensation, others that of perception and others again that of consciousness, though this last connection is, as we have seen, considerably weaker than the other two, because of the complete unawareness shown by Aristotle of the need to treat the problem of subjectivity within the general handling of the soul. Unfortunately, a similar vagueness affects the Aristotelian concept of *phantasia*, whose standard translation is 'imagination'. Here, however, it is much less clear that reflection on mental activity subsequent to Aristotle has yielded a satisfactory and coherent system of concepts. The imagination has certainly been a central topic of modern philosophy of mind, but from this it cannot be concluded that all those who have used the term or its nearest equivalent in other languages have been discussing quite the same thing. We are dealing with a 'family-concept', a congeries of notions with an assortment of mutual etymological and conceptual interconnections, and the family is neither a small nor an intimate one. It is thus possible to argue, with Schofield, that the incoherencies of Aristotle's account of *phantasia* in the *De Anima* are fertile for modern interests in this area and that the contours of his treatment reflect the terrain to be mapped by modern inquirers. I shall try, following Schofield, to exhibit the tensions in the Aristotelian account and then to show how the problem they reflect, that of uniting this concept, is one shared by the most important modern work, and indeed that it is in this area above all that the *De Anima* retains a practical utility for theorists of the mind.

The treatment of the subject of *phantasia* in the *De Anima* occurs in one chapter only, Book III, Chapter Three, and although *phantasia* is certainly mentioned in important contexts elsewhere in the work and beyond, yet it is in this chapter that Aristotle engages in the conceptual geography that is perhaps his most important contribution to the subject. The general account given here, then, is characterized by a tension between two latently distinct concepts, each of which is treated at different points of the chapter. What are the poles of this tension?

In the first half of the chapter (up to 428a1) Aristotle seems to be concentrating his thought on *phantasia* as an interpretative mental act in connection with perception. This is, of course, one familiar role for the concept. But it must be stressed that Aristotle's notion of the interpretative faculty connected with perception has none of the breadth of the conception of imagination in the Anglo-German Idealist tradition after Kant. It is certainly closer to the notion involved in Scruton's remark that 'imagination involves thought which is unasserted, and hence goes beyond what is believed'.[45] Relatively modest then as the interpretative conception of *phantasia* is, it nonetheless contrasts with the conception concentrated on by Aristotle in the second half of this chapter. For from 428a1 onwards he has within his sights another approach to imagination that has certainly found favour with some modern thinkers but which seems to lead inevitably to rather a different conception. This is the notion that imagination for us or *phantasia* for Aristotle should properly denote not a wide general faculty for the interpretation of the data of sense-perception but a specific faculty that we possess to produce in our minds imagery related to, but not identical with, that of the sense. There is clearly a strong temptation to take Aristotle in the second part of the chapter to be equating the notions of *phantasia* and that of the production of mental imagery. If this is so, however, it is seriously underacknowledged in the text. We have, indeed, a situation not dissimilar to that with sense-perception. There Aristotle, under the single heading of *aesthesis*, wandered in his treatment from the topic of sensation to that of perception and from that to the topic of awareness or consciousness. Here, under the single heading of *phantasia*, he wanders from the treatment of the interpretation of sense-perception to that of the production of mental imagery. In both cases, two legitimate subjects of philosophical study are under consideration but their related separateness is not acknowledged by Aristotle. In the case of *aesthesis*, this, as we have seen, has sometimes led to the mistaken ascription to Aristotle of a modern conception of consciousness. Are we then to conclude that in the case of *phantasia*, too, Aristotle has again produced a discussion too cryptically rambling to be helpful for our investigations? Or is there in this case either better justification for the rambling approach or some connecting theme?

Schofield[46] argues that the chapter exhibits both these features.

Reflection on the range of phenomena Aristotle assigns to *phantasia* and on the way he introduces them into his argument suggests a rather different physiognomy for the concept from that conveyed by 'imagination'. Aristotle seems to be concerned with a capacity for having what I shall compendiously call non-paradigmatic sensory experiences – experiences so diverse as dreams and the interpreting of indistinct or puzzling sense-data, which may be held to resemble the paradigm of successful sense-perception one way or another, yet patently lack one or more of its central features, and so give rise to the sceptical, cautious or non-committal *phainetai*.

The mention of the Greek word *phainetai* indicates the key, as Schofield sees it, to the interpretation of this chapter. Its connection with the abstract noun *phantasia* is of course much closer than is the case with the corresponding pair in English, 'seems' and 'imagination', and Aristotle suggests strongly at one point that we would be right to turn to the impersonal verb for the introduction to his concept. For one central use of *phainetai* in Greek is to give a hesitant or uncertain judgement, to indicate the existence of some grounds for the belief in a proposition but grounds that fall short of adequacy for full belief. The character of these grounds, their source and presentation, and their proximity or remoteness to what might license belief itself in their circumstances, will of course be varied, and this variety in the lexical behaviour of the verb will determine the range of the concept that, as it were, grows out of it. It is this etymological core that allows Aristotle to make his transition without apparently noticing even the danger of inconsistency from the notion of *phantasia* as interpretation to the notion of *phantasia*, as the production of mental imagery. For both these activities of *phantasia*, as presented by Aristotle, come under the scope of the central concept of that in virtue of which we give restricted assent to propositional claims.

Under Schofield's interpretation, Aristotle's chapter, far from being merely a muddled treatment of a difficult area where our greatly enhanced conceptual vocabulary has allowed us to bring a measure of order – a remark that would not be perhaps entirely unfair in application to the treatment of sense-perception for all its incidental merits – offers in fact an Andromeda's thread in a labyrinth where we too are immured. The Aristotelian concept of *phantasia* seems, because of its connection with the verb *phainetai*, in principle more capable of unification than our notion of imagination. If this is so it is not impossible that Aristotle could be used as a starting-point for the task of clarifying a major area of uncertainty in the philosophy of mind. For the untidiness of our conceptual framework for the imagination and its congeners is a scandal to analytic philosophy. In the words of Strawson, 'a perspicuous and thorough survey of the area is, as far as I know, something that does not exist'.[47]

Desire

After the treatment of perception and imagination, Aristotle passes to the topic of the intellect. So great is the amount of perverse ingenuity that has been devoted to the exegesis of his opaque remarks on intellect that I shall attempt a brief historical essay on the course of the debate. Before that, however, a few words must be said about the only remaining faculty of the soul examined in the *De Anima*. This is the motivation faculty, the need to account for which Aristotle has inherited from his predecessors, as he makes clear in Book I. His discussion of motivation is to be found in Chapters Nine to Eleven of Book III.

One of the more striking comments in Book I is the suggestion that Democritus' purely materialistic account of the soul's initiation of movement failed to do justice to its rational character. Here Aristotle seems to be very close to our modern recognition that the difficulty of the explanation of human spontaneous motion in particular, and perhaps that of animals in general, is that such motion seems to deserve the name of 'action'. The spelling out of this concept is not uncontroversial, but one thing that would seem to be integral to it is the notion that such movements are intentional, that they are done with some purpose in mind. Difficult as the explanation of human behaviour is on the assumption that it is intentional, there are notorious difficulties involved in supposing to the contrary, and if Aristotle has indeed, as the remark quoted from Book I suggests, realized the need to incorporate an elucidation of intentionality into any account of human action then he has certainly taken an important step forward. Furthermore, there is another passage where it seems that this modern analysis really is not far from Aristotle's thoughts. At 403a29f., he gives a much quoted indication of the relative spheres of operation of the dialectical and natural philosophers in connection with the affections of the soul: 'But the natural philosopher and the dialectician would give a different definition of each of the affections, for instance in answer to the question "What is anger?" For the dialectician will say that it is desire for revenge or something like that, while the natural philosopher will say that it is a boiling of the blood and hot stuff around the heart. And of these one will be expounding the Matter, the other the Form and rationale.'

Now this has caught the eye of recent commentators, as it seems to show an awareness of the need to account for states of mind such as anger both in the framework of a physiological system of explanation and in the quite different and probably irreducible framework of mental terms. This, together with the remark about Democritus, whets our appetite for a two-tier account of motivation. Yet, as Hamlyn remarks *ad loc.*, when we reach the appropriate section of Book III, we do not find anything of this kind.

How does Aristotle come to waste such promise? In the first place, we should resist the temptation to exaggerate the original promise. As Sorabji[48] has pointed out, the explanatory power of the parallel definitions of anger is diminished by the fact that the definition put into the mouth of the dialectician uses as the definiens another *pathos* or affection of the soul. Thus the dialectician will only be offering an account of anger that is not trivially reducible to the physiological account of his natural philosopher colleague if the salient term of his definition, *orexis* (desire), is more than a purely physiological term. The same can be said of the remark at Democritus' expense. It is preceded by the gibe that his account of psychic motivation has no more subtlety than that of the comic poet who makes the statue of Athena move by pouring into her a particularly fluid substance. In reality motions of animals must occur through some kind of thought and choice. But what Aristotle is stressing here is surely not so much the distinction between an account innocent of non-physiological terms and one dependent on them at least in part, but that between a more and a less sophisticated physiological account. The status even of thought (*noesis*) and certainly of choice (*prohaeresis*) is not beyond doubt. Aristotle would be surprised to be told that in this offhand remark he was committing himself to an entire explicative framework supplementary to, and not convertible into, his otherwise all-embracing physiological story.

Such an interpretation of the remarks on desire in Book I certainly makes them more easily compatible with the official treatment of Book III, Chapters Nine to Eleven. For this is a thoroughgoing exercise in physiological concept-analysis. It is preliminary to the detailed treatment of the problem of motivation in the *De Motu Animalium*. On the account here being offered, Hamlyn has the following to say:

> Aristotle's account of animal and human movement is vitiated by a failure to make a proper distinction between action or behaviour and the bodily movement which a physiologist might be concerned with. In consequence, for a great deal of the time he appears to be looking for the *causes* of movement, without making clear whether this is action or mere bodily movement. At other times he seems to be looking for the factors which will be necessary in any proper account of behaviour, and to be asking what psychological faculties are presupposed. But he also runs the two kinds of account together on occasion, so that the faculties in question appear to function as agencies of some kind. It is in general, however, the causal account that is uppermost in Aristotle's mind, and there is no doubt that his thinking on the matter is relatively crude.[49]

Here again, then, as with perception we see a failure by Aristotle to realize the full difficulty of integrating accounts of mental life, in this case of the origination of movement, that are couched in mentalistic terms into accounts phrased

quite physiologically. Yet it would be unreasonable to com-
plain of the failure of Aristotle to grasp a problem that has
only become a major philosophical concern in the modern
era. Rather we should admire the way that his inherently
aporetic approach leads him to confront those aspects of the
problem that are not most easily brought under the general
umbrella of his physiological account.

In any case, although no more here than anywhere else
does Aristotle show how the Form–Matter dichotomy,
central to his theory of the soul, can treat the problems of
consciousness which are what such a theory must deal with
for us, yet the notion of Form is by no means otiose within
the broader biological context in which the work should
properly be seen. To say that the notion of desire gives the
Form which, when put together with the Matter of boiling
hot material around the heart, yields anger is not to essay a
point in what we call the philosophy of mind. Rather it is to
show how, within a purely physiological context, natural
teleology can be evoked to account for a complex animal
function.[50] Unfortunately, however, even this more
authentically Aristotelian point is not really developed in
the course of the discussion of motivation in the *De Anima*.[51]
Sorabji has ingeniously suggested how the explication of the
formal and final causation of desire which is alluded to in the
De Anima might be extracted from discussions of motivation
in the *Metaphysics* and the *Nicomachean Ethics*. His reconstruction is in many ways convincing and may indeed
reflect the true course of Aristotle's thoughts, but the
temptation must be resisted to accredit the *De Anima* with
too great adequacy in answering the questions it raises itself,
and in the area of motivation and desire we should be content
to conclude that no view is offered in this work of the degree
of subtlety and system that characterizes the treatment of
the practical syllogism in the *Ethics*.

VI. Intellect

We have seen that Aristotle's account of sense-perception

can justly be called 'transitional', progressing as it does from a treatment of *aesthesis* in terms of the affection of the aesthetic faculty by an external object; (such treatment seems to bring the meaning closer to that of sensation than to that of perception) to a treatment of the same concept as a critical faculty, by virtue of its operation as a mean, which seems to align it rather with perception. We have seen, too, how Aristotle is seeking to establish a symmetry in his account of the various faculties of soul, such that the same conceptual apparatus can in different applications explain all the various psychic functions. These two tendencies combine in an unfortunate way in the treatment of the intellect. For Aristotle's account is manifestly open to the charge of attempting too great an assimilation of thinking to perception and especially to seeing. This would in itself diminish the possible interest for us of the account of the intellect to be found in these pages. But things are made worse by the fact that the aspect of the treatment of sense-perception with which Aristotle chooses to align his account of the intellect is the intrinsically less promising one, for us, of the treatment of *aesthesis* as a form of affection. In the circumstances it is to Aristotle's credit that he does not allow the unpromising simplicity of his schematic approach to thought to obscure certain real problems which are at least noticed. Of these the most interesting is the question whether thought is primarily of individual concepts or of judgements. Aristotle touches on this point in Chapter Seven of Book III, the third and easily the most interesting of the three chapters devoted to the topic of the intellect in the third Book. However, it cannot really be said that he arrives at any very clear answer to the problem and his remarks remain suggestive rather than programmatic. Many of the suggestions in this section, like much in the entire work, were moulded by Thomas Aquinas into a substantial new theory of the mind and soul in the thirteenth century, and Aquinas' ideas on this subject are certainly treated with respect by contemporary philosophers.[52] However, great as Thomas' debt is to the Stagirite, a cursory reading of both thinkers' disquisitions on the intellect will probably prompt the conclusion that Thomas can be credited with marked originality in producing an interpretation of Aristotle that achieves a far greater degree of system than anything in the text of the *De Anima*. Indeed, as far as the operations of the intellect are concerned, it would not be outrageous to rate Thomas' originality above that of the Stagirite – this of course without prejudice to the question whether the approach they have in common is likely in general to facilitate or obstruct the growth of conceptual clarity in this area.

I do not, therefore, propose to examine in detail the Aristotelian doctrine of the intellect, in terms of how it might be exploited today to shed light on its subject. It can now, I think, be considered a museum piece. This, however, is by no means the universal opinion of those who, through the centuries, have pored over this work. The history of the influence of the *De Anima* amongst those cultures whose general philosophical tone can be called Aristotelian – that is to say later Antiquity, the Arab world and Medieval Scholasticism – has indeed been very great, perhaps exceeded by no other single text except the logical and metaphysical writings. And of all the aspects of the work and of the theory of Entelechism, none, with the exception of the general entelechist conception of the soul itself, has been more fertile in controversy than the doctrine of the intellect. Thus to disparage the Aristotelian doctrine of the intellect, as presented in the *De Anima*, as most competent judges would wish to do today, is by implication to impute to the traditional discussions of the *De Anima* a certain missing of the point.[53] I think it is legitimate to accuse much of this tradition of inanity, and I think it is not contingently so. The concentration of later commentators and exegetes on the doctrine of the intellect in the *De Anima* was in no way fortuitous. All these later commentators had in common a curious circumstance. This is that they lived in ages in which philosophical discussion of all kinds was either permeated or wholly dominated by Aristotelianism, and yet in which the theological climate laid great emphasis on a article of faith not easily reconciled with the entelechist theory of the soul. This of course was the belief in the personal survival of the human soul after death. Evidently the view that the soul is but the Form of the body, if not flatly incompatible with any notion of disembodied survival, yet certainly militates strongly against it. Thus Aristotelians living in ages whose religious faith centred on the belief in the personal immortality of the human soul faced a major quandary. There was, however, one clear possible escape route. This lay through that part of the soul's functioning that is consistently treated by Aristotle in the *De Anima* as not wholly fitting into the general entelechist scheme. This of course is the intellect, and Aristotle's pious expositors felt that it would be here if anywhere that a link could be found between Aristotle and the requirements of theology. Their task, they must have felt, was made very much easier by the opaque but suggestive remarks that Aristotle makes in the short but very dense Chapter Five of Book III. This chapter has not without reason been called one of the hardest in Aristotle and it is certainly one of the most discussed.[54] In it Aristotle draws a distinction between an active and a passive intellect. I have sought to elucidate elsewhere[55] what he may have in mind by this, but on any account the passive intellect seems to embrace those aspects of thinking which in men seem most connected with mortality and the active intellect to embrace the remainder. The active intellect, then, seemed to offer the key to the retention within an Aristotelian framework of a doctrine of personal immortality. It was in the light of this possibility that the discussion proceeded.

I shall attempt very summarily to sketch the history of this now antiquated debate.[56] In doing so, I hope to indicate the general historical importance of the work – to do more would be, as Aristotle might say, for another discussion – but further I hope to point a moral. The whole protracted discussion of the doctrine of active intellect and the possibility of personal survival, which exercised some of the greatest minds from late Antiquity to the Renaissance, can now be seen, as I have said, to be empty of real philosophical substance. More importantly, however, we can object to this debate not that it was by our lights unphilosophical but that it was by anyone's lights unAristotelian. Aristotle himself was not directly concerned with the possibility of the survival of death by the human soul, and this issue makes no impact whatever on the *De Anima*. To scrutinize the work, therefore, for hints it might offer to a controversy to which its author was not party, and which he might indeed not fully have understood, can surely be characterized as perversity, and we need not be surprised if such an approach leads rather to rhetoric than to insight. Yet, as I shall try to show, the habit of trying to adapt Aristotle to disputes that are quite foreign to the philosophical problematic of fourth-century Greece by no means ceased with the waning of Scholasticism. Rather, as I shall also try to show, it is alive and well, and continues to obscure the real lessons that the Aristotelian writings on the soul have to offer us.

In surveying the history of the controversy excited by the doctrine of the active intellect, I shall confine myself, in the interests of tractability, to the major names. Of these the first is undoubtedly Theophrastus. He was Aristotle's successor as Scholarch of the Lyceum and, in addition to some original work of his own, seems to have been the first of a long line of expounders of the obscurities in the Aristotelian dogmata. Unfortunately, his critical work has survived only in fragments, but even from these we can conclude that many of the problems that were later to surround the treatment of the intellect by Aristotle were first expressly brought to light by Theophrastus and his colleagues. It was almost certainly they who added to the concepts of the active and passive intellects the notions of the mind in potentiality and the mind in actuality, which were destined to prove the foundation of an impressive scholastic edifice. It was perhaps also first at the time of Theophrastus that a connection was made, as it is not explicitly made by Aristotle himself, between the treatment of the intellect in the third Book of the *De Anima* and the discussions in two other important and influential Aristotelian passages. In the second Book of the *De Generatione Animalium*,[57] perhaps the last part of the lecture course of which, as we have seen, the *De Anima* may have formed the beginning, Aristotle advances his celebrated view that in conception the female contributes the matter of the future composite, and the male contributes the soul. The question arises whether even that part of the soul in virtue of which thought occurs enters the appropriate matter in this way and at this time. Aristotle significantly denies this and coins a phrase to describe the separate entry of the intellective soul, that was destined to have a long and perverse history. The phrase was *nous thurathen*, or 'intellect from without', and in view of the subsequent uses of the expression by some Aristotelians it is important to note its original introduction here in a context specifically connected with reproduction. It may well have been Theophrastus who first noticed the possibility of the adaptation of this phrase to the general psychological theory of the *De Anima*. The other Aristotelian passage that may also have first been collated with the *De Anima* at this time was the account of the divine intellect in the last section of *Metaphysics* Lambda.[58] In that notoriously vexed but undeniably important work, probably originally written by Aristotle as a separate treatise, the idea is introduced that the Supreme Being is perpetually engaged in an activity that Aristotle calls *noesis noeseos*, which on the surface appears to mean 'thinking of, i.e. about, thinking'. For various reasons, however, it seems more satisfactory to take the phrase to mean something like 'self-creating thinking'.[59] In any case, the implication is tantalizingly latent in the corpus as we have it that this *noesis noeseos* either is the same thing as, or is in some mysterious way closely linked with, the active intellect of the *De Anima* and the *nous thurathen* of the *De Generatione Animalium*. It is possible that the temptation to make the connection explicit was too strong for Theophrastus and his contemporaries, and certain that the religious significance of such a possibility was not lost on later ages. Thus, even though our evidence for Theophrastus' interpretation of the *De Anima* is fragmentary, it is interesting that even at this early stage it seems quite probable that most of the susbequently important problems had at least been formulated.

As is well known, from the death of Theophrastus at the end of the fourth century B.C. to the date somewhere in the middle of the first century when Andronicus brought out his great edition,[60] Aristotle's philosophical influence was minimal, no doubt not least because of the sheer unavailability of copies of his esoteric works. Even after Andronicus, the severity of the treatises prevented their exercising great influence until the neo-Platonic revival had got firmly under way and had, in effect, prepared the philosophical world for them. The cardinal figure in the general revival of Aristotelianism is the great commentator[61] Alexander of Aphrodisias, who lived around the turn of the second and third centuries A.D. His commentaries and original works were important both for the immediate impetus they gave to the study of the Stagirite and for their lasting effect on the interpretation of his doctrines by late Antiquity and by the Arab world. Unfortunately, Alexander himself lived in a neo-Platonic world and this seems to have affected his interpretation of a number of points of Aristotelian doctrine. This certainly applies to his handling of the doctrines of the intellect. In Alexander, as in some of his predecessors, the two-tier intellect of Aristotle has acquired a new level; instead of the dichotomy of active and passive mind, we are confronted with a passive mind such as we acquire at birth, an active mind which somehow enters us from without and a mind disposed to think which is what the active mind turns the passive, potential or material mind into. Of these three, it is clearly only the active intellect for which immortality is to be claimed, but Alexander, at least in his own *De Anima* if not in the later *De Intellectu*, seems to be suggesting that by thinking by the active intellect we somehow come to participate in its immortality.[62] If this was Alexander's view, it would have the important consequence that his conception of the immortality of the soul is not that of a personal immortality. Indeed, it was just for this reason that the interpretation he offered had relatively little historical influence, even at times when his general stock as an exegete was high.

The evolution of the treatment of the Aristotelian intellect towards the role of substitute, within the entelechist framework, for the Platonic immortal soul had, then, even by the time of Alexander, proceeded a considerable way. There was, however, to be further advance even among the Greek

schools before Justinian's closure of these institutions in A.D.
529. The primary importance of Alexander is as the first and
greatest of the commentators on the works of Aristotle, and
the tradition of commentary or paraphrase continued right
into the Scholastic era. Of Aristotle's paraphrasts the most
important that we have for the *De Anima* is the fourth-century
thinker Themistius. As a paraphrast he seldom feels entitled
to extensive digression from his text, but in the case of the
intellect he makes an exception. In this area his treatment
has affinities with that of Alexander but also interesting and
important divergences. In common with Alexander is his
tripartite conception of the mind, and as with Alexander it is
the active intellect that sets the merely potential mind into
its operative disposition. But in considering the mind
disposed to operate, Themistius, as against Alexander, argues
that this mind is individual and that its individuality pertains
to it in virtue of the fact that the active mind that puts it into
its operative disposition is the specific Form of the individual.[63] Thus Themistius' construal of the immortality of
the soul is noticeably closer to the notion of personal survival
that was becoming a theological requirement for philosophers in the fourth century. Already as between these two
late Greek exegetes we can see developing the polarity of
debate that was to characterize discussion of the active
intellect in the Middle East and in Europe down to the time
of Thomas.

As all educated people are aware, the descent of Greek
philosophical ideas to medieval Europe was through the
Arabs first of Abassid Baghdad and then of Ummayad Spain,
and through the Jewish philosophers of Toledo. Moreover, it
would be platitudinous to remark that these thinkers have
an importance of their own, quite independent of their historical connection with Latin Scholasticism. Profound as is the
influence of Aristotle over this whole age, space permits here
only the consideration of two great thinkers, Avicenna and
Averroes. Avicenna (980–1037) is most distinguished by his
colossal *Canon of Medicine*, but his adaption of all aspects of
Aristotelianism to the conditions and assumptions of his time
was second only to this in his life's work.[64] On the questions

of the soul and the intellect, he shows considerable debts to the exegetes of the past, but, no doubt through awareness of the precarious position of Greek studies in the Muslim world of his day, he is prudent to stress those aspects that are least likely to be a scandal to the faithful. He, like Themistius, was concerned to maintain the individual immortality of the soul, and he retained, though with some modifications, the tripartite arrangement of potential, dispositional and active soul that we have found both in Alexander and in Themistius. He advances on Themistius, however, in suggesting that the individuating feature of the composite intellect – the intellect in disposition – is connected with the body not the active intellect, and must therefore be made good on the death of the body. The question of how exactly this is to come about he evidently considers to fall within the scope of theology, not philosophy. Perhaps the most interesting feature of Avicenna's psychology is the progress it marks towards putting the nature of the intellect, not that of the soul as widely construed by Aristotle, at the centre of the debate about man's incorporeal or supracorporeal nature. In a later era, and at the Western end of the Arab world, Averroes (1126–98) was markedly bolder than his predecessors in emphasizing the true tendency of Aristotle's doctrine of the intellect. Availing himself of the more liberal climate of twelfth-century Cordoba, he took issue with Avicenna on the question of the personal survival of the soul after death. This, he thought, must be impossible. For the participation of the divine active intellect with the human potential intellect cannot yield a composite that is itself capable of immortality. Rather our participation in immortality is confined only to the presence in us of the active intellect itself. This alone will be preserved of us after our deaths, personal awareness of all kinds being for Averroes strictly dependent on the body and so coeval with it. We thus see that the issue as between Averroes and Avicenna is essentially that between Alexander and Themistius, though interestingly the order of evolution in the two cases was different. There is of course between the two pairs of thinkers the difference that the Arabians pretend not merely to the exegesis of Aristotle but to the establishment of the truth. Yet, it seems not unreasonable that the distinction between these two tasks was held to be in practice very much smaller both in late Antiquity and in the Arab era than it is now. Furthermore, we shall see the same polarity of debate on the intellect within the same Aristotelian framework flourish in thirteenth-century Paris. Indeed, it is Averroes who forms the direct link here.

The rise of Aristotelianism in Christian Europe from being, in the early twelfth century, the subject of repeated pontifical interdictions to being, in the mid-fourteenth century, the core of the examination syllabus at the University of Paris, is one of the great revolutions in intellectual history. It is well known that the man who, more than any other, contrived to render Aristotle respectable was Thomas Aquinas (1225–74). Opinions differ on the originality of Aquinas' system as against that of Aristotle, but it is not my task to adjudicate this difficult question. For present purposes we should remark that there were two issues above all that impeded the progress of Aristotelianism. One of these was the question of the eternity of the world, an issue that nicely focused the contrary tendencies of the Scriptures and Hellenic reason, but which lies beyond the scope of the immediate inquiry. The other was just that at which we have been looking, the question of the immortality of the individual soul. Now the immediate entry of Aristotelianism into France and England at this time was across the Pyrenees, and thus the psychological theory of Aristotle was encountered by the Scholastics very largely in the form in which it was presented by Averroes. As we have seen, his interpretation militated against the assumption of personal survival. It was just this interpretation of the Stagirite that played into the hands of the Augustinians opposing the new doctrine, and the Averroist interpretation was consistently frowned on by the Catholic Church. Although towards the end of the thirteenth century there did eventually emerge an Averroist School, Averroists excused their heterodox opinions as being no more than contributions to the unoffending activity of the exegesis of Aristotle, as contributions in effect to Classical scholarship without pretensions to establish truths that might rival the conventional wisdom of the age. Nonetheless, although the Averroist interpretation of Aristotelian doctrine on the soul and the intellect might thus be tolerated as a sideshow, it could hardly hope in this way to gain the centre of the stage. Thomas, however, conceived it as his life's work to accommodate the teachings of the Stagirite to Catholic orthodoxy, and for him therefore no flippantly Averroistic interpretation of the soul and intellect was possible. Rather, working from the Latin translation of the *De Anima* produced by William of Moerbeke,[65] he evolved the latest and most sophisticated of those interpretations of the entelechist thesis that seek to render it compatible with the personal survival of the individual soul. But Thomas is more ambitious than his predecessors and seeks to secure survival, not merely of the intellectual soul, but of the whole soul, so that his discussion does not hinge on a new interpretation of the doctrine of the active and the passive intellects, but on a reconstrual of the general doctrine of the soul and its substantiality. This evidently falls outside the scope of the immediate topic, though it suggests, what indeed might already have become apparent, that the remarks on the intellect are in themselves too diffuse and inchoate to bear any firm doctrine one way or another on the question of the possible survival of the soul, whether individually or not.

I hope that this extremely brief sketch will at least have suggested that the intensive study that the *De Anima* received in the millennium between Alexander of Aphrodisias and Thomas Aquinas was largely vitiated by being so much preoccupied with a question of only secondary interest to Aristotle. What I now hope to establish is that this tendency persists in a different form right into contemporary discussions of Aristotle's theory. Whereas the central question to medieval philosophy of mind in Europe was that of the nature of the soul's immortality, the central question in the philosophy of mind since Descartes has been that of accounting for our personal, subjective view on the world. It is the question of how the phenomena of consciousness, which seem somehow to be internal to ourselves, are to be reconciled to our general scientific conception of the external world that has most preoccupied philosophers since Descartes. As is well known, since the 'linguistic turn' in philosophy around the beginning of the twentieth century, interesting new lines of approach to these difficult questions have emerged.[66] However, it is my contention that Aristotle is not conversant with the problems of consciousness as they have struck post-Cartesian thinkers, and that attempts to invoke his authority to settle questions of this kind one way or the other are equally inappropriate.

Modern philosophers of mind divide mostly into two broad camps, that of the Phenomenologists and that of the Physicalists. I intend to look at the use made of Aristotle by a representative of each of these groups and try to show why that use is tendentious. I shall begin by looking at a thinker who has many claims to be considered the father of the modern Phenomenological school, Franz Brentano.

VII. Entelechism in the Modern Debate

Brentano

Franz Brentano (1838–1917) is now considered one of the most important philosophers of his era, even though his thinking is in many ways antagonistic to that tradition that has come, above all through Wittgenstein and Ryle, to dominate the Philosophy of Mind in the twentieth-century English-speaking world.[67] The reason for Brentano's importance is that he was the first to evolve a conceptual apparatus which seemed, and still does seem to many, to offer the possibility of an independent description of the content of mental experience, a description not parasitic on our descriptions of the reality with which that experience purports to be correlated. This is a hotly controversial matter, and the possibility of such a description has yet to be definitively vindicated or repudiated, but the criteria on which the legitimacy of such a description must be determined are of a conceptual subtlety far removed from anything familiar to

Aristotle in the area of mental philosophy. Yet Brentano, in introducing his conception of the hallmarks of the content of experience, presented these as being already present, if only latently, in the Aristotelian view. In doing so he was, as I shall try to show, guilty of pressing Aristotle into the role of witness in a dispute which was beyond his ken.

Two publications of Brentano are relevant to this inquiry, *Die Psychologie des Aristoteles* (1867) and *Psychologie vom empirischen Standpunkt* (1874).[68] The second of these is perhaps Brentano's most important book and in it he introduces his most important single idea. This is the concept somewhat opaquely labelled 'intentional inexistence' which Brentano conceives as a feature of mental as opposed to physical items. In saying that the objects of the mind have intentional inexistence, Brentano means that mental phenomena are directed on to an external world but their objects have no actual existence themselves within that world. This subtle conception greatly influenced the thought of Brentano's two greatest pupils, Edmund Husserl and Alexius Meinong, and through them it continues to play a role in the current controversy over the possibility of a pure Phenomenology. However, as we have seen, the validity of the claim that mental phenomena are characterized by intentional inexistence is one that must be settled on grounds a long way from anything within Aristotle's conceptual scheme. Yet in the first of the two books mentioned, Brentano, who was in general an exceptionally acute commentator on Aristotle, went so far as to see in the *De Anima* itself at least the embryo of his own theory. He adduced three reasons for holding that Aristotle already subscribed in effect to the intentional inexistence theory. All the reasons alleged connect with the treatment of the perceptive faculty, though we might concede to Brentano that if they could be upheld for sense-perception then they could also be upheld, under Aristotle's theory, for intellection. Brentano's first reason for ascribing his own theory to Aristotle, then, was that the Stagirite at various points describes sensation as the reception by the organ of sense of the Form but not the Matter of the object of sense. This, Brentano argued, corresponded to the distinction that he himself was drawing between the real existence of the external object itself and its merely intentional existence, its existence only as directed on to the external world not as in it, in the mental phenomenon. Secondly, he took as a further hint Aristotle's remark that sensation is not an ordinary affection of the sense-organ. Thirdly, Brentano pointed to Aristotle's claim that the actualization of the object of sense coincides with the actualization of the sense faculty within the subject.

Of these three arguments, the first two obviously hang closely together, and the refutation of the first will suffice for them both. The first is, however, if not easily refuted, at least easily exposed as being foreign to the general spirit of Aristotle's psychology. I owe this point entirely to Sorabji.[69] It is his claim that Brentano is making an unwarranted assumption in supposing that, when Aristotle says that an act of sensation is constituted by the reception by the sense-organ of the Form but not the Matter of the sense-object, he must be construed as claiming that the act of sensation is not something that occurs exclusively in the physical, material world. It is quite possible to construe Aristotle's remarks in a purely physiological way and without any implication of the sort of 'world' in which Brentano's inexistence phenomena could occur. There is no good reason to doubt that when Aristotle held that the sense-organ takes on the Form but not the Matter of the sense-object he meant anything other than that the eye, in seeing a green object, itself becomes green. As Sorabji has shown, hostility to this interpretation usually rests on a misconstrual of Aristotle's physiological jargon that makes it seem absurd. In the physiological account of sense-perception it is the *kore* of the eye that acquires the formal but not the material properties of the object. If this word is taken to mean 'pupil', then, the interpretation is demonstrably not only false but absurd. If, however, it is taken to mean the 'jelly' or liquid within the eye-ball, then the interpretation is one that would have to await the rise of modern medical techniques for refutation. Thus it is quite arbitrary for Brentano to hold that, by saying that in perception the Form but not the Matter is received, Aristotle

must have meant that something other than a purely physiological process is involved. Here it is obvious that too much is
being read into the Aristotelian text.

Brentano is being similarly high-handed in his treatment
of the third ground that he adduces for seeing Aristotle as a
precursor of his own view. On the surface, the claim in the
De Anima that in an act of sensation the sense-object is
actualized in the subject may look strikingly similar to the
claim by Brentano that in an act of sensing the mental
phenomenon exists in the individual and not in the world.
But, as Sorabji[70] again points out, Aristotle stresses that
while in actuality the sense-object exists in the subject, it
exists in potentiality outside in the world. It cannot, then, be
a hallmark of the sense-object as such, as Brentano needs it
to be, that it exists only in the individual. To be sure, the
interpretation of the Aristotelian doctrine is by no means
easy, and perhaps no commentator has yet been able to
make full sense of it. But that circumstance cannot be taken
to license the reading into the text of ideas drawn from quite
a different stage in the development of philosophical reflection.

It is interesting, then, that close study of the *De Anima*
should have led Brentano to his undeniably important but
clearly quite original discovery – and it is perhaps worth
remarking that Aristotle might well be the only philosopher
to whom a man who had made so original an innovation
might wish to ascribe his discovery – but none of this bears
out Brentano's historical claim that Aristotle 'got there first'.
Furthermore, the obvious penalty of misascription is that it
tends to hinder the extraction from texts written like the *De
Anima* within remote conceptual frameworks of insights to
which unfamiliarity might blind us.

I have argued that Aristotle's approach to the soul is quite
different from that of the post-Cartesian era. The problem of
integrating personal consciousness, and the first-personal
perspective, into our general view of the world does not loom
large in the *De Anima*, or indeed anywhere else in Aristotle's
work, or the entire extant body of ancient philosophical
writing. With the exception of Brentano, it seems to me

that the post-Cartesian tradition has respected this fact. Frequent reference to the *De Anima* is not to be found in the works of the Rationalists, Empiricists or Idealists. This is appropriate in that Aristotle's views cannot indeed be brought to support those of the schools mentioned, but regrettable, perhaps, in that Aristotle's approach might have given them pause for thought, and specifically for the thought that the emphasis they laid on the first person might have been misplaced. However, in fact Aristotle's psychology, like most of the theories in the corpus, lay neglected during this period.

In our century, however, the Cartesian problematic has itself come to look, to some at least, old fashioned. The orthodoxy of our day eschews the Cartesian postulation of a mental realm and is intent on the reduction to the physical of the subjects of mental terms. We live in the era of Physicalism, which seeks to construe language about the mind as being only talk of a rather special kind about the body. The ontology of this school is more sternly monistic even than Aristotle's. We have seen that Entelechism equivocates as to the physical nature of the intellect. But for the Physicalist thought gives absolutely no more reason than sensation for the postulation of entities that might be labelled 'mental' and whose correlation with the physical world might be problematic. Thus the conclusions about the world arrived at by the modern Physicalist are indeed much closer to those of Aristotle than they are to those of Leibniz, Hegel or, for that matter, Plato. Thus for the modern Physicalist the temptation is much greater than for his opponents to press Aristotle into service as a lost leader of their tribe. Yet the exercise is illegitimate. For although Aristotle arrives at a similar position to that of the Physicalist, he starts from a very different point and this crucially affects the legitimacy of the parallel. I shall now try to illustrate this claim in the case of a recent and interesting attempt to align Aristotle with a Physicalist explanation of the soul.

The De Anima *and Functionalism*

We have seen how Franz Brentano's attempt to enlist Aristotle's support for his own interesting theory of sense-perception and the mental amounts to an overstretching of the meaning of the text of the *De Anima*. This is made less surprising by the reflection, with which we are familiar, that Aristotle's general approach to the soul is unsympathetic to the postulation of items intended to constitute the content of experience. I will now, however, seek to show that a recent attempt to use Aristotle to lend authority to an exercise in psychological explanation in principle much closer to his thinking, also encounters the objection that Aristotle is being called to witness in a dispute that is beyond his ken, and further that thereby insights of real value that Aristotle can offer are obscured.

Wilkes, in her recent outline of a Functionalist account of the soul, ends by suggesting that the account for which she has been arguing amounts in all essential to the thesis of the *De Anima*.[71] She ends by calling for a return from Cartesian epistemological and ontological dualism to an Aristotelian Functionalist monism. She is indeed swift to concede that this interpretation is not easily to be reconciled with the doctrine of the active and passive intellects as expounded in the *De Anima* Book III, Chapter Five, but this feature she, along with many commentators, regards as an anomalous intrusion into the generally empirical and biological pattern of the work of Aristotle's wholly separable theological, metaphysical and ethical interests.[72] The intrusion was an unhappy one and its notorious obscurity, the source of such a prodigious amount of debate among Aristotle's various theistic opponents and apologists, reflects for Wilkes the philosopher's own half-realization of its inappositeness. If, she claims, we can ignore this, we are left with an account which is in all essentials a direct antecedent of her Physicalism.

Wilkes bases her case on eight points of similarity between Aristotle's view and her own. These merit individual scrutiny. For Wilkes, Aristotle's account of psycho-biological functioning consists in the aligning of certain capacity analyses with certain structure analyses. This she not implausibly sees as being analogous to her own search for a coordination on a systematic basis of the r-terms of her psychological explanation and the x-terms of her physiological one. Her first point of similarity with the Aristotelian view is that in neither system is it required that there be a one to one correlation of capacity and structure, of r and x. This is, I take it, to say, in Aristotelian terms, that the operation of a bodily function of whatever degree of complexity need not depend on the structure of any one bodily part. This claim seems open to attack on two grounds: first, its inherent vagueness, especially as to the delimitation to be applied to the sense of the word 'part', and secondly, as to its extricability from the text of Aristotle. If an r is to be tied neither to a specific x nor to any specifiable group of xs, then we are surely entitled to wonder just what degree of correlation has in fact been achieved. What seems to be lacking from Wilkes' own account, and thus, if she is right, from Aristotle's, is any clear principle for deciding in any given case of either series of explicative term what is to be a natural area, as it were, of description, what is the natural unitary scope to which either term-system should be adjusted. Why should it be, for instance, that the process of vision in the eye should be psychologically simple but physiologically multiple? Or is this an arbitrary whim of our practical everyday psychological theory? It seems to me that this is a question that can much more effectively be urged against Wilkes than against Aristotle.

Wilkes' second point of claimed similarity between her view and Aristotle's is the related one that neither theory is committed to an exhaustive correlation of the psychological and physiological explanations of any given case. 'Aristotle would not count as a relevant identifiable substance within his theory any item of which the form is merely a certain shape or design, rather than something specifying an ability or a function.'[73]

Now it certainly is open to the modern Physicalist to adopt any criterion he likes for the admission of physiological explanata as possible correlanda with psychological explanata – or perhaps this is a little too strong, but in any case there is considerable range for him to manoeuvre in here – but Aristotle is committed to the view that soul is in general the Form of the organic body, not that it is, in some way, selectively so. There can on his view, then, be nothing that admits of a physiological explanation or, in his terminology, is the Matter of the natural body potentially having life, but that it also admits of a psychological explanation. Otherwise it is quite simply unformed Matter, and the admission of this liberally distributed about a composite substance is unthinkable. Indeed, as Ackrill[74] has shown, one of the great problems of the use that Aristotle makes of the Form–Matter distinction in his psychology to explain the function of structures is just that he seems thereby to pre-empt the only conceptual tool that he has for even introducing in his physiology an 'item of which the Form is *merely* a certain shape or design' and which is therefore innocent of psychological significance. Just as no part of the axe can fail to contribute to its being an axe, so can no part of the organic body fail to contribute, in the human case, to its being an ensouled human being.

Wilkes in any case considers these two points to be relatively minor, and apparently uncontroversial. In her third point of comparison, she turns to consider a physiological component that clearly does have psychological significance, the water of which the eye is composed.

If we hope to explain how the eye is capable of seeing, we must look at the constituent material element, water; this, too, is a substance (it has matter and form), and part at least of its form is its capacity to take on any colour. To give this capacity as part of the form of water is to go some way towards showing how it is that the eye sees.

But is it? Evidently, if the eye were composed of non-transparent stuff, precisely by Aristotle's discussion of light, transparency and seeing, and generally by common sense, sight would be impossible. But this is not to come near to explaining why it is – and this is surely the salient point – that the water in the eye sees while that in the ocean, say, does not. Of course both types of water, if that is the right way to put it, are receptive of colour, indeed it is impossible for that which is transparent not to be; but the crucial point surely is that they receive colour in quite different ways – the one by merely becoming coloured the other by being affected in a way that amounts to sensation and perception. Aristotle reveals his grasp of the clear difference here in the discussion of smell in the second Book of the *De Anima*.[75] And obviously, insofar as it is the same water that is both in the eye and in the ocean, no general explanation of the concept of water in itself will help us to elucidate what is peculiar to the water in the eye. It may well be the case that Aristotle does not feel that we are in a position to spell out more fully at all the physiological concept, the watery structure of the eye, to which the psychological concepts of both potential and actual sight relate. If this is so, however, it is mistaken generosity in Wilkes to attribute to him an implicit explication of whose intrinsic improbability he himself gives elsewhere convincing evidence of his grasp. It is uncontroversial that Aristotle does not seek the elucidation of psychological functioning by penetrating physiological analysis; it should be clear that he cannot, and knows it.

Wilkes' fourth point of comparison is just that the Form–Matter dichotomy, in its psychological application, prevents Aristotle from being classed as an identity theorist. Aristotle is indeed not an identity theorist, but this point he surely has in common with a wide range of philosophers of mind and it is not clear in quite what way Wilkes wants us to take this as showing any very *special* affinity between her and Aristotle. (However, she makes one remark on this subject that is worth quoting for its own sake: 'The truth of the matter is that he considers it so obvious that matter and form are categorically distinct, so obvious that they are not to be identified, that at times he simply does not bother to stress their non-identity.')

Wilkes calls her fifth parallel 'particularly important'.

In each account the subject-matter is man *qua* purposively acting agent; each is trying to account for man's most characteristic and most fundamental activities. Aristotle must evidently insist upon this, since for him these capacities for action are precisely those that spell out what it is to be a person. All other capacities of a human being are subordinated to this activity; hence the only interest in *explaining* them lies in the help this would give in explaining rational purposive activity ... Whether the *analysandum* is a person, an animal, or a plant, it is the most characteristic activity, and hence its highest-order capacity, that is to be explained; and everything else is explained in terms of its contribution to that.[76]

Now these claims seem very bold. Wilkes, however, does not support them with a single reference to any Aristotelian text, except a very vague one to the notorious problem of the identification of speculative reason as man's function in the tenth Book of the *Ethics*. Now whatever is to be made of that identification, the interpretation that Wilkes is urging on us for the purely psychological theory – and why not be as strictly scientific about this matter as about the exclusion of the active intellect from relevance? – seems not to be justified by anything that Aristotle says or implies; indeed, it seems to run against the general structure of the *De Anima* and to amount to a misconstrual of the significance of Aristotle's hierarchical arrangement of the psychic faculties.

This is perhaps most clearly seen in the light of the sixth point, which Wilkes rightly considers closely allied to the fifth and which indeed is her real motivation for introducing the intrinsically improbable fifth point in the first place. This sixth point, then, is that Aristotle is like the Physicalist in being more interested in explaining sapience than sentience,[77] and indeed in being only interested in the latter insofar as its explanation is subsumed in that of the former. But this seems a very strange claim to advance on Aristotle's behalf. Consider Kahn's following remark:

The soul must be understood by reference to its specific powers of nutrition, sensation, desire, locomotion, and rational thought. The exposition proper consists of a discussion of these five faculties: the nutritive in II 4; the sensory in II 5–12 and III 1–2; the intellect in III 4–8; the motive and desiderative in III 9–11. Three chapters fall outside this simplified scheme. Omitting them from our reckoning, we see that there are ten chapters in the *De Anima* devoted to sensation, whereas the other three or four faculties together account for only nine. In terms of fullness of treatment there can be no doubt: Aristotle's work on the soul is primarily a treatise on sensation.[78]

Now it is true that the *De Anima* deals with the whole range of sentient life and not just man, and thus can be expected not to concentrate on that faculty that is most characteristically human. But even so there is no suggestion that the perceptive faculty in man is any less autonomous than that in animals, still less that this faculty is a necessary prerequisite for thought. On the contrary, it appears that there may well be various beings superior to men who think but do not feel. What is peculiar about man is that he is an animal that thinks, that is, that he is something that both perceives and thinks, and there is nothing in the *De Anima* to suggest that the former of these, though indeed less special to man, has any less entitlement to explanation in its own right. It is absurd to claim that the *only* interest Aristotle has in explaining perception is the help this gives in explaining rational purposive activity; help, one might add in passing, whose precise character is in any case the subject of very considerable debate.[79]

Wilkes' seventh and eighth points are that Aristotle, by immunity to the Cartesian temptation to deify mental events, sensational or propositional alike, frees himself from the danger of having to admit either the Cartesian mind or the Cartesian body. Here, as with the point against the identity theorists, we must agree with Wilkes. But as also in the case of that point, we may legitimately ask why this assimilates the Aristotelian view especially to Wilkesian Functionalism. Thus, although Aristotle is a direct precursor neither of Descartes nor of the Materialists, the case for assigning him to Wilkes' camp, at least as argued by her, is not convincing.[80]

VIII. Conclusion

Close analysis of the affinities of Aristotle either to the Phenomenology of Brentano or to the Functionalism of Wilkes has revealed the connection to be slender in both cases. This confirms, though it does not indeed prove, the claims advanced at the start of this Introduction that the doctrine offered in the *De Anima* contains insights that it does not share with any other psychological theory, with the qualified exception of Thomism. The prospects for the assimilation of Aristotle to any position in the modern debate have been surveyed expertly by Sorabji, whose conclusion is also that Aristotle's account is *sui generis*. To make this claim for Aristotle does not, of course, imply rejection of two additional criticisms that might be made of the work, that the entelechist case is only of independent philosophical interest if the central Form–Matter dichotomy, on which we have seen it to depend for its significance, can be upheld in the twentieth century, and that in any case Aristotle does not remain loyal to the original structure of his explanation. I do not intend to argue against these objections, as I believe them to be substantially correct. But how seriously they diminish the interest for contemporary inquirers of the *De Anima* is much more open to question. Even someone disposed to reject the thesis of the *De Anima* on the grounds that it borrows all its content from the larger concept of Form, which is to be repudiated as a paradigm figment of bogusly substantial metaphysics, might yet derive from the *De Anima* the insight that the Attribute Theory of the Soul, from which I have argued that the entelechist thesis is distinct, will remain descriptive rather than explanatory until supplemented by some notion that will play the role of the Aristotelian Form, though in a less extravagantly reifying style. From this perspective the merits of Aristotle's thesis are best described as schematic. He offers us an outline of how a middle way might be found between the conception of the soul just as a substance, which now seems unpromising, and the conception of the soul as a set of attributes, which though currently popular is surely open to updated versions of the points scored by Aristotle in the first Book against the Harmony Theory. Even if the outline actually offered should come to seem unpromising, yet the offer itself draws attention to the unsatisfactory character of either pole. We see, most notably, that the history of the philosophy of the soul has by no means been that of a mere alternation between various attribute and various substantialist theories, the latter tending to predominate. This might induce a salutary caution as the contemporary debate moves into the post-Dualist era.

On the other hand, the objection that the actual argumentation of the *De Anima* deserts the structure of account implicit in the initial thesis is of a kind almost out of fashion among Aristotelian scholars. After the explosion of the bogus over-assimilation of the corpus in the first half of this century,[81] and especially in the anti-systematic climate of much Anglo-Saxon philosophizing, the current orthodoxy, almost, is to point to those features of his work that are usually labelled aporetic.[82] These are essentially the features in which we see the triumph of philosophical instinct and integrity over system, of the Socratic over the Platonic legacy. Those who have sought such features in the corpus have been rewarded to a surprisingly large extent. And there is no more happy hunting ground for them than the *De Anima*. In the three most difficult areas – perception, thought and motivation – we see Aristotle resisting firmly the temptation to abide by a programme that is under pressure from the evidence.[83] The consequent inconclusiveness of the accounts may diminish the substantial contribution that the work makes to the totality of valuable reflection on its subject, but it remains an exemplary monument to Aristotle's intellectual honesty. It is intriguing to ponder how different the world would be if the aporetic Aristotle had been as influential as the systematizer.

Barnes has aptly remarked recently that contemporary moral philosophers treat the author of the *Nicomachean Ethics* as a 'brilliant colleague'.[84] It would be audacious to claim the same for the author of the *De Anima*. Yet for all its conceptual simplicity the work remains, as Hamlyn has said,[85] the first systematic attempt to account for all the activities of soul and mind under a single theoretical umbrella. Its successors have indeed been more refined but none has entirely risen to the comprehensive character of the brief, and all are marked by conceptual infelicities of their own. The greater relevance of the *Ethics* to current moral philosophy than of the *De Anima* to current philosophy of life and mind throws light on the respective state of development of those two subjects. We feel that in the harder studies of science and metaphysics we have progressed more rapidly than in the softer subjects of ethics, politics and literary theory. Yet it is perhaps in the study of the soul, the softest area of the hard studies, that this claim is most open to dispute. It is not excessive to suggest that scrutiny of what Aristotle has to say here may serve as a corrective to the illusion of too great advance. Even, however, if we persist in feeling that to the extent that Aristotle's conception of the soul is not an attribute one, to that extent it is an anachronism, yet we may derive profit from the method with which Aristotle approaches his subject. For it is arguable that the most striking peculiarity of his genius was his ability to adapt an initially unpromising conceptual framework to evidence of ascending orders of complexity. This, surely, is notable in the *De Anima*, reflection on whose method might lead us to conclude that, if the Stagirite's status as the master of those who know might long have been open to review, he can now be appreciated properly as the master of those who inquire.

IX. The Translation

The *De Anima* is not characterized by a lack of architecture. From the bombsite of the traditional theories, whose demolition we witness in Book I, there rises in Books II and III the structurally sound if ornamentally wayward edifice of the entelechist thesis. Here, however, we reach the period of the literary merits that Aristotle displays in this text. As mentioned in the *Life of Aristotle*, the treatises are for the most part lecture notes, either Aristotle's own or those of an attentive pupil. Contentious perhaps for some works, this conclusion seems safe for the *De Anima*. It is unlikely that lecture notes in any language can be made to sound much like anything except lecture notes in any other language, but the ease of reproducing clarity might be supposed usually to compensate the translator for the impossibility of generating elegance. In the case, however, of the lectures delivered by the founder of the Lyceum to serious students, this compensation does not readily obtain. The treatises, and conspicuously the *De Anima*, are uncompromisingly 'esoteric'. They make constant unapologizing use of a complicated 'in-house' jargon, and they evidently feel under no obligation to expand points whose brevity, if not content, renders them of dubious intelligibility to the uninitiated. In my opinion, there is no systematic solution to these problems for the translator.[86] It is not, for instance, possible to match Aristotle's jargon case by case with constant English equivalents. I have, however, tried to mitigate for the beginner the repellent effects of jargon by providing a glossary setting out the variants that in my version stand for most of the key Aristotelian terms. The problem of ellipse has been solved pragmatically, within the bounds, I hope, of what seems to me philosophically legitimate interpretative licence.

A more general problem has confronted me in the form of pitch. Traditionally, the *De Anima* has been subjected, like the other treatises, to scrutiny of a closeness that yields only to that reserved for Holy Scriptures.[87] There are certainly passages of the *De Anima* that continue to merit very close verbal examination. To render this possible, however, it is necessary to follow the contours of the Greek text in a manner incompatible with continuous readability for more than short stretches. Alternatively, readability can be achieved only too easily at the price of tendentious amplification. My policy has been to seek a middle way. I have striven to produce a translation that can be read through without intolerable discomfort by the reader who, as yet innocent of the profounder problems of the subject, wishes for a superficial feel, but which will still be found reliable and perhaps even illuminative in places by those whose ruminations on the text must be more strictly tied to the *ipsissima verba*. If I have erred in favour of the latter group, I hope it will be allowed that the nature of the work makes this the more permissible lapse.

I have prefaced each chapter with brief introductory remarks. They do not aim to be more than an indication of the core of the subject-matter in the ensuing section. If inexperienced readers find them occasionally illuminating, I shall be consoled for their striking the specialist consistently as epexegetically empty.

The text followed throughout has been that of Ross, though I have occasionally adopted suggestions of Hamlyn. These I discuss in the notes.

GLOSSARY

The Glossary, without any pretensions to being comprehensive, attempts to survey the most important meanings attached by the translation to the central terms of Aristotle's general explanatory jargon as well as those whose use is peculiar to his psychology. It is thus advisable that the reader unfamiliar with Aristotelian jargon preface his reading with a general inspection of the Glossary, which its brevity is intended to make feasible.

account, formula, ratio: *logos*. This is the hardest single word for the Aristotelian translator. The reason is that it is used by Aristotle, who does not here differ sharply from general Greek practice, both to denote the account that an inquirer might want to give of a particular thing and the principle of arrangement really responsible for that thing's being as it is, which the account merely reproduces, as it were, in the verbal mode. There is of course no modern English term that can play these two roles consistently, though sometimes the words 'formula' and 'ratio' or even 'rationale' can be used to catch this real sense. The position is not made any easier by the fact that *logos* can also have the very wide sense of 'reason' in general.

actuality, employment: *energeia*. This literally means a 'putting into use', an 'employment', but is often translated as 'actuality'. It usually contrasts with *dunamis* (capacity) or some cognate word, and is close in sense to *entelecheia*.

affection, emotion, property: *pathos*. This can be translated in a wide variety of ways, ranging from 'property' to 'emotion'. The essential feature of the sense of the term is that it must denote something that is done to the thing of which it is predicated, not something that that thing does.

appetite: *epithumia*. This is Aristotle's basic word for irrational craving, as distinct from *orexis* (desire) which can be both rational and irrational.

being, essence, substance: *ousia*. The translation of this word is crucial to the proper understanding of Aristotle's whole conception of the soul. It is conventionally translated 'substance', but it has a much wider sense in Aristotle's metaphysics than this would suggest. It is thus possible on the surface to ignore Aristotle's explicit claim that the soul is an *ousia*, and insist that he holds a non-substantialist view of the soul. I have tried in the Introduction to assess the merits of this interpretation.

belief, opinion: *doxa*. This word means an established opinion either of the Platonic tradition or of more general thought, but also sometimes 'belief' as such as opposed to other mental states, such as those involved in imagination.

capacity, faculty, potentiality: *dunamis*. This term, coupled with one or other of the terms for actualization, is a key part of Aristotle's explicative method and constantly deployed in the *De Anima* both to explain the general relation of body and soul and to elucidate particular psychological and biological processes.

cause: *aition*. This is the main Greek word for 'cause' and plays a large role in Aristotelian science. Aristotle holds that there are four causes for any thing or event: a final cause which constitutes its end, a formal cause which gives its terminus of development, an efficient cause which sets in motion the process that produces it and a material cause which constitutes the matter of which it is made.

consciousness, perception, sensation: *aesthesis*. This is a word of wide meaning both in Greek in general and for Aristotle. It encompasses the sense of the three modern terms 'sensation', 'perception' and 'consciousness', though it is only to a very etiolated sense of the latter that it corresponds. It can also mean a particular sense, or even loosely the sense-organ.

desire: *orexis*. This word is conventionally translated 'desire' and is of wider sense than *epithumia* (appetite) in that it can as equally easily mean rational as irrational motivation. It emerges as the key to Aristotle's general conception, as here presented, of animal movement.

difference: *diaphora*. This is either the difference between two things or the properties of one thing in virtue of which it can be distinguished from other members of the same species.

division: *diairesis*. This is a division either conceptually of some inherently complex subject-matter or physically of a complex item, such as the dissected insects discussed in the first Book. Division was an important part of Aristotelian logical method, as before it had been for Plato in his latest phase.

element: *stoicheion*. It is from the elements that the particular objects of science are composed. This term is surprisingly wide in application, indicating equally easily material and non-material items.

emotion: see under 'affection'.

employment: see under 'actuality'.

entelechy: *entelecheia*. This word is used much more frequently in the *De Anima* than in any other treatise. Its literal meaning is something like 'intrinsic possession of end', and seems to have struck Aristotle as especially appropriate for the description of the soul. It is, as noted, close in sense to *energeia* (actuality).

essence: see under 'being'.

faculty: see under 'capacity'.

first principle: *arche*. This is the first principle or starting-point from which an inquiry or an ordered series of entities stems. It is a central idea of the scientific system of the *Posterior Analytics* that the grasp of the *arche* is in each case the first step to the mastery of a whole subject.

form: *eidos*. This is another central Aristotelian term. It has two main meanings: on the one hand, in the sense in which it is usually translated 'form', it means the principle of organization of a thing which leads it to have its particular existence: on the other, in the sense that is usually translated 'species', it means a sub-group of a genus or kind.

formula: see under 'account'.

function: *ergon*. This is another Platonic word adapted by Aristotle to mean 'function' in a rather theoretically non-committal sense.

genus: *genos*. This is a word for a type or kind of thing, but it would be overtranslating to render it 'class' or 'group'.

imagination: *phantasia*. This term, standardly translated 'imagination', combines all the difficulties of that concept with peculiar ones derived from its extensive use in Aristotle's biology in connection with motivation.

intellect: *nous*. Apart from a few uses in the first Book when he is criticizing Anaxagoras, Aristotle uses this term not to denote a wide Cartesian concept of the mind as a general abode for the entire content of experience but much more narrowly to mean the intellective capacity. Sometimes in this work, and more notably in the *Ethics*, it seems almost to be best to translate the word as 'intuition', the capacity for unreasoned grasp of the first principles of science.

intellection: *noesis*, *dianoia*. This is the process of intellection, the entertainment or utilization of a concept.

kind: see under 'genus'.

knowledge: *episteme*. This is a word that Aristotle inherited already invested with significance by Plato. He, however, most often, at least in this work, uses it in distinction from the more active state of *theoria*.

movement, process: *kinesis*. The literal meaning of this word is 'movement' and it is often right to translate it so, but it has a much wider sense for Aristotle, denoting a process in general, sometimes distinguished from an *energia* in having an end outside itself.

nature: *physis*. This is a complex term, usually translated as 'nature' whose many uses and ramifications Aristotle investigates in the first two Books of the *Physics*.

object: *antikeimenon*. This is the object of a sense or thought, which for Aristotle is partly definitive of that faculty.

opinion: see under 'belief'.

perception: see under 'consciousness'.

potentiality: see under 'capacity'.

process: see under 'movement'.

property: see under 'affection'.

puzzle: *aporia*. This is the standard word for any puzzle or general incongruity between a doctrine and either the evidence or common sense or both.

ratio: see under 'account'.

sensation: see under 'consciousness'.

separation: *chorismos*. This important theoretical concept is usually rendered as 'separation' and it can be either of a conceptual or of a physical kind. Aristotle draws in his general system deep consequences from a thing's being or not being separable in either of these ways.

soul: *psyche*. A Greek word conventionally translated 'soul', ideally, but impossibly, rendered 'principle of animation'.

species: see under 'form'.

state: *hexis*. This is the ancestor of the modern word 'habit'. It is used by Aristotle to mark an intermediary state between mere potentiality and actuality. Its use in the treatment of the soul is made clear in Book Two, Chapter Three.

subject: *hupokeimenon*. This word has more than one technical sense for Aristotle. It can mean both a logical subject of predication, or, more controversially it must be said, a mere substrate, perhaps to be identified with matter itself.

substance: see under 'being'.

ON THE SOUL

BOOK I

The Traditional Background

Chapter One: The Scope of the Work

Aristotle opens the work by setting the study of the soul in its scientific context. It merits our attention for the accuracy of which it is suscep- tible, which it has in common with the general study of the sub-lunary world, and for the superior value of its object, which it shares, for instance, with the study of the stars. Indeed, it enjoys a key position within the whole study of reality (aletheia) *and especially within that of the province nature* (physis), *as soul stands in the position of principle* (arche) *of all living things. These opening remarks make clear the general meta-biological standpoint of the work.*

Aristotle then passes to a preliminary discussion of how the soul is to be fitted into the general conceptual and taxonomic framework of the Categories *and the* Posterior Analytics. *It is here that the ques- tion of the soul's substantiality is first raised. It is to be answered in a clear affirmative at the opening of the second Book. Connected with the task of conceptually locating the soul is the need to uphold or repudiate its purported unity. This comes under strain, if, in a way that Aristotle rightly implies to be new, we avoid the temptation to think in effect only of the human soul. If the soul does indeed turn out not to be a single thing – and at this stage Aristotle leaves the question firmly open – we must try to find the differentiating criteria either for the parts of a single soul or for the species of a genus.[1] In any case, the event- ual definition of soul must be such that the attributes and the sub- stance* (ousia) *are mutually illuminative. This is clearly a feature that Aristotle holds to distinguish his own account from that of his predecessors.*

In the second part of this opening chapter, Aristotle passes to the pathe *of the soul. This word admits of a vexatiously wide range of possible translations. It can mean, widely, 'properties', more narrowly, 'passive properties', or, most narrowly, 'emotions'.[2] The standard translation of* pathe, *here adopted, is 'affections', in the sense of those things that something undergoes, the things that are done to it, as opposed to the things that it does. Aristotle's general position is that these* pathe *are features common to both body and soul, and his illustration of this doctrine with the case of anger has recently been thought to bring him close to modern physicalist accounts of mental states. Even here, however, it should be noted that Aristotle suggests that the general account of the* pathe *may not cover the problematic case of thinking. It is this general account, however, that leads to a digression on the relative competences of the sciences which comes towards the end of this chapter. Finally, in a difficult sentence, Aristotle restates his claim that the* pathe *of the soul are inseparable affections common to both body and soul.*

Chapter One

402a Supposing that knowledge is one of the things that is fine and valuable, and one kind rather so than another either for its accuracy or by its being of better or more wonderful things, on both these grounds we would be right to place the inquiry into the soul among the first kinds of knowledge. But knowledge of the soul is also held to make a great contribution to the complete understanding of the truth and especially towards that of nature. For the soul is, so to speak, the first principle of living things. We seek to contemplate and know its nature and substance and then the things that are accidental to it. Of these some are held to be affections peculiar to the soul itself, others belong to the animal as well in virtue of the soul. In general, and in all ways, it is one of the hardest of things to gain any conviction about the soul.

Now, since the inquiry is one that is common to many other subjects as well – the inquiry, that is, about substance and what a thing is – perhaps someone might think that there is some one method for application to all subjects whose substance we wish to know, similar to the demonstration of individual accidental characteristics, so that it would be this method that we would have to seek out. But if there is not some single common method for the investigation of particulars, then putting our inquiry into practice becomes still more difficult. For we will have to grasp in each case what the method of inquiry is to be. But even if it is clear whether our method is to be demonstration or division or some other, there remain many problems and confusions as to the starting-points of the inquiry. For the starting-points of different subjects are different, for instance those of numbers and plane figures.

But perhaps it is necessary first to distinguish in which of the kinds it is and what it is, that is to say whether it is a particular and substance, or a quantity or quality or some other of the categories that we have distinguished, and again whether it is one of the things that are in potentiality or rather some actuality. For this makes no little difference. *402b* We must also consider whether or not it is with parts, and whether or not every soul is of the same character; and if not, whether they differ in species or in genus. For at the moment those who talk or inquire about the soul seem to consider only the human case. But we must be very careful not to overlook the question whether there is a single account to be given of soul, as that of an animal in general, or a different one to be given in each case, for instance those of the horse, dog, man and god, there being either no such thing as the animal in general or only in a secondary way. In the latter case the situation would be the same as for any other common predicate. But further, if there are not so much many kinds as many parts of the soul, then we must decide whether we should first investigate the soul as a whole or its parts. But with these too it is hard to determine which of them are by nature different from each other. And it is hard to know whether we should investigate the parts of the soul first or their functions, for instance thinking first or the intellect, perceiving first or the perceptive faculty, and so with all the other parts and functions. But if it is the functions that we should look at first, someone might again question whether it is the objects of these functions that we should first look into, for instance the object of perception before the perceptive faculty and the object of thought before the intellect. But it would seem that not only is knowledge of what a thing is useful for the contemplation of the causes of those things that are attributes of the substances – just as in mathematics, knowledge of what the straight and the curved are, or the line and plane figure, are useful for seeing to how many right angles the angles of a triangle are equal – but conversely knowledge of the attributes contributes a great deal to knowledge of what the particular is. For when we can give a demonstration, in accordance with the appearance of the attributes, either all or most, then will we also be in the best position to talk about the substance in question. What a thing is is the starting-point for any demonstration. Thus all those definitions from which we do not get to know the accidental 403a properties of the thing, and in fact not even to guess easily about them, are obviously all given quite vacuously as mere debating points.

The affections of the soul also present a difficulty. It is unclear whether all these are shared also with the ensouled thing or whether some one of them is peculiar to the soul itself. This we must decide, but it is not easy. It seems indeed to be the case that with most affections the soul undergoes or produces none of them without the body – being angry, for instance, hoping, desiring and perceiving in general. But thinking particularly is like a peculiar affection of the soul. If, however, this too turns out either to be imagination or to be impossible without imagination, then not even this would admit of occurring without body. But if there is some one of the functions or affections of the soul that is peculiar to it, then the soul would admit of being separable, whereas if there is not one that is peculiar to it, it will not be separable, but there will be a parallel with the way in which a straight line has, in virtue of its straightness, many attributes, such as that of touching a bronze sphere at only one point, while the straightness itself, if separated, would not so touch the sphere. For straightness is inseparable if indeed it is impossible without a body. But in the case of the soul too it seems that all its affections are of it with body, as anger, mildness, fear, pity, hope and even joy and loving and hating. For in all these cases the body is affected in some way. A clear indication of this is the fact that sometimes when strong and marked afflictions occur men are not at all exasperated or cowed, while they are on occasion moved by small and slight sufferings, when the body is in a state of rage and in the same physical condition as when the man is angry. But there is an even clearer sign in that when nothing frightening at all happens men find themselves among the affections characteristic of one who is afraid. But if this is the case, it is clear that the affections are formulae in matter. Definitions, therefore, of the affections will be of the following kind: 'Anger is a kind of movement of a body of the given kind or of a part or capacity of such a body because of one thing and for the sake of another.' Thus it is already within the province of the natural philosopher to have a theory about the soul, either quite generally or about the given kind of soul. But the natural philosopher and the dialectician would give a different definition of each of the affections, for instance in answer to the question 'What is anger?' For the dialectician will say that it is a desire for revenge or something like that, while the natural philosopher will say that it is a boiling of the blood and hot stuff about the heart. And of these the one will *403b* be expounding the matter, the other the form and rationale. For the rationale of the thing is indeed the one given, but it is necessary that this be in matter of the appropriate kind if it is to occur. It is the same as is the case with a house; the rationale will be something like 'A covering preventative of destruction by wind, rain and sun'. But while one philosopher will say that the house is composed of stones, bricks and beams, another will say that it is the form in these things for the given purposes. Who, then, is the natural philosopher among these? Is he the one who defines the house in terms of its matter and knows nothing of its rationale, or the one who defines it only in terms of its rationale? Or is he rather the one who defines it on the basis of both? In which case how should we label each of the other two? Or is it rather that it is the province of no philosopher to treat exclusively either of those affections of the matter in question that are inseparable or of the others insofar as they are so, but that the natural philosopher treats of all the functions and affections of the appropriate body and matter, while someone else treats of all things that are not of this kind, in some cases, it may be, a craftsman, such as a carpenter or doctor, but in the case of those things that are inseparable but which are treated as the affections of no particular kind of body, but in abstraction, it is the mathematician, while in that of those treated as actually separated it is the first philosopher?[3] But we must return to where we left the argument. We were saying, then, that the affections of the soul, insofar at least as they are such things as anger and fear, are in this way inseparable from the natural matter of living things, rather than inseparable only in the way that a line or surface are.

Chapter Two: Some Earlier Theories

It is characteristic of Aristotle to preface the exposition of his own view on a subject with a survey of the positions of his predecessors.[4] So he does here, opening with the remark that all have been agreed that the things with soul are distinguished from those without it by two capacities, that of instigating movement and that of sense-perception. Starting from this common ground, philosophers have arrived at various theories, which Aristotle here presents, mainly without comment, and in a slightly confusing order. A feature of all the views mentioned that at once strikes a modern reader is that they are all what can broadly be labelled 'substantialist accounts'; that is, accounts that seek to explain the special capacities attributed to the soul in terms of its composition from some appropriate substance. Since all the substances here mentioned, with perhaps one exception, are material, the views can all be called 'materially substantialist', as opposed to the positions of Plato and Descartes, and, more shadowily, the Pythagoreans. These thinkers, while agreeing that the soul is a substance, have felt that its properties could only be explained by supposing it to be none of the material substances, nor any compound of them, but rather a substance of a non-material kind, such as is usually dubbed 'spiritual'. It is significant that Aristotle does not draw attention to this fact, however obliquely, given that, as we shall see, there is a temptation to ascribe to him the first full-blooded non-substantialist account of the soul. The first views discussed are those of the atomists Democritus and the earlier Leucippus. They held that the atomic composition of the soul was the same as that of fire, and that it was in virtue of this fact that the soul was productive of movement in the animal. Tantalizingly, Aristotle connects this idea with two schools of thought within Pythagoreanism, but without giving us either position in any detail. Anaxagoras is also credited with the view that the soul is the source of movement, but in his case no attempt is made to explain this in terms of the material composition of the soul. With this exception, however, these theories are all materially substantialist. They take the soul's capacity to produce movement as that which is chiefly to be explained, and simply explain it by supposing that the soul is the most mobile substance. Aristotle then turns to those theories whose target is the other main traditional feature of the soul, its responsibility for perception. The theories considered all assume that perception is of like by like. This thought combines the reasonable idea that perception must occur in virtue of some common feature of both object and subject with the much less evident claim that the common feature must be their material composition.[5] Aristotle has little difficulty in raising serious doubts about the second part of the assumption later in this Book. Here, however, the universal assent to the assumption by all the thinkers considered means that these theories too are materially substantialist, with the exception of the difficult view put forward in Plato's Timaeus *and in Aristotle's own early work* On Philosophy. *The* Timaeus *tries to account for the phenomena associated with the soul in terms of numbers and their properties. Interest in the magical or mystical properties of numbers had been inherited by the Academy from the Pythagoreans, and is perhaps the area of Academic thought least attractive to modern readers and indeed least attractive to Aristotle. Although he may have dabbled in number theories himself in his youth and although he is respectful to the* Timaeus, *Aristotle reveals his contempt for this approach in his treatment of the theory of Xenocrates, third head of the Academy, that the soul is a moving number.[6] In this chapter, he includes the* Timaeus *view amongst those that aim to explain the soul as a producer of perception.[7] He is not, however, trying to be very consistently systematic, as he returns rather confusingly to the theories of Democritus and Anaxagoras, which are at least in part aimed at the explanation of the soul's production of movement. He then gives without much comment a very heterogeneous list of the other views that have been put forward. It is interesting that he does not remark on the rather different character of Alcmaeon's view of the soul. It is fairly clear that he considers the Atomists and Academicians his real rivals among the theorists here referred to by name or otherwise, and it is interesting that he does not introduce the Harmony Theory at this stage.*[8]

Nor is consistency greatly helped when Aristotle announces at 405b11–12 that the fundamental features of the soul are not in fact two but three, the third, in addition to those of movement and perception, being that of 'bodilessness' (to asomaton). This term is suggestive and might prompt the supposition that Aristotle is about to consider views that are either not materially substantialist or not substantialist at all. This supposition, however, is disappointed, as asomaton turns out to mean little more than 'particularly fine-grained' for which Aristotle already has a word, leptomeres. *In any case, at the end of the chapter he concentrates on the close connection between the thought that the soul is material and the thought that perception is of like by like, and, consistently, takes Anaxagoras to task for supposing the mind to be unaffected* (apathes) *and thus excluding the only explanation of its cognition that Aristotle here considers, its affection by its like in external objects. The concluding etymological remarks are a fair sample of Aristotle's usually unhappy excursions into this science.*

Chapter Two

Now in our investigation of the soul, if we are in doubt about those things of which we should gain clear knowledge as we proceed, it is necessary that we collate the opinions of as many of our predecessors as have given a view about the soul with the aim of adopting all sensible proposals and of guarding against anything that may have been not so sensibly suggested. And the beginning of the inquiry is to put forward the most widely held beliefs as to what pertains to the soul by its nature. Well then, that which is ensouled is held to be different from that which is unsouled above all in two ways, in producing movement and in perceiving. These two are pretty much the things that we have received from earlier thinkers as main characteristics of the soul. For some hold that especially and primarily the soul is that which

produces movement. And thinking that what is not itself
moved does not admit of moving something else, they have
supposed the soul to be one of those things that is moved. On
this basis Democritus asserted it to be a kind of fire and hot
stuff. Given an unlimited range of atomic shapes he says that 404a
the spherical atoms are fire and soul (like the things in the
air called 'motes' which can be seen in rays of light through
windows). The mixture of all the atoms forms the elements
of the whole of nature (and here Leucippus agrees), while it
is the spherical ones among them that make up soul for the
reasons that this sort of shape is particularly able to permeate
through everything and move the rest, being themselves
moved, and this is on the supposition that it is the soul that
produces movement for animals. For this reason, too, they
say that respiration is the mark of life. For the surrounding
atmosphere compresses bodies and squeezes out of them those
of the atoms that produce movement for animals by never
—being at rest themselves, and then in breathing assistance
comes from without through the entry into the body of other
atoms of the same kind. These in fact even prevent the ones
in the animal from being forced out by joint resistance to the
compressive and constrictive force. And the animal's life
lasts just as long as it is capable of this. And it seems also
that the view expressed by the Pythagoreans reflects the
same thinking, as some of these said that the soul was the
motes in the air and others that which produces their
movement. The reason why the motes are chosen is that
they appear to be in constant motion even if there is a
complete calm. And the same tendency of thought is shown
by those who say that the soul is that which moves itself.
For a feature of all these theories is the supposition that the
production of movement is the most characteristic feature
of the soul and that while it is through the soul that all
other things are moved the soul's movement is produced by
itself. And this is based on our seeing nothing move that is
not itself moved.[9]

In the same way Anaxagoras too says the soul is what
produces movement, as must anybody else who has said that
mind moves the universe. But he is saying this in a different

way from Democritus. For Democritus simply asserted the identity of soul and mind. For he equated the true with the apparent and for that reason approved of Homer's expression 'Hector, as he lay there, grasped different thoughts'.[10] So that it is indeed clear that he did not treat the mind as a kind of faculty to do with truth, but rather asserted the identity of 404b soul and mind. Anaxagoras, on the other hand, is much less clear about these points. In many places he says that the mind is the cause of fine acting and correct thinking, but then says elsewhere that this is the soul. For it is indeed his view that mind is present in animals great and small, noble and less so. But the mind in the sense of intelligence at least would not seem to be present in the same way in all the animals – nor even in all men.

All those, then, who have looked on the ensouled thing from the point of view of its moving have supposed the soul to be that which is most productive of motion. But all those who have looked on it from the point of view of its knowing and perceiving entities say that the soul is the principles.[11] Those who hold there to be many of these claim the soul to be them; those who hold there to be one say that it is that. Accordingly, Empedocles composes the soul out of all the elements, though he also says that each one of them is soul. He puts it thus:

'For Earth we see by Earth, Water by Water,
By Air the holy Air, pernicious Fire
By Fire, and Love by Love, Strife by harsh Strife.'

And in the same way Plato in the *Timaeus* also composes the soul out of the elements. For he holds that knowledge is of like by like and that things are composed from the principles. And the same definition is given in the book *About Philosophy*, that is, that the World-Animal comes from the form of Unity and the primitive length, breadth and depth, and that the other things arise in a similar way. Still another version of his, however, is that mind is the One, knowledge the Two (there being only a single line between single points), opinion the number of the plane figure and perception that of the solid body.[12] For it is the numbers that are said by him to be the forms themselves and the first principles, though they are in fact made from the elements. And some things are judged by intuition, some by knowledge, some by opinion and some by perception, and it is the corresponding numbers that are the forms of the respective things.

But since in this way the soul is held to be something both productive of movement and cognitive, some have combined it from the two features, declaring the soul to be a self-moving number. Yet they differ on the subject of the first principles, both as to what they are and as to how many, especially as between those who hold that the first principles are embodied and those who hold that they are not, and as between these and those who admit both and declare the 405a first principles to be of both kinds. There are also the differences as to the number of them. For some say that there is only one first principle, others that there is a plurality. And in conformity with these positions are their views on the soul, as they have assumed, and not unreasonably, that productivity of motion is the nature of the primary bodies. And this has been the ground for the view of some of them that the soul is fire. For indeed this is the most fine-grained and disembodied of the atoms and it is also in a primary way that it both is itself moved and moves other things.

But Democritus has asserted the reason for each of these two things rather more perspicuously. Soul and mind are the same. And mind is composed of the primary and indivisible bodies and is productive of motion through the smallness of these parts and their shape. The spherical is the most mobile of shapes. Mind, then, as well as fire, is composed of spherical atoms. Anaxagoras, however, seems to be saying, as we remarked earlier, that the soul is different from the mind, and yet he treats both as of one nature, except when he says that when it really comes down to it mind is the first principle. For he does say that mind is the only one of the existing things that is simple and unmixed and pure. Yet he expounds from the same first principle both cognition and the production of motion, in saying that it is mind that moves the universe. (And even Thales seems, from what is recorded of him, to have supposed that the soul is something productive

of movement, if he really said that the magnet has a soul
because it produces movement in iron.) Now Diogenes and
some others say that the soul is air, thinking that this is the
most fine-grained thing of all and the first principle. And he
holds that this is why the soul both has cognition and
produces movement, having cognition by virtue of its being
the first thing and everything else's coming from it, and
being productive of motion by being the most delicate and
fine thing. But in fact Heraclitus also holds that soul is the
first principle, if indeed this is the same as his *emanation*, from
which he constructs everything else. This is also something
very much disembodied and in continual flow and *knowledge
is for that which moves by that which moves*. For he shared with
the common man the thought that the things that exist are
in motion.[13] Alcmaeon's supposition about the soul seems
also to have been similar to these. For he says that it is
immortal through its resemblance to the immortals, which
comes from its being always in motion. For the divine bodies
also are in continuous everlasting motion, the moon, the sun,
405b the stars, and the heaven as a whole. Now from among the
bulky elements there are also some who have declared the
soul to be water, such as Hippo. They seem to have been so
persuaded by considering sperm as this is wet in all cases.
Indeed, Hippo actually takes to task those who assert that
the soul is blood, on the grounds that the sperm is not blood
and that it is sperm that is the primary soul. Still others, for
instance Critias, have said that the soul is blood, on the
assumption that it is perception that is the most peculiar
characteristic of soul and that this belongs to it through the
nature of blood. All the elements have found their advocate
then, except earth; no one has actually claimed this to be
soul, except insofar as some have said that the soul is
composed out of all the elements or is all of them.

The soul seems to be universally defined by three features,
so to speak, the production of movement, perception and
incorporeality, and a connection is made between each of
these and the first principles. Accordingly, those who define
the soul by *cognition* make it out to be an element or composed
from the elements. They all argue in much the same way as

each other except one of them,[14] that is they hold that *cognition* is of like by like; for it is because the soul has *cognition* of all things that they compose it from all the elementary principles. All those then that say that there is one cause of things and one element also posit the soul to be one thing, such as fire or air, while those who admit a plurality of first principles compose the soul too of many things. But Anaxagoras is alone in claiming the mind to be unaffected and to have nothing in common with any of the other things. But as to how and through what cause, if it is so constituted, it comes to know things, neither has he himself vouchsafed nor is it clear from his remarks. All those, too, that hold there to be oppositions among the first principles compose the soul out of opposing pairs as well, while those who say that it is one of a pair of opposites that is the first principle, such as the hot or the cold or some other such, consistently enough assert the soul too to be one of these. In the same spirit, they follow out the names of the principles, so that those who say that the soul is the hot will say that it is also for this reason that life is so called, while those who say that it is the cold derive the word 'soul' from the cooling effect of respiration.[15] Such then are the views that have come down to us about the soul and the reasons for which they have been held.

Chapter Three: Comments on Earlier Views (I)

After completing his survey, Aristotle turns to critical assessment. He begins by attacking the ascription to the soul of the property of causing motion in itself, from its constitution. His argument is, first, that if the causation of movement is an essential property of the soul then the soul must be a spatial item, and, secondly, that, in addition to other difficulties, the picture of animal movement offered by theories of a spatially extended soul is absurdly like the comic idea of a playwright, that Daedalus made a statue move by the infusion into it of a particularly mobile substance, molten silver.[16] (The force of this point he turns specifically against Democritus, and it is not hard to see how it could be adjusted to fit the views of his modern descendants.) As against that picture, animal movement seems to come about as the result of some kind of thought or at least choice. This is a good example of Aristotle's pioneering approach to conceptual clarification. However, the present work does not develop this point, and Aristotle's other discussions of action all seem to skirt the difficulty at least apparently involved in the causation of physical by mental states.[17]

After his general discussion of the soul's production of movement, Aristotle turns to the psychology of the Timaeus. *In that work the word 'soul' is used very generally to mean both the world soul and that of men, and it is in this wide sense that Aristotle here criticizes the Platonic view.[18] After extensive discussion of the* Timaeus *theory, a short paragraph makes the important and characteristic point that all the theories so far discussed have supposed that the connection of soul and body is contingent. This, says Aristotle, is not correct. For this claim he here gives no grounds, but since exhibiting the necessary connection between soul and body is to be a conspicuous feature of his own view, giving grounds for the necessary connection will be part of the general defence of Entelechism in Books II and III. Its mention here, in any case, paves the way for the discussion of the last two theories of the soul to be considered and rejected.*

Chapter Three

Let us first, then, look at the soul's production of movement. For perhaps it is not merely not the case that the soul's 406a substance is as those suggest who say that it is that which produces its own movement or that which can set other things in motion, but in fact an impossibility that it should be characterized by the production of movement. It has already been remarked that that which produces movement need not be itself moved. Now everything that is moved is so in one of two ways, either, that is, in connection with something else or in itself. (Something is said to be moved 'in connection with something else' just when its being moved is occasioned by its being *in* something else that is moved. Oarsmen are an example – they are clearly not in motion in the same way as the boat is. The boat is in motion 'in itself', they by virtue of being in that moving thing. Consider the parts of their bodies. It is the peculiar motion of the feet, namely walking, that is the intrinsic way for men to move, and clearly the oarsmen are not walking as they move in the boat.) Motion, then, is spoken of in two ways. So let us now take up the case of soul and ask whether it is in itself that it is moved and participates in the production of motion.

There are four types of movement – locomotion, altera-tion, decay and growth.[19] If, then, it has motion, the soul will move either in one of these ways, or several, or all of them. Also its movement, if not accidental, will belong to it by nature, and in this case it will have a spatial location, as all the types of movement we have listed occur in space. But if the substance of the soul just consists in moving itself, then its being moved will not be an accidental feature of it, as it is of whiteness or being three cubits long, which also come to be moved but only accidentally, i.e. by the movement of that to which they pertain, the body. Thus while they do not have spatiality, the soul will have it, if it is of its *nature* that it partakes of movement. And in this case it will also be mov-able by force, and vice versa. And it will be in the same situation as regards its being at rest – it will be at rest of its nature at that very point to which it is moved of its nature and in just the same way it will come to rest by force at the point to which it is moved by force. However, just what these force-produced movements and states of rest of the soul will turn out to be, it is not easy to say, even if we are happy to conjecture. Again the soul's moving upwards will indicate its being fire, downwards its being earth, such being the charac-teristic movements of these bodies, and the same argument applies to the intermediate movements.

Since, then, it is clear that the soul does move the body, it seems reasonable that it should produce in it just those types of movement through which it itself moves. And if this is so, it will be no less true conversely to say that the type of move-ment through which the body is moved will also be that through which the soul is moved. But since the body is moved *406b* through locomotion, it would follow that the soul too, either all of it or by a rearrangement of its parts, would change place. And if it admits of this, it would also admit of departure from, and re-entry into, the body, from which the return to life of dead animals would follow.

Now while accidental movement can be produced by

something else, as when the animal is moved by a force, it is not possible for that whose substance comprises self-movement to be moved by anything else, except accidentally. There is a parallel with the way that what is good in itself cannot be so because of anything else and what is good for its own sake cannot be so for the sake of anything else. But the most obvious way in which one might say that the soul is moved, if one accepts that it is, would be by the objects of perception. But also, plainly, if it produces its own movement, then it comes to be moved, and so, if we take all movement to be a displacement of what is moved, insofar as it is moved, and if it is not accidentally that the soul moves itself, if this movement is of the substance of the soul in itself, then the soul too would, of its substance, come to be displaced. And some thinkers do in fact say that the soul moves the body in which it is in exactly the way that it is itself moved. The position of Democritus, for instance, bears a curious resemblance to that of the comic poet Philippus. Philippus has Daedalus make the wooden statue of Aphrodite move by pouring molten silver into it. But Democritus hardly seems to be saying anything different when he asserts that spherical atoms, through their naturally being never at rest, pull the body along with them and thus produce its movement. But our question will be whether this same effect brings the body to rest. How indeed it should do this it is hard, perhaps impossible, to say. But quite generally, this does not seem to be the way in which the soul moves the body. Rather it produces the motion through some kind of choice and thought process.

In the same way the *Timaeus* too puts it forward as a physical theory that the soul produces the body's motion. For it claims that it is by its being moved itself and by its being connected with the body that the soul moves the body as well. For according to this view, God made the soul out of the elements and then divided it according to the harmonic numbers, so that it may have a perception that is of the same nature with harmony and that the universe be moved in harmonious motions, and then bent the straight line into a circle. He then took from the single circle two circles that

touched at two points and again divided one of them into 407a
seven circles, on the grounds that the travels of the heaven
were the same as the motions of the soul.[20] But, to begin
with, it is not right to say that the soul is a quantity. For
Plato is clearly wanting his 'world soul' to be of the same kind
as that which is ordinarily called the intellect. (At least, he
cannot be wanting it to be like the perceptive or desiderative
faculties, as their movement is certainly not circular.) But
the intellect is a single and continuous thing as is thinking,
and thinking just consists of thoughts. But these are one by
being in sequence, as is the case with numbers, and not in
the way that a quantity is one thing. Thus it cannot be in
this latter way that the mind is continuous; rather it must
either be without parts or continuous but not in the way that
a quantity is. In any case, how is it to think, if it is a quantity?
Perhaps we would say that it is by each of its own parts. But
will it have parts in the quantitative sense, or only as points?
(To assume that we can talk about parts in the latter sense.)
But if it is with the parts in the sense of points, and if there is
an infinity of these, then the mind will never complete its
thought. If on the other hand we mean parts in the quantitative sense, then the mind will think the same thoughts
many times, perhaps an infinite number of times. Yet it
would seem possible for the mind also to think something
only once. In any case, if it is enough that the mind make
contact with some one of its parts, what need is there for it to
be moved in a circle, or in general to have quantity? If, on
the other hand, thinking requires contact with the whole
circle, to what does contact by the parts correspond? There
is a further puzzle as to how, if the mind is without parts, it
will think that which has parts, and vice versa. Yet, says
Plato, it must be the case that the mind is this circle. For the
movement of the mind is thinking, and that of the circle is
circular motion, so that, if thinking is a circular motion,
mind would then surely be the circle of which the appropriate
kind of motion is thinking. But, then, does that mean it will
always be thinking (as it should, if, as we assume, circular
motion is eternal)? Yet all practical thought processes have
termini – they are all *for* some purpose – and all contem-

plative thought processes are similarly limited by their arguments.[21] Now every argument is either a definition or a demonstration, and of these a demonstration is both from a starting-point and in a way has an end in the syllogism or rather its conclusion (and even if they do not reach a conclusion they certainly do not bend back again towards their starting-point, but at each stage take a new middle or final term and carry on in a straight line, while bending back on its starting-point is just what circular motion does do), and all definitions are obviously limited. Another objection is that if the same rotation occurs many times, then the mind will have to think the same thought many times, and another is that thinking is more like a kind of rest and standing still than a movement, and the same goes for the syllogism. 407b Furthermore, something that happens not easily but perforce can hardly be blissful, and the soul would be moved against its nature, unless its movement belonged to it of its substance. And a further source of hardship for the soul would be its indissoluble admixture with the body; and indeed we must actually avoid this, if it really is better for the mind to be without the body, in the popular cliché. Finally, the reason for the heaven's rotation is obscure. It is not the substance of the soul that is the cause of this rotation, as the soul is moved by accident in this way. But neither can the body be the cause, as the soul must rather be a cause for *it*. Nor is this motion argued for on the grounds that it is better than any other, yet surely this would be a suitable reason for God to make the soul rotate, on the grounds that motion is better for it than rest and motion in this way than in any other.

However, this inquiry is really part of another subject-matter, so let us leave it for now. But there is one absurdity that this argument has in common with most theories about the soul. The soul is connected with the body, and inserted into it, but no further account is given of the reason for this *nor of the condition that the body is in.* Yet this would seem to be required. For it is by their partnership that the body acts and the soul is affected, that the body comes to be moved and the soul produces motion. And none of these is possible for things whose mutual connection is contingent. But most theories only try to say what sort of thing the soul is, making no further specifications at all about the recipient body. Thus in the stories of the Pythagoreans it is possible for the soul to be inveigled into the body quite haphazardly. The point is, however, that each body has its own form and shape. There would be no difference between these theories and a theory that said that the art of carpentry became inveigled into flutes, for there is a parallel between the skill's need to use tools and the soul's need to use the body.

Chapter Four: Comments on Earlier Views (II)

The Harmony Theory is sometimes ascribed to the heterodox Pythagorean Philolaus. It is attacked by Plato's Socrates in the Phaedo, *as also, to judge from fragmentary evidence, by Aristotle's own early work, the dialogue* Eudemus, *in both cases because it was supposed to entail the mortality of the soul. The arguments that Aristotle here gives are sound as against the theory as it stands, but they can be met to some extent by emendation. The same can be said of the similar view here ascribed to Empedocles that the soul is the rationale (logos) of the body. What is clearly absent from Aristotle's treatment is any acknowledgement that the Harmony Theory involves a radically different approach to the soul from those assumed by the substantialism of either the materialists or the Academicians and orthodox Pythagoreans. This is certainly surprising if, with some commentators, we take Aristotle's own view as being little more than an elaboration of the Harmony Theory.*

After disposing of this view, Aristotle returns to the soul's production of movement, just the feature that the Harmony Theory had most clearly failed to explain. He restates his view that the soul produces movement not in itself but incidentally and thus avoids the difficulties raised earlier. To claim, however, that the soul produces movement incidentally is not to claim that the soul is not a substance, and the remark that it would be better not to say that the soul pities, learns or thinks but that the man does so with the soul, which has often been held brilliantly to anticipate Ryle's linguistic approach to mental items, leaves it open whether the soul is or is not a substance.[22] We should note, however, that Aristotle reminds us that the imperishability of the mind suggests that it, at least, is inseparable and substantial, and no clear distinction is drawn in this respect between the mind and the soul in general.

Aristotle now turns to attack the curious view of Xenocrates that soul is a moving number, which he considers the height of absurdity. Xenocrates, whom Aristotle does not mention by name, succeeded to the Scholarchy of the Academy on the death of Speusippus, Plato's nephew and successor. It is thus quite probable that Aristotle's rather splenetic rejection of this admittedly unpromising view is coloured by a certain rancour.[23] In any case the traditional chapter break interrupts the course of the refutation of Xenocrates, as marked in the text, and I have departed here from the standard division of the work.[24]

Chapter Four

Now there is another opinion that has been handed down about the soul, not yielding in popular persuasiveness to those already mentioned but which has rather acquitted itself successfully at its hearing before the bar of common sense. This is the thesis that the soul is a kind of harmony. This assumes that harmony is a mixture and composition of opposites and that the body is composed from opposites. However, the harmony itself is a kind of ratio or composition of the ingredients in the mixture, and the soul cannot be either of these. Nor can the production of movement be a feature of a harmony, and yet it is to the soul that all theories assign this above all, so to speak.

408a It would be more 'harmonious' to use the word harmony in connection with health and the successful performance of bodily functions in general than to use it of the soul. This becomes pretty clear to anyone who tries to expound the affections or functions of the soul in terms of some kind of harmony. 'Harmonizing' theory and facts is not easy.[25]

Now there are two things that we refer to when we use the term harmony. The main use is to denote the composition of quantities in things that have motion and position, when these are so fitted together as to admit nothing of the same kind, and the secondary use is to denote the ratio of ingredients in a mixture. In neither sense is it reasonable to call the soul a harmony. In particular the claim that the soul is the composition of the parts of the body is easily disposed of. There just is more than one composition of bodily parts and in more than one way. Of what parts, then, and in what ways are we to suppose the intellect to be a composition, and of what the perceptive and desiderative faculties? And it is no less absurd to call the soul *the* ratio of the mixture.[26] The mixture of elements that yields flesh by no means has the same ratio as that which yields bone.

The upshot will be that there are many souls and everywhere in the body, if all parts of the body are indeed composed from mixtures of elements and the *logos* of a mixture is a harmony and thus soul. (One could also ask Empedocles his view on this. After all he says that every part of the body has a certain ratio. Is this ratio then the soul, or is the soul rather something else that comes to be in the limbs? And is love the cause of a contingent mixture or a mixture in accordance with a ratio, and indeed is it itself the ratio or something else in addition to the ratio?) Such are the difficulties that these claims raise. But if the soul is a different thing from the mixture, what then is it that is destroyed at the same time as what it is to be flesh and the other parts of the animal? Furthermore, if each bodily part does not in fact have a soul, that is, if the soul is not just the ratio of their mixture, what is it that is destroyed when the soul leaves the body?

It is clear from these considerations that the soul can neither be a harmony nor be in rotation. And as we said, it is possible for the soul both to be moved accidentally and to produce its own movement, that is, that which contains the soul can be moved and its motion be produced by the soul. There is no other way in which the soul can have spatial movement. But one might derive a more reasonable difficulty about the soul as something in motion from the following thought. We say of the soul that it is sad and happy and *408b* cheerful and fearful and that it both gets angry and perceives and thinks. And all these things are held to be movements. They might then be grounds for thinking that the soul is in motion. But we do not have to say this. Let being sad and being happy and thinking be movements as much as you please and let each of them be in motion, yet if the motion is produced *by* the soul, if, for instance, being angry or afraid consists in the heart's being moved in the appropriate way, and if thinking is no less a movement of this part or of some other (some of the movements will occur in connection with the spatial movement of something in motion, others in connection with an alteration, but we will give their character and manner elsewhere), then saying that it is the *soul* that gets angry will be rather like saying that the *soul* weaves or builds a house. Perhaps indeed it would be better not to say that the soul pities or learns or thinks but that the man does *in virtue of the soul*. And by this we would mean not that the motion is *in* the soul but rather sometimes towards the soul and sometimes from it, perception being from the appropriate sources towards the soul, memory from the soul towards the states of movement or rest in the sense-organs.

On the other hand, the mind seems to be a substance that comes to be in the animal and to be imperishable. For the most likely cause of its perishing would be the decay of old age but it in fact seems to be in the same situation as the sense-organs. For if an old man were to acquire a young man's eye, he would see just like a young man. Thus old age does not consist in the soul's being affected in some way. It is an affection of what contains the soul as with intoxication and disease. Thought and contemplation are indeed diminished when some other internal part decays, but in themselves they are unaffected. But thinking and loving or hating are not affections of the mind but of the visible possessor of the part insofar as he possesses it. Thus when the possessor decays the mind no longer remembers or loves, these never having been affections of itself but of the body in general which has perished. But this leaves open the possibility that the mind is something more divine and unaffected.

All this has made it clear that the soul cannot be in motion, and if in general it is not in motion, obviously it is not moved by itself. But by far the most irrational of the accounts that have been given is that to the effect that the soul is a number that moves itself. This confronts the impossibilities attendant on the soul's being in motion and those peculiar to it that are occasioned by the claim that the soul is a number. For how *409a* are we to think of a unit as moving, if it is without parts or distinctive features? By what will it be moved and in what way? For insofar as it is a thing that moves and is moved it must have distinctive features. What is more, given that the movement of a line is said to produce a plane figure, and that of a point a line, the movements of units also will be lines. For the point is a unit that has position, so that, on this reasoning, the number of the soul will be in a certain place and have a position. Again if one takes from a number a number or a unit, one is left with another number, while the plants and many of the animals continue to live after being divided and seem to have the same soul in form.

It would in fact seem to make no difference whether we talk about units or tiny particles. For suppose that we convert the atoms of Democritus into points only leaving them as quantities,[27] then just as with a continuous body there will be a part of them that moves and a part that is moved. This is a feature of them not in virtue of their being of a particular size or smallness, but in virtue of their being quantities. There must thus be something to move the units. But if it is the soul that produces movement in the animal, then it will be the soul that produces movement in the number, so that the soul will not be both that which produces movement and that which is moved, but only the former. Is it then somehow possible that this be a unit? It must have some feature that distinguishes it from the other units, but what distinctive feature could a unitary point have except position? So on the assumption that there is a difference between the units in the body and the points in the body, the units will be in the same place as the points, as each unit will take up the space of a point. Yet if two things are to be in the same place, what is to stop an infinite number so being? For things whose space is indivisible are themselves indivisible. But if it is the number of the *points* in the body that is the soul, why do not all bodies have a soul? For there are believed to be points in every body, indeed an infinite number. We might also ask how the points are to be separated and freed from the body, if lines cannot even be broken down into points.

The result is, as we were saying, that in one way this theory says the same as that to the effect that the soul is a fine-grained kind of body, and in another it has its own 409b absurdity like that besetting Democritus' view that the body is moved by the soul. For if we accept that the soul is in every perceptive body, then if the soul is a body, there must be two bodies in the same place. But if one says that the soul is a number, then there must be many points in the same point or every body must have a soul, unless there is some distinctive number that comes into the soul and is different from the number of the points in the body. In either case the result is that the animal has to be moved by the number, just as we saw that Democritus makes it move. What difference will there be between talk of minuscule spheres or large units or moving units at all? On either view the animal's motion has to be explained by the movement of these things. Any theory then that identifies movement and number encounters these and many other similar difficulties – it is not just impossible that this should be the definition of the soul; it could not even be an attribute. This would be obvious if one were to try to explain the affections and functions of the soul on this theory, such as reasonings, perceptions, pleasures, pains and so forth. As we said before, one would be hard put even to guess.

Chapter Five: General Remarks

Stating that his criticisms are now complete of the claims that the soul directly moves the body and that it is the most fine-grained and most incorporeal body, Aristotle turns to consider the argument that it is composed from all the elements. He ascribes this view to Empedocles, although it is not easily rendered compatible with the 'Empedoclean' view associated with the Harmony Theory.[28] In any case, Aristotle's main point is that the perception of particulars must involve the perception of their form and not merely of their matter. This feature is not explicable on the mere assumption that the soul is composed of all the elements, even if this is allowed to account for the perception of the elements.

Aristotle next raises the objection that the traditional accounts have missed the gradations of soul, that even the supposition that like perceives like does not require the supposition in the soul of every element, and that it is absurd to hold that soul is immixed with the whole universe. Finally, he poses the question whether the soul has faculties, and, if so, how it is that these come to have a unity. These problems are connected with the fact that none of the traditional views has in Aristotle's opinion been able to explain all the functions of soul. By the end of the chapter and Book, Aristotle has accepted without argument the division of the soul's labour among faculties and this paves the way for his own hierarchic view of the soul. The last part of the chapter clearly suggests that this is what Aristotle thinks new in his work.

Chapter Five

There are then three features by which the soul has been traditionally defined. Some, on the grounds that it moves itself, assert that it is the thing most productive of motion. Some say that it is the most fine-grained and non-bodily body.[29] I think we have pretty well covered the difficulties and contradictions of these views. It remains to consider how it is argued that it is composed from the elements. The point of this claim is that the soul should have perception of the things that exist and know each particular one, but from it many logical impossibilities must flow.

The holders of this view suppose that knowledge is of like by like, just as though they were supposing that the soul and external things are the same. But the elements are not the only external things. There are many others – perhaps they are infinitely many in number – in the things that are composed from the elements. Even, then, if we grant that it is possible for the soul to know and perceive those things from which these particulars are composed, we can ask by what faculty the soul will know or perceive the entire entity, so as to know, for instance, what God is or a man or flesh or bone, or any other of the composites. For each particular *410a* consists of the elements arranged not just anyhow but by some formula and principle of composition. For instance, Empedocles says of the bone:

> 'But the kind Earth in her broad channels took
> Two portions out of eight of gleaming Moisture,
> Four of Hephaestus – and there were white bones.'

There will be no advantage then in the elements' being in the soul, unless these formulae and principles of composition are so too. For each element will perceive its like, but there will be nothing to perceive a bone, say, or a man, unless these are in the soul too. It would be superfluous to remark on the impossibility of this. Who would seriously ponder whether there is in the soul stone or man? Nor is it different with the good and not good or any of the other things.

Now that which exists is spoken of in many ways – it can mean a particular on the one hand or, on the other, a quantity or quality or some other of the categories we have distinguished. Is the soul, then, composed of things that are in all these ways? The elements, however, are not common to all these things. Or is the soul perhaps composed from as many of the things that are as are substances? How, in that case, will it also know each of the other things? Or are our friends to say that there are elements and proper first principles for each genus, and compose the soul from these? The soul would then consist of quantity, quality and substance. However, it is impossible that from the elements of quantity there should be composed not a quantity but a substance. Such and others like them are the difficulties for those who make the soul consist of all things.

However, it is also absurd to say that the like is unaffected by the like, but that the like perceives the like and that knowledge is of like by like. Perception is *ex hypothesi* a form of affection and being moved, and the same goes for thinking and knowing. And that there are many problems and difficulties in saying with Empedocles that the soul knows particulars by the bodily elements, and with reference to the like, is attested by what I shall now say. All those things in the bodies of animals that are composed simply of earth, such as bones, sinews and hair, are not thought to have _{410b} perception of anything and so not of their like, as the argument would require. Also each of the elements will have much more ignorance than understanding, as each will know one thing and be ignorant of many, because ignorant of all the rest. And it is also a consequence at least of Empedocles' view that God is the most unintelligent thing. For he alone is ignorant of one of the elements, namely strife, whereas mortal creatures are familiar with them all, each one being made from all. But in general on this view what reason have we to deny that all existing things have a soul, as everything either is an element or is formed either from one element or from several or from all? It follows from the theory that everything must know one thing or several things or all things. One might also raise a question as to what it is that unites the constituents of the soul. For the elements are like matter, and that which is continuous, whatever it may be in each case, is responsible for their unity. But it is impossible that there should be something responsible for and administrative of the soul, and still more impossible that there should be of the mind; for it is very reasonable to suppose that this is the most primitive and effective thing by its nature, despite the view that the elements are the primary things that exist.

All those, however, who say that the soul is composed from the elements on the grounds of its having knowledge and perception of the things that exist, as well as all who say that it is the thing most productive of movement, are not offering an account to cover every type of soul. On the one hand, there are some things that perceive but do not move – there seem to be some animals incapable of locomotion, which is thought to be the one type of motion in which the soul moves the animal. And on the other, there is a similar problem for those who construct the mind and the perceptive faculty out of the elements, as the plants seem to live without partaking of perception and many of the animals seem not to be capable of thinking. But suppose these objections were sidestepped and the mind were simply asserted to be a part of the soul and the perceptive faculty treated in the same way. Not even this would make the account one of every type of soul, nor of any one type as a whole. (This objection also applies to the account given in the so-called Tales of Orpheus.[30] For this states that the soul enters the body from the universe as the animal breathes, being borne along on the breezes, despite the impossibility, which eluded the framers 411a of this account, that this should happen to plants or even, if it is right that not all animals have respiration, to all animals.) If, however, the soul must be composed from the elements, it is not at all necessary that it be composed from all of them, one half of an opposing pair being sufficient to discriminate both straightness and curvature, the ruler being a judge of both, while curvature is a judge neither of itself nor of straightness.

The soul has also been asserted by some to be immixed in the whole universe, the grounds, perhaps, of Thales' view that all things are full of gods. But this position is not unproblematic. Why, for one thing, does the soul not produce an animal when in air or fire but only when in mixtures of the elements, even though it is held to be in a better state in the pure elements? (A further question might be why indeed the soul in air is better and more immortal than that in animals.) Either way of answering leads to absurdity and nonsense. It is nonsense of a higher degree to call fire or air an animal, yet absurd to deny their animality if they contain a soul. The grounds for the supposition of the presence of soul in these elements seems to have been the resemblance of homogeneity for the parts of the soul with the whole, if it is by fragmentation of the surrounding air into animal bodies that the animals become ensouled. But if the fragment of air is of one form, but the soul not homoeomerous,[31] it is clear that part of it will be present and part not. The soul must either be homoeomerous or not be present in any chance part of the universe.

It is thus clear from what has been said that neither does the soul have cognition from being composed from the elements nor is it correct or accurate to say that it is moved. Now the soul comprises cognition, perception and belief-states. It also comprises appetite, wishing and the desire-states in general. It is the source of locomotion for animals, as also of growth, flourishing and decay. Is each of these things the business *of the whole soul*? Is it with the whole soul $411b$ that we think and perceive and are moved and perform and are affected by each of the others? Or do we do different things with different parts? And indeed is life located in one of these parts or several or all of them? Or is there for this some other cause? Now it is indeed held by some that the soul has parts, with one of which it thinks and with another of which it has appetites. But, if it does have parts, what then can it be that holds it together at any time? It will certainly not be the body at least. For the contrary is more widely accepted, that the soul holds the body together. If then there is some other thing that unifies the soul, then this will be that which in the strictest sense *is* soul. We will then have to ask in turn of this thing whether it is single or has many parts. And if it is single, why not just make the soul single in the first place? But if it has parts, the argument will pose the question what it is that holds this together and, surely, we will have an infinite regress.

But about the parts of the soul as well one might ask what capacity each one of them has in the body. For if it is the soul as a whole that keeps the entire body together, it would be appropriate for each of its parts to hold together some part of the body. But this would seem to be impossible. What part the mind would hold together, and in what way, it would be hard even to guess. It also seems to be the case that plants and, among animals, some of the insects go on living when they have been divided so that they must have a soul of the same kind in each part even if numerically different – each of the parts has perception and moves spatially for a certain period of time. Nor is there anything odd in this period's being limited, as they do not have the organs necessary to preserve their nature. This does not detract from the fact that in each of the two parts all the parts of the soul are present. The parts of the soul are thus of the same kind as each other and as the whole. They are like each other because they are not separable from each other and like the whole in that it is not divisible.

It also seems that the first principle in plants is a kind of soul, being uniquely common to both animals and plants. While it can occur separately from the first principle of perception, nothing that does not already have it has perception.

BOOK II

The Nature of the Soul

Having surveyed, in Book I, the opinions of his predecessors, Aristotle is ready at the beginning of Book II to begin expounding his own view. In the first three chapters of this Book he outlines the account of soul as Form that is the core of his theory and establishes the hierarchy of psychic functions that arises from this conception. This hierarchy is to provide the structure for the rest of the work. The nutritive faculty of the soul is discussed rather briefly in the fourth chapter of Book II. Then, from Book II, Chapter Five to Book III, Chapter Two, Aristotle analyses the faculty of sense-perception. It is clear that his practical interest is greatest in this area, to which he also devotes the longest treatise in the Parva Naturalia. *After a short discussion of the imagination in Book III, Chapter Three, Aristotle passes to his much discussed theory of the intellect in Chapters Four to Six of that Book. The notoriously untidy Chapter Seven forms a jackdaw appendix to the treatment of sense and intellect, and the general theory is summarized in Chapter Eight. Chapters Nine to Eleven deal with desire, the ability to cause movement, that is the other feature of animals traditionally to be explained in terms of the soul, and the last two chapters of the work, devoted to the consideration of certain aspects of animal life from a teleological perspective, seem perhaps designed to tie the work in to a larger course of biological study.*[32]

Chapter One: Soul as Form

Although in Book I Aristotle has raised rather inchoately the possibility that soul might be non-substantial, he does not do this again at the start of Book II. Rather he begins by reminding us of the three types of substance admitted by the Metaphysics, *Substance as Matter, Substance as Form and Substance as the composite of these. Dismissing the first and last, Aristotle concludes that soul must be substance in the second way, as Form. Thus everything hangs for this psychological theory on whether the conception of different kinds of substance can be made acceptable. I have tried, in the Introduction, to give grounds for understanding Aristotle to be hoping to be taken at his word in his clear assertion here that the soul is substance.[33]*

Having told us that soul is substance in the way that form is, he goes on to say what distinguishes the soul from other such substances. This is done, as we would expect, by stating more exactly of what it is that the soul is the Form and in what way it is its Form. The full definition is given at 412b4: 'If then we must say something in general about all types of soul, it would be the first actuality of a natural body with organs.' I have tried in the Introduction both to bring out the way that Aristotle is here using the word 'actuality' (entelechy), and to defend this definition against the charge that it leaves no way open independently to specify the matter that is to correspond to the entelechy here defined.[34] The illustrations provided in the second half of the chapter, while perhaps stopping short of pellucidity,[35] bring out the teleological character of Aristotle's conception of the soul.

Chapter One

412a Let these then suffice as the opinions handed down to us about the soul by our predecessors, and let us go back again as from the beginning in the attempt to define what the soul is and what might be the most general account of it. One kind, then, of the things that there are we call *substance*, and part of this group we say to be so as matter, that which is not in itself a particular thing, a second part we say to be so as shape and form, in accordance with which, when it applies, a thing is called a particular, and a third as that which comes from the two together. Now matter is potentiality, and form is actuality, and this in two ways, one that in which knowledge, the other that in which contemplation, is actuality. And it is bodies that are most believed to be substances, and of these natural bodies, which are the origins of the others. Now of natural bodies some have life and some do not, life being what we call self-nourishment, growth and decay. Every natural body, then, that partakes of life would be a substance, and a substance in the way that a composite is. But since the natural body is still a *body* of the kind in question, that, of course, which has life, the soul would not be a body. For the body, far from being one of the things said of a subject, stands rather itself as subject and is matter. It must then be the case that soul is substance as the *form* of a natural body which potentially has life, and since this substance is actuality, soul will be the actuality of such a body. But there are two ways in which actuality is spoken of, on the one hand as knowledge, on the other as contemplation, is spoken of, and it is accordingly clear that soul is actuality in the way that knowledge is. For sleeping and waking are a part of the soul's being present, and waking is like contemplation, sleeping like having but not employing knowledge. And since knowledge is in the individual case prior in origin, soul is the *first* actuality of a natural body which potentially has life. Now this kind will include any body that has organs – and even the parts of 412b plants are organs, though completely simple, as for instance the leaf is a covering for the pod and the pod for the fruit, while the roots are like the mouth in that both draw in food.

If then we must say something in general about all types of soul, it would be the first actuality of a natural body with organs. We should not then inquire whether the soul and body are one thing, any more than whether the wax and its imprint are, or in general whether the matter of each thing is one with that of which it is the matter. For although unity and being are spoken of in a number of ways, it is of the actuality that they are most properly said.

We have then said what soul is in general, substance in accordance with the account of the thing. And this is the 'being what it was' for a body of this kind. In the same way, if some tool, say an axe, were a natural body, its substance would be being an axe, and this then would be its soul. And if this were separated from it, it would not continue to be an axe, except homonymously, whereas as it is it is an axe. But it is not of that sort of body that soul is the being what it was and the account, but a natural body of the right kind, having itself the principle of movement and rest. But we must consider what we have said in connection with the parts of the body as well. For if the eye was an animal, then sight would be its soul, being the substance of the eye that is in accordance with the account of it. And the eye is the matter of sight, so that when sight leaves it it is no longer an eye except homonymously, in the way of a stone or painted eye. Now we should take that which applies to the part and apply it to the living body as a whole. For just as each part of perception stands to each part of the perceiving body, so does the whole of perception stand to the whole perceiving body as such. So it is not that which has cast off its soul that is potentially such as to be alive, but that which has its soul. And the seed and the fruit are potentially the body of the appropriate kind. Waking, then, is an actuality in the way that cutting and 413a seeing are, while the soul is like sight or the potentiality of a tool. And the body is what is in this potentiality. So just as pupil and sight *are* the eye, so, in our case, soul and body *are* the animal. It is quite clear then that the soul is not separable from the body, or that some parts of it are not, if it is its nature to have parts. For with some of the parts of the soul the actuality is of bodily parts themselves. Not that there are not some parts that nothing prevents from being separable, through their not being the actualities of any body. But it remains unclear whether the soul is the actuality of a body in this way or rather is as the sailor of a boat. We have thus given an outline definition and sketch of the soul.

Chapter Two: The Psychic Hierarchy (I)

At the start of this section, after a methodological remark to the effect that the adequacy of a definition is revealed by the transparency with which the explanation of the definiendum shines through it, Aristotle proceeds to identify having a soul with being alive, and since there are various ways in which life can manifest itself, this leads to the argument that a peculiar faculty of the soul is responsible for each of the ways of life. It is in this chapter, therefore, that the doctrine of the soul as a hierarchy of parts emerges. This idea suggests the possibility, introduced in the second half of the chapter, that some one or more of these faculties might be capable of independence from the body, or, as Aristotle would put it, of separation. Aristotle does not tell us whether this is a real possibility, and indeed in the case of intellect his position remains equivocal throughout the work, leading to the distinction between the active and passive intellects. For other faculties of the soul, he seems here clearly to lean towards the idea that they are not separable.[36]

Chapter Two

Now since from the things which though obscure are yet relatively obvious there arises that which is clear and more intelligible in accordance with an account, we must try to go over again in this spirit what we have said about the soul. For our definitional account should not only show what it is, as the majority of definitions do, but must also contain the reason for its being as it is, which must shine through it. (In present practice, definitional accounts tend to be like conclusions. For instance: 'What is squaring?' – 'An equilateral rectangle's being constructed equal to a non-equilateral one.' But a definition like this is an account of a conclusion, whereas the man who says that squaring is the finding of the mean proportional gives the reason for the affair.)[37] Let us then, taking up the starting-point of our inquiry, say that the ensouled is distinguished from the unsouled by its being alive. Now since being alive is spoken of in many ways, even if only one of these is present, we say that the thing is alive, if, for instance, there is intellect or perception or spatial movement and rest or indeed movement connected with nourishment and growth and decay. It is for this reason that all the plants are also held to be alive – for they clearly have within themselves a potentiality and principle of the right kind, through which they take growth and decay in opposite directions. For it is not that they grow upwards but not downwards but in the same way in both directions, indeed in all directions, as many of them, that is, that are regularly nourished and so go on living as long as they are able to take nourishment. Now *this* faculty can be separated from the others but the others cannot be separated from this in mortal things. And this is obvious in the case of plants, as they have no other 413b potentiality of the soul. All living things then have life in virtue of this principle, but they are not animals unless they have perception. For indeed of those things that without moving or changing place yet have perception, we say not just that they are alive but that they are animals. Further, the most basic of the senses, touch, all animals have, so that just as the nutritive faculty is separable from touch and all perception, so is touch separable from the other senses. (We call nutritive that part of the soul in which even plants partake, while it is clear that all animals have the sense of touch. But for what reason these two things should be so we will say later.) [38]

For the moment we may be taken to have made the following claim, that the soul is the principle of these things that we have mentioned and is defined by these things, the nutritive, perceptive and intellective faculties and movement. Now as to whether each of these is a soul or a part of soul, and, if it is a part, whether in such a way as to be separable only in account or also spatially, in the case of some of these it is not hard to see, but some present a difficulty. For just as it is quite clear with plants that some will still be alive if divided up and separated from each other, because the soul in them is in actuality one in each plant but in potentiality many, so we see this happening too with another characteristic type of soul, in the case of insects, with those that are being dissected. For each of the parts has perception and spatial movement, and if perception then also imagination and desire. (For where there is perception there is also pleasure and pain, and where there are these, of necessity also appetite.) But nothing is yet clear on the subject of the intellect and the contemplative faculty. However, it seems to be another kind of soul, and this alone admits of being separated, as that which is eternal from that which is perishable, while it is clear from these remarks that the other parts of the soul are not separable, as some assert them to be, though it is obvious that they are conceptually distinct. [39] For what it is for something to have perception and what for it to hold beliefs, are different if indeed perception is different from believing, and so with each of the other things that we have mentioned. And again some of the animals have all these, some some of them, and others one only (this produces the variation among animals). But why this is so, *414a* we must consider later. And it is much the same situation in the case of the senses, as some animals have all the senses, some some of them, and some the one most necessary, touch.

Now that by which we live and perceive is spoken of in two ways, just as with that by which we know (for by this we mean on the one hand knowledge and on the other soul, for we say that we know in virtue of both of these things), and in the same way by that by which we are healthy we mean on the one hand health and on the other some part of the body or a whole body. Of these knowledge and health are indeed shape and a kind of form and an account, and as it were activity of the recipient, knowledge of the knowing faculty, health of the healthy faculty (for it is held that the activity of the productive faculty is present in the thing that is affected and disposed), but soul is that by which primarily we live and perceive and think. So it too will be a kind of account and form and not matter and the subject. For substance is, as we said, spoken of in three ways, as form, as matter, and as the composite, and of these matter is potentiality, form actuality, and since the composite is in this case the ensouled thing, it is not that the body is the actuality of the soul but that the soul is the actuality of some body. And for this reason they have supposed well who have believed that the soul is neither without body nor a kind of body. For it is not a body but belongs to a body, and for this reason is present in a body and a body of the appropriate kind, and not in the way that our predecessors attached it to a body, making no additional determination as to what body or what kind of body, although it does not even seem to be the case that any thing receives any thing else contingently. But the present account meets this condition, as it is the nature of the entelechy of each thing to be in what is potentially it and in its own matter. It is clear then from all this that the soul is a kind of actuality and account of that which has the potentiality to be of the appropriate kind.

Chapter Three: The Psychic Hierarchy (II)

In this chapter the hierarchic conception of the faculties of the soul is further developed and an analogy is drawn with the sequence of shapes. The elucidatory value of this is not immune to controversy, but it is intended to underline the importance of the particular over the general definitions of soul, and to bring out the dependence of each faculty of the hierarchy, at least in mortal things, on the faculty that stands below it.[40] Hamlyn, perhaps, brings out the true force of the analogy: 'An account of figure in general or soul in general (just as for being in general) will be uninformative about figures or souls, not just in the way that any general definition is uninformative about the details of the things to which it is applied, but also because it will omit the crucial point that figures and souls form a progression.'[41]

Chapter Three

Now of the faculties of the soul, some living things have all those that we have talked of, as we said, some have some of them, and some only one. The faculties we spoke of were the nutritive, perceptive, desiderative, locomotive and intellective, plants having only the nutritive, other living things 414b both this and the perceptive. But if they have the perceptive faculty they have also that of desire. For desire is appetite, passion or wish, all animals have at least one of the senses, namely touch, and for that for which there is perception there is also both pleasure and pain and the pleasant and painful, and for those for whom there are these there is also appetite, the desire for the pleasant. And they also have perception of their food (for touch is the sense of nourishment, all animals being fed by things that are dry and wet and hot and cold and the sense of these being touch) and they have perception of the other sense-objects incidentally. For neither sound nor colour nor smell contribute anything to nourishment, while flavour is one of the tangible objects. For hunger and thirst constitute appetite, hunger being for the dry and hot, thirst for the wet and cold. (Flavour is as it were a kind of relish to these things.) We must get clear about these later;[42] for the moment let the following remark suffice, that those living things that have touch also have desire. The situation with imagination is unclear and must be discussed later on.[43] And some animals have also in addition to these faculties that of locomotion, still others also the thinking faculty and intellect, such as man and any other creature there may be like him or superior to him.

It is clear then that there will be one account of soul in the same way that there will be one account of shape. For in the case of shape there is no shape in addition to the triangle and those in series from it, and in this case there will be no soul in addition to the ones we have mentioned. Yet even in the case of the figures there would be a general account, which will fit all but be peculiar to no one figure. And so it is also with the souls that we have mentioned. And for this reason it is absurd in both these and other cases to seek out the common account that will be the peculiar account of no one of the things that there are nor fit the proper individual species, and neglect the sort of account that will do this. (The situation with the figures is similar to that with the things that have soul, the earlier member of the series always being present in the later in both cases, the triangle for instance in the square and the nutritive faculty in the perceptive.) We must, then, seek out in each case what the soul of each thing is, what for instance is the soul of a plant and what of a man or a beast, and we must consider for what reason it is that they stand thus in series. For while there is never the per- 415a ceptive faculty without the nutritive, in plants the nutritive is separated from the perceptive. And again without the sense of touch none of the other senses is present, but touch can be present without the others, many of the animals having neither sight nor hearing nor the sense of smell. And of those creatures that perceive, some have the locomotive faculty, others do not. Ultimately and most rarely, some have reasoning and thinking. For those of the perishable beings that have reason have all the other faculties but not all of those that have each of them have reason; indeed, some do not even have imagination, while others live by this alone. About the contemplative mind, however, another account will be needed.[44] In any case, it is clear that the account of each of these things will be the most appropriate account for the soul too.

Nutrition

Chapter Four: Methodological Remarks; Nutrition

In this chapter, after remarking that each faculty of the soul must be separately examined, Aristotle stresses that the objects of the various faculties must be used to establish clear distinctions between them. He then turns towards the most elementary of the faculties, nutrition. However, before we actually reach the discussion of nutrition, there is a further digression on the idea of the soul as Form. Though this digression may at first sight seem somewhat arbitrary, it prepares the way for the discussion of nutrition. For Aristotle reminds us that the soul is the cause of the body in three of the four ways admitted in his system. The soul is final and formal cause, but also the motive cause or efficient cause, and this aspect is no less evident in the processes of growth and decay than in those of locomotion in which plants, and some animals, have no share. In the case of growth, soul also clearly functions as a formal cause, taking the part, it has been suggested, of DNA in modern biology.[45]

The discussion of nutrition itself, although shorter than those of sense-perception, intellect and desire, is in fact closer than them to the central ideas of the work. Characteristically, Aristotle sees his theory as reconciling a traditional dispute in this area. It is very likely that Aristotle gave the ideas broached here rather more shape in his lost treatise on Nutrition to which reference is made at the end of this chapter.[46]

Chapter Four

But he who intends to hold an inquiry into these things must first grasp what each one of them is and then in the same way make a further inquiry into its secondary aspects and then into the other features. But if we have to say what each of them is, such as what the intellective faculty is or the perceptive or the nutritive, then even before that we must say what thinking is and what perceiving is, for conceptually prior to potentialities are activities and actions. And if this is so, then even before these we should first make definitions about them, about nutriment, that is, and the sense-object and the thought-object.

We must then speak first about nourishment and re-production. For all the other living things as well as plants have the nutritive faculty which is the first and most general faculty of the soul, in virtue of which all creatures have life. Its functions are to reproduce and to handle nourishment. For this is the most natural of the functions of such living creatures as are complete and not multilated and do not have spontaneous generation, namely to make another thing like themselves, an animal an animal, a plant a plant, so that in the way that they can they may partake in the eternal and the divine. For all creatures desire this and for the sake of this do whatever they do in accordance with their nature. But that 'for the sake of which' is in two ways, on the one hand that 'for the purpose of which' and on the other that 'for whose sake'.[47] Now the living creature cannot have a share in the eternal and the divine by continuity, since none of the mortal things admits of persistence as numerically one and the same, but in the way that each creature can par-ticipate in this, in that way it does have a share in it, some more some less, and persists not as itself but as something like itself, not numerically one, but one in species.

The soul, then, is the cause and principle of the living body, and as these are talked of in several ways, so is the soul the cause of the body in the three ways we have distinguished; for it is the cause as that from which the movement itself arises, and as that for whose sake it is, and as the formal substance of ensouled bodies.[48] Now that it is so as substance is clear, for for all things the reason for their being is their substance, and living is the being of living things, and the soul the cause and principle of this. Again the actuality is the rationale of that which potentially is something. But it is also

clear that the soul is the reason for the body as that for which
it is; for just as the mind acts for the sake of something, in the
same way does nature, and this is its end. And in animals the
soul is naturally such, all natural bodies being the soul's
instruments, those of plants in just the same way as those of
animals, and existing, then, for the sake of the soul. But that
for the sake of which is in two ways, that for the purpose of
which and that for whose sake. But it is also the soul from
which first comes locomotion, although not all living things
have this faculty. Change and growth too are in virtue of the
soul; for perception is thought to be a kind of alteration, and
nothing perceives that does not participate in soul. And it is
the same situation with growth and decay, as nothing
naturally decays or grows that is not nourished, and nothing
is nourished that does not have a share of life. Empedocles
then spoke incorrectly in making the further suggestion that
growth happens in plants when they extend roots downwards
through its being the nature of earth so to be carried and
416a when they grow upwards through it being the nature of fire
to move thus. He did not in fact even correctly grasp 'upwards' and 'downwards' (for 'upwards' and 'downwards'
are not the same for all things as for the universe, rather the
roots in plants are as the head in animals, if we should
distinguish and identify the organs by their functions); but
on top of these objections, what is it that holds together the
fire and earth as they tend in different directions? For the
plant will be torn apart if there is nothing that prevents this,
and if there *is* such a thing, this will be the soul, and this will
be the cause of its growing and being nourished. Some, however, believe that it is simply the nature of fire that is the
cause of nourishment and growth; for this seems to be the
only one of the bodies or elements which is nourished and
grows, and for this reason both in plants and in animals one
might suppose this to be what effects these processes.[49] But
this is somehow an ancillary cause, and not the cause pure
and simple, which is rather the soul. For the growth of fire is
not limited as long as there is something to be burnt, but of
all those things that are put together in nature there is a
limit and formula of their size and growth, and these things

come from soul rather than fire, from their rationale rather than matter.

Now since it is the same faculty of the soul that is nutritive and reproductive, we must first come to a definition about nourishment; for the faculty in question is distinguished from the other faculties by this function. Now nourishment is believed to be of opposite by opposite, and not by every pair of opposites but only those that have not only their origin from one another but also growth; for many things arise out of each other but not all of them as quantities, for instance the healthy out of the sick. But even the pairs in question do not seem to be nourishment for each other in the same way, rather water,[50] for instance, is nourishment for fire, but fire does not nourish water. In simple bodies especially, then, there is contrariety between the nourishment and the recipient of nourishment. Yet there is a problem. For some say that nourishment is of like by like, as is the case with growth, while others, as we have said, hold the opposite view, that it is of opposite by opposite, the like being unaffected by the like, while nutriment undergoes a change in being digested, and for all things change is to the opposite or the middle state. Again, while the food is affected by its recipient, the recipient is not affected by the food, any more than the carpenter by his material, though it is affected by him, the carpenter only changing from inactivity to activity. Now it makes all the difference whether the nutriment is the last thing added or the first. If, on the other hand, it is both these, the one before digestion the other after it, then we could speak of food in both ways; for insofar as it was undigested we would say that nourishment would be of opposite by opposite, but insofar as it was digested we would say that it was of like by like. Thus it is clear that both parties are in a way right and in a way wrong. But since nothing is nourished that does not partake of life, it would be the ensouled body, as ensouled, that is nourished, so that nutriment too is non-accidentally related to the ensouled thing. But being nutriment is different from being productive of growth; for while it is in virtue of the fact that the ensouled thing is a quantity that the food is productive of growth, it is in virtue of the fact that it is a particular and a substance that it is nutritive, for the creature preserves its substance and persists just as long as it is fed. It is also productive of generation not of the thing being fed but of something like it – for its own substance already exists, and nothing produces, but only preserves, itself. This principle then of the soul is the faculty that preserves that which has it as of the kind that it is of, while nutriment prepares it for activity. Thus, deprived of food, it is not capable of existing. Since, then, there are three things involved, the recipient of nourishment, that by means of which it is nourished and the nourisher, that which nourishes is the primary soul, that which is nourished is the body which has this, and that by means of which it is nourished is the food. But since it is right to label everything on the basis of its end, and the end here is to generate something like itself, the primary soul would be the soul generative of its possessor's like. Now that by means of which it is nourished is in two ways, as with that by means of which a boat is steered, which can be both the hand and the tiller, the one moving as well as being moved, the other only being moved. And it is necessary that all nutriment be capable of being digested, and this is effected by heat, for which reason all ensouled things have heat. What nourishment is then has been said in outline – we must get clear about it later in a special treatise.

Sense-perception

Chapter Five: Sensation

With this chapter we move to the discussion of the perceptive faculty which continues until Book III, Chapter Two and has rightly been identified as the principal business of the De Anima.[51] *Some of the problems introduced here are taken up again in the* De Sensu, *the first treatise of the* Parva Naturalia. *Chapters Five and Six discuss sense-perception in general and they stand to the subsequent discussion of the particular senses in much the same relation as the general remarks about the soul stand to the treatment of the particular faculties.*

*Sense-perception is here presented as a kind of alteration. It is not clear
how this is to be reconciled to his subsequent treatments of it as being
the reception of Form without Matter from the object and judgement in
virtue of a critical mean. The explanation offered here, however,
shares with the two other thoughts about perception an exclusive concentration on physiological aspects. Aristotle reveals throughout this discussion no clear interest in the modern notion of consciousness. He is
clearly more concerned, as Hamlyn has pointed out,[52] to achieve conceptual clarification in this area. This is in keeping with the general
scope of the* De Anima *within the biological works of providing a
schematic account of the common properties of living things. As in the
previous chapter, there is a digression, in which Aristotle reminds us of
necessary refinements in his conception of the potential–actual distinction. The cardinal idea here is that of the* hexis, *habitual state,
which is, as explained, more active than a mere capacity but more
potential than activity itself.*

Chapter Five

Now that these things have been defined, let us talk in general
about all perception. Now perception arises, as we have said,
in the animal's being moved and affected – for it is held to be
a kind of alteration. Now some would add that it is the like
that is affected by the like, but we have stated the way that 417a
this is possible or impossible in the general account of action
and affection. But there is a difficulty as to why it is that
there is not also a sense *of the senses themselves*. There is also a
difficulty as to why the senses do not produce sensation without external bodies, there being in them fire, earth and other
elements, which are objects of sensation either in themselves
or by their accidents. But it is clear that the perceptive faculty
is not in activity, but only in potentiality and for that reason
does not perceive on its own, just as the combustible thing
is not burnt in itself without the thing that burns. (Otherwise
it would burn itself and have no need of that which is in
actuality fire.) And since we speak of perceiving in two ways
(for of that which potentially hears or sees we say that it
hears or sees even if it happens to be asleep and we also say
this of that which is in fact in these activities), perception

too would be spoken of in two ways, both as in potentiality
and as in activity. And in the same way the sense-object too
will be spoken of both as being in potentiality and as being
in activity. At first, then, let us speak as if being affected,
being moved and being active are the same thing. (As we
said in another work, movement is a kind of activity, but
incomplete.) But all things are affected and moved by that
which is productive and in activity. There is then a way in
which things are affected by their like and a way in which
they are affected by their unlike, as we said.⁵³ For it is what
is unlike that is affected, but on being affected it becomes like
what has acted on it.

But we should draw some distinctions as regards potentiality and actuality, for up to now we have been talking
rather simplistically about them. First then there is, say, a
knowing thing just in the way that we would say that a man
is knowing in that man is one of those things that know and
have knowledge; and then there is a knowing thing in the
way that we (in fact) say that a man who has learned
grammar is knowing (but each of these two is potentially
knowing not in the same way, rather the first is so in that his
genus and matter are of the right kind, the other in that he
has the potentiality to contemplate whenever he will, providing no external factor prevents him); and thirdly there is
the man who is in fact contemplating, being in actuality and
in the truest sense knowing the particular before him. Now
both of the first two, being in potentiality knowing, become
so in actuality, but the first one does so by changing his state
through learning and through often changing from the opposite condition, and the second by changing from having
417b arithmetic or grammar, but not employing them, to the
employment of them, a different change. Being affected is
also not simple; on the one hand it is a kind of destruction by
the opposite, on the other rather a preservation of what is in
potentiality by what is in actuality, and of what is like what
acts on it in the way that a potentiality is like its actuality;
for that which has knowledge becomes that which contemplates, and this is either not to change state at all (for the
progression that occurs is towards the thing itself and towards

its actuality), or is another kind of change of state. And for this reason it is not right to say that that which understands, whenever it is understanding, is changing its state, any more than it would be right to say this of the builder whenever he is building. It would be right, then, that to take what has intellect and understanding from a condition of potentiality to one of actuality should not be called teaching but have some other name, while we should say either that that which from a condition of potentiality learns and takes knowledge from what is in actuality and teaches is not affected at all, as we said, or that there are two ways of changing state, the change to privative dispositions and the change to natural states. Now in the case of the perceptive faculty the first change occurs through the father and when the creature is born it already has perception and knowledge in one way. And actually perceiving is spoken of in the same way as contemplation. Yet there is a difference between them in that those things that are productive of actual perception are external, the visible and the audible and in the same way all the other sense-objects. And the reason for this is that perception in activity is of particular things, knowledge of universals, which are in a way in the soul itself. Thus it is for a man to think, whenever he will, but not so for him to perceive, because for that the presence of a sense-object is necessary. And this applies in the same way even to our knowledge of the sense-objects, and for the same reason, namely that the sense-objects are among the particular and external things.

But there will be another opportunity to get clear about these matters later on. For the moment let the following definition suffice, that, just as that which is spoken of in potentiality is not simple, but is on the one hand spoken of in the way that a child is potentially a general, and on the other in the way that we would say this of someone of the right age, so is it with the perceptive faculty. But since in this *418a* case the difference has no name, though we have defined about it that the ways are different and indeed how they are different, we must use the terms 'affection' and 'alteration' as though they were the right ones. And, in the way we have said, the sense faculty is like the actual sense-object – it is affected as being unlike but on being affected it becomes like and is such as what acts on it.

Chapter Six: The Types of Sense-object

This chapter is much shorter than its predecessor, but it contains an important classification of sense-objects into the three kinds — special, common and incidental.[54] The discussion of the particular senses will obviously treat of the sensation by each sense of its special object, but Aristotle will return thereafter to this framework in order to elucidate some general problems about perception. Here Aristotle draws a distinction between the two sense-objects that are essential and the one that is incidental. Both the special and the common sense-objects are essential in that they contribute to the definition of the sense or senses to which they correspond. The special sense-objects, especially, are conceptually integral to their sense faculties. In their case Aristotle seems open to the accusation that out of love of theory he has assimilated too much the heterogeneous objects of the various senses.[55]

Chapter Six

Now in the case of each sense we must speak first about the sense-objects. The sense-object is spoken of in three ways, of which we say that we perceive two in themselves and one incidentally. Of the first two, one is that special to each sense, the other that common to all. Now I call that sense-object special that does not admit of being perceived by another sense and about which it is impossible to be deceived, as sight is connected with colour, hearing with sound and taste with flavour. (Touch, on the other hand, has a wide range of objects.) Each sense then judges about the special objects and is not deceived as to their being a colour or sound, but only as to what the coloured or sounding *thing* is or where it is. It is, then, such objects as these that are called special to each sense. The common objects, on the other hand, are movement, rest, number, shape and size, such being not special to any one sense but common to all. For of course a movement will be perceptible to both touch and sight. Finally, those sense-objects are called incidental that are like the white thing's being the son of Diares. For this we perceive incidentally, for it is incidental to the white thing we perceive. And for this reason we are not affected at all by this sense-object as such. And of the things perceived in themselves it is the special ones that are most strictly speaking sense-objects, and it is in natural relation to them that the formal substance of each sense stands.

Chapter Seven: Sight

We now embark on the survey of the particular senses, which are less confusingly known as the special senses as their objects are general qualities. In these chapters the tone of the discussion is even more markedly physiological than before. The only nod in the direction of consciousness is the suggestion at the very end of the Book that the nose's reaction to the smell might be distinguished from that of an inanimate thing by its possessor's consciousness. This, however, is no more than a nod at the very most.[56] Most of the conceptual analysis of sense-perception has already been done by Chapters Five and Six, and neither they nor the continuation of the general discussion after that of the special senses can be said to encourage the consideration of sense-perception from the Cartesian, first-personal perspective.

Unfortunately, as an essay in physiology, Aristotle's account of the special senses is only too obviously antiquated. The notions of the actuality and potentiality of the sense-organ are consistently employed, and in the case of the remote senses (sight, hearing and smell) the need is stressed of a medium between object and sense-organ. In the case of sight the medium will be light, which Aristotle accordingly discusses.

Chapter Seven

That which is the object of sight is the visible, and this comprises both colour and something which though it can be given by an account has no name. (What it is that we are referring to will become clear as we proceed.) For the visible is colour and colour is what is on the surface of the thing visible in itself, and that not from its rationale but in that it has within itself the cause of its being visible. Now all colour moves that which is transparent in actuality, and this is its _{418b}

nature. Thus colour is not visible without light but the whole colour of the particular thing is seen in the light. We must then first say what light is. We can take for granted the existence of something transparent. And I call that transparent which is visible but not, to put it simply, visible in itself, but through the colour of something else. Of such a kind are air and water and many of the solid bodies. For it is not *as* water or air that these things are transparent but in that there is within them a nature that is the same in both these and in the eternal upper body.[57] And light is the activity of this thing, of the transparent as transparent. And wherever this is there is potentially also darkness. But light is as the colour of the transparent, when it is rendered transparent in actuality by fire or something of the same kind as the upper body (for this too has one and the same property). We have said, then, what the transparent is and what light is, that it is not fire or in general a body or an effluence from any body (for in this case it would still be a body of a kind), but the presence of fire or something like it in the transparent. (Also since it is not possible that two bodies be in the same place at the same time, and light is believed to be the opposite of darkness, darkness is in fact the removal of the condition in question from the transparent; so it is clear that it is the presence of this that is light.) Empedocles, then, and anyone who may have followed him in this, was wrong to say that light is conveyed and arrives at some time between the earth and its surround and that we do not notice this. This is counter both to clear reason and to appearances. Over a short distance we would not notice this, but it is too much to claim that we would not notice it the whole way from East to West.

Now the uncoloured is the recipient of colour, and the unsounding of sound. The uncoloured comprises the transparent and the invisible or scarcely visible, as the dark is believed to be. And the transparent is of such a kind, not whenever it is transparent in actuality, but whenever it is so potentially. For the same nature is at one time darkness, at 419a another light. But not all visible things are in light, but only the proper colour of each particular. For some things are not

seen in the light but produce the sensation in darkness, such
as fungus and horn and the heads, scales and eyes of fish. But
it is not the proper colour of any of these that is seen. For
what reason these are seen requires another account; for the
moment this much is clear, that that which is seen in light is
colour. And for this reason it is also not seen without light –
for this was what it was for it to be colour, to be productive
of movement in that which is transparent in actuality. And
the actuality of the transparent is light. And there is a clear
indication of this. If someone puts what has colour on the
sight-organ itself, he will not see it. In fact, colour moves the
transparent, the air, say, and by this if continuous the sense-
organ is moved. Democritus got this wrong. He thought that
if the medium was void then we would see clearly even an
ant in the sky. This, however, is impossible, because it is
from the perceptive faculty's being affected in some way that
sight arises and it is impossible that it should be affected by
the observed colour itself. The remaining possibility is that it
be affected by the medium, so that it is necessary that there
be something as a medium. If the medium becomes void, so
far from a thing's being seen as accurately as possible,
nothing will be seen at all.

We have now given the reason why it is necessary that
colour be seen in light. Now fire is seen in both darkness and
light, and this of necessity, as it is by this that the transparent
becomes transparent. And the same account can be given in
the case of sound and smell. For none of them produces the
sensation by touching the sense-organ, rather it is the
medium that is moved by smell and sound and each of the
sense-organs by this. And when anyone puts the sound or
smell source on to the organ itself, this produces no sensation.
It is the same situation, only not so apparently so, with
touch and taste, and for a reason that will be clear later.
Now the medium of sounds is air, but that of smell has no
name. For there is a common affection in air and water
which relates to that which has smell just as the transparent
relates to colour, and this is present in both of them. For it
seems that even those of the animals that live in water have
the sense of smell. Man, however, and as many of the land *419b*

animals as have respiration are unable to smell without breathing, and the reason for this too will be given later on.

Chapter Eight: Hearing

Here, as with sight, so with hearing, the apparatus of potentiality and actuality is central to Aristotle's account. He digresses to discuss the subject of voice, but although he distinguishes this as a sound with meaning, he does not investigate at all what the consequences of this may be. He is a long way from the problems of intentionality, the difficulty of accounting for our understanding of sentences without existential import.[58]

Chapter Eight

But now let us first determine about sound and hearing. Now sound is in two ways, one in actuality, the other in potentiality. For there are some things that we say not to have sound, such as sponge and wool, and others which we say to have a sound, such as bronze and everything that is hollow and smooth, so as to be able to give sound, that is to produce sound in actuality between itself and the hearingorgan. Now sound in actuality is always of something and against something and in something. For it is a blow that produces it. Thus it is impossible for sound to occur if there is only one thing, for that which strikes is different from that which is struck. The sounding thing, then, sounds against something, and no blow can come about without movement. But, as we said, sound is the striking of the right kind of things. For wool, if struck, would make no sound, but bronze would, and the things that are smooth and hollow. Bronze, by being smooth, and hollow things by reverberation produce many blows after the first one, as the air that has been moved cannot escape. The sound is also heard in air, and also, though to a lesser extent, in water, but it is neither air nor water that is responsible for sound; rather there must be a striking of solid bodies together and against the air. And this occurs whenever the air being struck remains in place and is not dispersed. Thus if something strikes swiftly and hard, it makes a sound; the striker's movement must anticipate the dispersal of the air, just as if something travelling swiftly were to strike a pile, or, better, eddying cloud, of sand. And an echo occurs in the following circumstances: some air is brought together by a cavity which encloses it and prevents its dispersal and from this the rest of the air bounces back like a ball. It seems that an echo always occurs, though not a clear one, since in the case of sound the same thing happens as in that of light. For light is always reflected (otherwise there would not be light everywhere but rather darkness outside the area lit by the sun), but not so reflected as from water or bronze or some other of the smooth things, so as to cast a shadow, by which we demarcate the light. But the void is correctly called responsible for hearing. For the air is believed to be a void and this it is that produces hearing, whenever it is moved as a continuous and unified thing. But because of its discrete character it makes no noise unless that which strikes it is smooth; in this case the surface of the *420a* object, which if the object is smooth will be single, makes the air come together at the same time.

That which sounds, then, is that which produces motion in such air as is one in continuity up to a hearing-organ. And air is of one nature with the hearing-organ, and since this is in air, when the external air is moved so is the internal air. For this reason, the animal does not hear everywhere any more than the air permeates everywhere. For the part which will move and produce sound does not have air all around it. The air itself, which is easily dispersed, is not productive of sound, but its movement, whenever it is prevented from dispersing, is sound. But the air in the ears is so set in as to be unmoved, so that it may accurately perceive all the characteristics of the movement in question.[59] And we can hear even in water as the water does not penetrate through to the connate air itself. Indeed it does not reach even into the ear, because of its involved structure. But whenever this does happen, the animal does not hear. Nor does it when its drum is damaged, as with the membrane over the pupil of the eye. But a sign of whether or not hearing is occurring is the persistent echoing of the ear like a horn, for the air in the ears is always moving with a certain proper movement of its own, while the sound is the movement of other air not of the internal air itself, which is why it is said that we hear by what is hollow and echoing – we hear by that which has confined air within it.

But is it that which is struck or that which strikes which makes the sound? Or is it both, but in different ways? For sound is a movement of that which can be moved in the way of things bouncing back from smooth surfaces when someone has struck them. But as we said, it is certainly not the case that everything that is struck or that strikes produces a sound – think of a pin striking a pin – but that which is struck must be flat-surfaced so that the air bounces back bunched together and reverberates. But the characteristics of the sound-sources are revealed in the actualized sound; for just as colours are not perceived without light, so without sound the sharp and flat are not perceived. These last are spoken of by metaphor from the touch-objects. For the sharp moves the sense to a great extent in a short time, the flat to a small extent in a long time. It is not of course the case that the swift is the sharp and the slow the flat, but the movement of the one becomes what it is because of its speed, and that of 420b the other because of its slowness. And this seems to have an analogy with the tactile sharp and blunt; for the sharp as it were pricks, and the blunt as it were pushes, because the one moves in a short time, the other in a long time, so that it is incidental to the one to be swift and to the other to be slow.

Let the above account stand then for sound. Now voice is a kind of sound of an ensouled thing. For none of the things without soul gives voice, though some are said by analogy to give voice, such as the flute and the lyre and whatever other of the things without soul have the production of sustained, varied and articulate sound. For voice also has these features and so there is a likeness. But many of the animals do not have voice, such as the bloodless ones and, of the ones with blood, the fish. And this fits our account, if indeed sound is a certain movement of air, while those that are said to give voice, such as those in the Achelous, make a sound with their gills or some other such part. And since everything gives sound by something striking and against something and in something, and as this last is air it is reasonable that only those things that admit air should give voice. We now see that nature uses what has been breathed in for two tasks – just as she uses the tongue both for taste and for speech (and of these taste is a necessity – which is why more animals have it – while meaning is for the sake of living well). And in the same way nature uses the breath both for the internal warmth of the animal, which is a necessity (for a reason that will be given elsewhere), and for the voice, so that it may have the chance to live well. And the organ of breathing is the throat, and it is the lung for which this part is there. And by this part the land animals have more heat than the others. And first of all it is the area around the heart that has need of the in-breathing, so that it is necessary that the air when inhaled go within the body. It is then the striking of this inhaled air by the soul in these parts of the body against the so-called windpipe that is voice. For it is not every sound of an animal that is voice, as we said (for it is possible even with the tongue just to make some sound and to make a sound like those coughing), rather it is necessary that that which strikes be ensouled and have a kind of imagination, as voice is a kind of sound *with meaning*, and not, like a cough, just of the in-breathed air, though it is with this that it strikes the air in the windpipe against the windpipe.[60] And an indi- *421a* cation of this is our inability to give voice when either breathing in or out, but only while holding the air, for as one holds it in one produces a movement with it. And it will also be clear why fish are without voice – they have no throat, and it is because they do not receive air or breathe in that they lack this part. And why this is so will receive separate treatment.[61]

Chapter Nine: Smell

'*There is little that requires comment in Aristotle's treatment of smell (v. further* De Sensu, *5). He is right about the close connection of smell with taste and about the poverty of the human sense of smell.*' (*Hamlyn*)[62]

Chapter Nine

But with smell and the object of the smell-faculty the situation is less well defined than with what we have so far been discussing; for it is not clear what sort of thing smell is as it is clear with sound and colour. The reason is that we do not have this sense in an accurate way but worse than many animals. For man smells badly and perceives none of the smell-objects except the painful and pleasant ones, as his organ is not accurate. And it is reasonable to suppose that it is in this way that the hard-eyed animals perceive colours, and that varieties of colours are not apparent to them beyond the deterrent and non-deterrent. Man, then, is in the same situation as regards smells. There seems also to be an analogy with taste, and the species of flavour are analogous to the species of smell, but our sense of taste is more exact through its being a kind of touch, the sense that is at its most accurate in man. For in the other senses man is outstripped by many of the animals, but in point of touch his accuracy exceeds that of the others by a long way. And it is also for this reason that he is the most intelligent of the animals, an indication of which is the fact that even within the race of men it is in accordance with this sense-organ that individuals are well or badly endowed by nature, and in accordance with no other. For those with hard skin are intellectually poor natured, those with soft skin the opposite.⁶³ And just as some flavours are sweet and some bitter so is it with smells. But some things have the same smell and flavour – I mean for instance a sweet smell and sweet flavour – and some have the opposite. And smells like flavours can be acrid, bitter, sharp and greasy. But as we said, because smells are not very clearly distinct to us, as flavours are, they have taken their name from 421b these in accordance with their similarity in reality. For the sweet smell is that of saffron and honey, the acrid smell that of thyme and such things. And it is the same with the other varieties. And just as hearing is of the audible and inaudible, sight of the visible and invisible, and so with each of the senses, so is smelling of the odorous and the odourless. And the odourless is either that which cannot have smell at all, or that which has smell but slight and weak. And the tasteless is spoken of in the same way.

And smell too is through a medium, such as air or water. For even the animals in water are thought to perceive smell, whether they are with or without blood, as also those animals in the air. And indeed of these last, some track their prey from a distance guided by their smell. And so there would seem to be a puzzle, if all animals smell in the same way, while man does smell when breathing in, but when breathing out or holding his breath and not breathing in, he does not smell an object either at a distance or nearby, or even if it is put inside his nostril. Now the imperceptibility of that which is placed on the organ itself is common to all animals but not perceiving without breathing in is a peculiarity of man. But this is clear to those who make the experiment. The bloodless animals, then, since they do not have respiration, would appear to have some other sense in addition to those mentioned. But this is impossible as they do perceive smell, for smell is the perception of the smell-source and of the pleasantly or unpleasantly smelling thing. Furthermore, some of them seem to be damaged by the same strong smells as man is, such as bitumen and sulphur and such like. It is necessary then that they smell but without breathing in. But this sense-organ seems to differ in men from that in the other animals, in the way that our eyes differ from those of the hard-eyed animals; for some animals have the eyelids as a screen and as it were a protective case without moving or parting which it does not see. But the hard-eyed animals do not have any such thing, but simply see directly what is happening in the transparent. In the same way for some animals the smell-organ is uncovered, as with the eye, *422a* while those that take in air have a covering for it which is opened when they breathe in, the veins and pores being dilated. And for this reason the animals that breathe in do not smell in water, for they must breathe in to smell, and this it is impossible to do in water. Smell is also of the dry in the way that flavour is of the wet, and the smell-organ is potentially of the appropriate kind.

Chapter Ten: Taste

Taste must be distinguished from the three previously treated senses in view of the fact that, like touch, it has immediate contact with its object and does not operate, as Aristotle puts it, at a remove. It thus becomes important to distinguish taste from touch in general, and Aristotle seeks to do so in this and the subsequent chapter.[64]

Chapter Ten

Now the taste-object is a kind of touch-object, and this is the reason for its not being perceptible through the medium of any other body, for this is not the case with touch either. And the body in which the flavour is, the taste-object, is in the moist as its matter, and this is a kind of touch-object. And for this reason even if we were water-dwellers, we would perceive if something sweet were thrown into the water. But our perception would not be through a medium, but by its being mixed with the water as though in a drink. But colour is not seen in this way by being mixed, nor by its effluences. In the case of taste, then, there is no medium; and as colour is the visible, so is flavour the tastable. But nothing produces the perception of flavour without moisture, but that which does so must have moisture either in actuality or in potentiality, as salt does. (It dissolves easily itself and together with the tongue it dissolves other things.) But just as sight is of the visible and invisible (for darkness is invisible, but sight judges of this too), and in the same way hearing is of sound and silence, of which the one is audible and the other not, and also of the great sound as sight is of the bright (for as the small sound is inaudible, in a way so is the great and forceful sound), and something is said to be invisible on the one hand generally, and in the way that a thing is said to be impossible in other respects, and on the other if despite its nature it is not visible or only weakly, as with what is said to have no foot or no kernel — in just this way, then, taste too is of the tastable and the untastable, and this last is that which has small or weak flavour or is destructive of taste. But the distinction between the drinkable and the undrinkable is considered to be the key here (there is after all a kind of taste of both, but the taste of the one is foul and inhibitive of taste, that of the other in accord with nature); the drinkable too is something that is common to both touch and taste. And since the tastable is moist, it is necessary that the organ for it be *422b* neither moist in actuality nor incapable of becoming moist. For the taste is affected in a way by the tastable insofar as it is tastable. It is necessary then that the taste-organ be not moist but capable of surviving becoming moist, and that it become moist. And an indication of this is the fact that neither when it becomes entirely dry does the tongue taste nor when it is too moist. For in the latter case the tongue makes contact with the water already on it and it is as when someone having first tasted a strong flavour then tastes another, and like the fact that everything seems bitter to those who are ill because they perceive everything with their tongue full of the moisture that then occurs. Now the species of flavour, as it is with the colours, are simple and opposite. There is the sweet and the bitter, and adjoining the one the greasy and the other the salty, and between these there are the sour, rough, acrid and sharp. These are more or less all the varieties of flavour there are held to be. The taste-faculty then is that which is potentially of the appropriate kind, and the taste-object is that which makes it so in actuality.

Chapter Eleven: Touch

Aristotle comes finally to the discussion of touch. He has already told us that this is the most necessary of the senses in that, if the animal did not have it, it would not be able to preserve its existence.[65] It has the further distinguishing feature of having no obvious organ. Aristotle is especially keen to show that flesh must be the medium and not the organ of touch.

Chapter Eleven

But we will give the same account about what is tangible and about touch. For if touch is not a single sense but many, then it is necessary that the things that are tangible are the objects of the many senses. But whether sense *is* many or one is a problem, as is the question what the sense-organ of the touch-faculty is, whether it is the flesh or corresponding part in other animals, or not, this being rather the medium, while the primary sense-organ is something else within. For every sense is believed to be of a single opposition, as sight is of the white and black, hearing of the sharp and flat, and taste of the bitter and sweet. But in that which is tangible there are many oppositions, hot and cold, dry and wet, rough and smooth and all of the others that are of this kind. But a solution of a kind is afforded to this riddle by the fact that in the case of the other senses too there are many oppositions. In voice, for instance, there is not only the opposition of sharpness and flatness, but also that of loudness and softness, and smoothness and roughness of voice and other such oppositions. And there are other analogous varieties in the case of colour. But what is not clear is what is the single underlying thing which is to touch as sound is to hearing.

But as to whether or not the sense-organ is within, or 423a whether it is the flesh, directly, no indication is held to be afforded by the fact that the sensation arises immediately on contact. For as it is, if someone were to make, as it were, a membrane and stretch it around the flesh, it would in just the same way indicate the sensation immediately on touch. And yet it is obvious that the sense-organ would not be in this membrane. And if indeed it were naturally attached, the sensation would come through all the more quickly. This part of the body thus seems to be in the same situation as if the air grew naturally around us in a circle; for in this case it would be by a single faculty that we would be held to perceive sound, colour and smell, and sight, hearing and smell would be a single sense. But as it is, because of the distinction of that through which the movements arise,[66] it is obvious that the sense-organs we have mentioned are different from one another, while in the case of touch this is unclear. For it is impossible that the ensouled body be composed of air or water, for it must be something solid. It remains then possible for it to be something mixed from earth and these things, after the tendency of flesh and similar parts. And so it is necessary

that the body be the ongrown medium of the touch-faculty
and that the sensations (which are indeed many) take place
through it. The fact that they are many is made clear by
touch in the case of the tongue, for this perceives all the
tangible objects with the same part as with flavour. And so if
the rest of the flesh also perceived flavour, taste and touch
would be believed to be one and the same sense. As it is, the
impossibility of interchange makes them two.

But someone might pose the following problem. Every
body has depth, which is its third dimension, and where
there is a body between two other bodies, the two are not
able to touch each other. Furthermore, the wet and the
moist are not without body, but both must either be or have
water. But the things that touch each other in water, their
edges not being dry, must of necessity have water between
them, with which their extremities will be full. But if this is
so, it is impossible that anything should touch anything else
in water, and this would apply in the same way for the air.
(For air stands in the same relation to those things in it as
water to the things in water, but we notice this less, in just
the same way that the animals in water notice less if two
moist things touch.) Is perception, then, of all things in the 423b
same way, or of different things in different ways, in the way
that taste and touch in fact seem to work by contact, the
others from a distance? But this is not the case; rather we
perceive both the rough and the smooth through other
things, just as with the audible and the visible objects and
the smell-source. But while we perceive this last group at a
remove, we perceive the first two nearby and so miss this.
We indeed perceive everything through some intermediary,
but in the case of the contact senses we fail to notice this.
And yet, as we also said before, even if we perceived all the
tangible objects through a membrane without realizing that
it separated us from them, we would be in the same situation
as we are in fact in as regards water and air. For we think
that we in fact make contact with things directly and that
there is no intermediary. But the tangible object is different
from visible things and sound-sources, for these we perceive
because the medium has an effect on us, whereas with the

tangible things we are not affected by the medium but at the same time as the medium, like a man struck through his shield. For it is not that the shield, when it is struck, hits the man, but that it happens to both to be struck at the same time. And in general it would seem that as air and water are to sight, hearing and smell, so are flesh and the tongue to each sense-organ to which they are connected in the same way. But neither in the one case nor in the other would sensation arise when the sense-organ itself is touched, if, for instance, someone were to place a white object on the edge of the eye. From this it is clear that the sense-faculty of touch is within. For in this case the situation would be the same as with the other senses, which do not perceive objects put on the sense-organ, while we do perceive objects put on the flesh.

The characteristics of body as body are tangible, those characteristics I mean that define the elements, the hot and cold, and the dry and wet, about which we have spoken earlier in our discussion of the elements. And the sense-organ of touch, which deals with them, and is that in which the so-called sense of touch primarily subsists, is that part which is 424a potentially like them. For perception is being affected in a certain way. Thus the active thing makes that which is potentially like it like it in actuality. And it is for this reason that we do not perceive what is equally hot or cold or rough or smooth, but rather the excessive degrees, sensation being as it were a kind of mean of the opposition in the sense-objects, and thus a judge of them. For it is the mean that judges, being the opposite to each of the two ends of the scale, and, just like that which is to perceive white and black, it must be neither in actuality but both in potentiality, and so with the other senses, and in the case of touch, neither hot or cold.

And again, just as in a way both the visible and the invisible are objects of sight, and opposites were in the same way the objects of the other senses, so is touch too of the tangible and the intangible. (An intangible thing is either what has only very slightly the characteristic of tangible things, as is the case with air, or the excessively tangible things, such as the destructive things.) We have given our outline account, then, of each of the senses.

Chapter Twelve: Perception as the Reception of Form without Matter

It is in this chapter that Aristotle introduces the idea that perception is the taking by the subject of the Form but not the Matter of the object. This could be seen as a refinement of the idea that perception is a Form of alteration.[67] It is far from clear, however, that Brentano was right to see here in embryo the idea that in perception the object has intentional inexistence within the subject. The idea that perception consists in the reception of Forms without Matter from its objects is connected with the idea that perception is a kind of mean between extremes and thus capable of judgement as between the extremes. We thus clearly see that Aristotle, perhaps at the price of consistency, is here stressing those aspects of his conception of sense-perception that align it best with the intellect, to be discussed after the imagination in Book III. In the present chapter, Aristotle uses the idea that the perceptive faculty receives only Form, not Matter, from the object to elucidate the distinction between the effect of a sense-object on a percipient and on a non-percipient receptor. As we have seen, this leads at the end of the Book to one of his rare flirtations in this work with the idea of consciousness.[68]

Chapter Twelve

But we must grasp in general in connection with perception as a whole, that the sense is the recipient of the perceived forms without their matter, as the wax takes the sign from the ring without the iron and gold – it takes, that is, the gold or bronze sign, but not *as* gold or bronze. And in just the same way the sense is affected in each case by that which has colour or flavour or sound, but not as they are said to be each of these things, but as they are of a certain kind, and in accordance with the account of them. And the primary sense-organ is the thing in which this capacity is located. It is therefore the same as the capacity but different in point of what it is for it to be this. For that which perceives would be some thing extended, but what it is to be perceptive will certainly not be extended nor the sense; rather, they will be a formula and capacity of what perceives. And it is also clear from all this why the excesses of the sense-objects destroy the sense-organs. For if the movement is too strong for the sense-organ, its formula [69] is destroyed – and it was this that was the sense – just as the congruence and pitch are lost when strings are too vigorously struck. And it is also clear why it is that the plants do not perceive, though they have a psychic part and are in some way affected by the touch-objects. 424b After all, they become cold and hot. The reason, then, is that they do not have a mean, nor such a principle as can receive the forms of the sense-objects, but are affected by the matter as well. But someone might puzzle whether that which cannot smell is affected in any way by smell, or that which cannot see by colour, and so on with the other senses. But if the smell-object is a smell and if it has an effect, then the effect that smell will have will be smelling – thus it is impossible that any of the things that cannot smell be affected in any way by a smell, and a similar account can be given of the other senses. Nor indeed can any of the things that can sense be affected except insofar as it is perceptive, as is clear from the following consideration too. Neither light nor darkness nor sound nor smell has any effect on bodies but rather that in which they are, just as the air with thunder is what splits wood. But the tangible objects and the flavours do affect them directly; for if not, by what would the things without soul be affected and altered? But will the other sense-objects also have an effect on such bodies? Or is it that not every body is affected by smell and sound, and that such as are are indeterminate, and do not persist, like the air, which smells indeed, as though affected in some way? But then what *is* smelling beyond being affected in a certain way? Or is it that smelling is also perceiving, but the air on being affected immediately becomes itself a perceptible object? [70]

BOOK III

Sense-perception

Chapter One: General Problems of Perception (I)

In the first two chapters of Book III, Aristotle continues and completes the discussion of sense-perception, and, as in the last chapter of Book II, concentrates on aspects of sense-perception that take him away from the relatively simple analysis of it in Chapter Five of Book II. Aristotle opens the Book with a piece of baroque argumentation to show that there being five senses is not a contingent matter. Hicks cites as a parallel Hegel's proof, unfortunately occurring in the year of the discovery of the first asteroid, that there must be seven planets.[71]

In the second half of the chapter, Aristotle elucidates our perception of the common sense-objects that have been introduced in Chapter Six of Book II and ignored since then. These sense-objects are not essentially available to any special sense, but are incidentally perceived by all of them though not quite in the way that each perceives another's special sense-object. But though not essentially available to any special sense, they are essentially available to a common sense, whose essential objects they are. With the perception of the common sensibles by their proper sense is contrasted the incidental perception by each sense of another's special object. This latter is only possible, it eventually transpires in the De Sensu, Chapter Seven, in virtue of the unity of the entire sense faculty. As Block and Hamlyn [72] have shown, the unity of senses is to be carefully distinguished in this theory from the common sense.

Chapter One

That there is no other sense besides the five (which I take to be sight, hearing, smell, taste and touch) the following argument might be found convincing. If we have in fact sensation of everything of which the sensation is a type of touch (for all the affections of the tangible, as tangible, are perceptible to us by touch), and if from the lack of a sense the lack of a sense-organ in us necessarily follows, and if all those things that we perceive by direct contact we perceive by touch, which we happen to have, and all those things that we perceive not directly but through a medium we perceive by the simple bodies such as air and water, and if, further, it is the case that if more than one kind of sense-object is perceptible to us through a single medium, then he who has a sense-organ of the appropriate sort can necessarily perceive both objects (for instance, if the sense-organ 425a is made of air and air is the medium of both sound and colour), while if there is more than one medium for the same sense-object, as air and water are both media of colour, both being transparent, then he who has only one or other of them will perceive that which is perceptible through them both, and if in fact sense-organs are made from only two of the simple bodies, air and water (the eye-jelly is made of water, the hearing of air, and smell of both these), while fire is either of none or common to all (as nothing can perceive without warmth) and earth either of none or involved in a particularly characteristic way with touch, so that the possibility does not remain of there being any sense-organ made from any body other than water and air, of which are made the sense-organs that some of the animals in fact have, *then* all the senses will be possessed by animals that are neither incomplete nor deformed – as indeed even the mole evidently has eyes under its skin. Thus, if there is no other body and no affection characteristic of none of the bodies in the environment, no sense will be missing.[73]

And indeed it is not possible that there should be some sense-organ special to the common sensibles, which we perceive incidentally with each sense. Such are movement, rest, shape, size, number and unity. All these we perceive by movement. For instance, we perceive size by movement (as also shape which is a kind of size), and we perceive a thing at rest by its not moving. Number we perceive by the denial of continuity and by the special sensibles, since it is *one* thing that each sense perceives. It is thus clear that there could not possibly be some special sense of such common sensibles as movement. The situation would be like our present *visual* perception of sweetness. This occurs because we happen to have a sense for both objects in such a way that we recognize them even in their coincidence.[74] (Were this not so, we would be able to perceive them only incidentally, in the way, that is, that we perceive not that Cleon's son is Cleon's son but that he is a white man to whom it is incidental to be Cleon's son.) But of the common sensibles we do in fact have a common sensation that is not incidental. This shows that there is no special sense for them – otherwise, there would be no other way in which we could see them except that in which it was said that we see Cleon's son. Now it is not as *themselves* that the senses have incidental perception of each other's special objects but insofar as sensation is a *unity*, and this occurs whenever there is simultaneous perception of the same object. For instance, our perception of bile is that it is *425b* bitter and that it is yellow, and it is at any rate not the function of some *other* sense to say that it is one thing that is both these. This also is the reason for illusion, when something's being yellow prompts us to think that it is bile.[75]

A possible line of inquiry would be into the question for what purpose we have many senses and not just one. Is this to improve our awareness of the accompaniments of the special sensibles, the common sensibles, such as movement, size and number? Suppose we just had sight and that whiteness was its object. We would have much less awareness of the common sensibles – in fact we would think that they were all the same, as size always accompanies colour. In fact it is the presence of the common sensibles in more than one special sensible that makes clear that each one of them is something different.[76]

Chapter Two: General Problems of Perception (II)

This chapter is extremely disorganized, which is the more unfortunate in that it deals with some very important problems connected with sense-perception. It is indeed here, as in the previous chapter, that Aristotle comes closest to the modern notion of consciousness, as Block has demonstrated.[77] There remains, nevertheless, a great distance between him and Descartes.[78] Aristotle's approach to consciousness in this chapter is via two questions. He asks first how it is that we perceive that we are perceiving, how, to take his example, we see that we are seeing, and secondly how we know by which special sense each special object is perceived. The answer to the second difficulty takes us back to the ground opened up in the first chapter of the Book, the unity of the sense faculty as a whole. Aristotle answers the first difficulty, that of how we see that we are seeing, characteristically, by suggesting that sight is not a simple sense but comprises both seeing itself and the sense by which one perceives that one is seeing. What is absent, as Hamlyn points out,[79] is any notion of a subject of perception in the modern introspective style, and the absence of this entails the absence of a modern notion of self-consciousness.

Between these two consciousness-adumbrating problems, Aristotle devotes considerable space to further development of the complementary application of the potential–actual distinction to sound and hearing, thus in his favourite way resolving a debate among his predecessors.

Chapter Two

Now since we perceive *that* we are seeing or hearing, it must either be by sight that something perceives that it is seeing or by some other sense. But given the consequent identity of the sense that perceives sight and that which perceives the colour that is the object of sight, there will either be two senses with the same object or the one sense will perceive itself. Further, if the sense that perceives sight were some other sense than sight, the only alternative to an infinite regress will be that there be *some* sense that perceives itself. Why not let this be a feature of the first of the series?

Yet there is a problem. If perceiving by sight is seeing, and it is either colour or the coloured thing that is seen, if there is

to be seeing of seeing, then seeing in the first place will be
coloured.[80] However, it is quite clear that perceiving by
sight is *not* some single thing. For when we are not seeing, it
is by *sight* that we discern [though in a different way],
darkness and light. And anyway the thing that sees is as
though coloured – each organ receives the sense-object without its matter, after all. (That is why even after the removal
of the sense-objects perceptions remain in the sense-organs,
and imaginings.)

Now the activity of the sense-object and that of the sense-
organ are one and the same, but what it is for each to be it is
not the same. Take sound in activity and hearing in activity.
The man with hearing can of course not be hearing and that
which has a sound is not producing sound all the time. But
whenever that which can hear is activated and that which
can give sound is doing so, then the activated hearing coincides with the activated sound. The first of these one might 426a
dub 'harking', the second 'sounding'.[81] If then the movement
and productive activity occur *in* what is acted on, activated
sound and activated hearing must be *in* the potential hearing,
the productive and motive activity being in the thing acted
on (whence the possibility that what produces movement be
not itself moved).[82]

The activity, then, of the sound-productive faculty is sound
or sounding, that of the hearing-productive faculty hearing
or harking, both hearing and sound being in two ways, and
this account holds no less for the other senses and sense-
objects. For in just the way that both action and affection
are in the thing that is affected not in that which acts, the
activity of the sense-object and the sense faculty are in the
sense faculty. But while in some cases this has a name, as
with sounding and hearing, in others both activities are
unnamed. Seeing, for instance, is what we call the activity of
sight, but there is no name for the activity of colour. Tasting
is the activity of the taste faculty, but there is no name for
the activity of flavour. But since the activity of the sense-
object and of the sense faculty are the same but their being
so different, hearing and sounding in this way must be preserved or put an end to together, as also with flavour and

taste and the others. But it is not necessary that this happen with these things as potentialities. The earlier natural philosophers, however, expressed this point badly, thinking that nothing could be either white or black, without sight nor have flavour without taste. In one way what they said was right, but in another wrong. Both sense and sense-object are talked about in two ways, as in potentiality and as in actuality. In the latter case what is claimed occurs, in the former not. They spoke in one way of things that are spoken of in two.

Now if the voice is a kind of concord, and if voice and hearing are as one (and also not as one), and if the concord is a formula, it is necessary that hearing too be a kind of formula.[83] This is also why hearing is destroyed by each excess, the excessively high and excessively low in pitch, in the 426b same way as taste is destroyed by excesses of flavouring, sight by colours that are extremely bright or dark and smell by a strong smell, either sweet or bitter. For there is a kind of ratio of sensation. Thus, although things are pleasant when brought pure and unmixed to the ratio of sensation – for in such circumstances high pitch, sweetness and saltiness are sweet – yet it is in general rather the mixture that is pleasant, the concord, than either high or low in pitch or in the case of touch than what can be made either warmer or colder. So sensation is a formula, dissolved or destroyed by excesses.

Each sense, then, is of the sensible thing that is subject to it, is present in the sense-organ *as* sense-organ and discerns the variations in the sensible thing that is its subject. (For instance, sight discerns whiteness and blackness, taste sweetness and bitterness, and in this respect the other senses are similar.) But since we discern both whiteness and sweetness and the object of each sense by contrast with an object of that sense, what is it whereby we further perceive that they are the objects of different senses? It must indeed be by sensation, as these are sensible things. In this way it also becomes clear that flesh is not the ultimate sense-organ; to suppose that it is requires the supposition that on contact with the object the sense-organ itself discerns *what is doing the discerning*.[84] No more, indeed, is it possible that it should be

by separate things that we perceive that sweetness and whiteness are the objects of different senses. Rather it must be to
some single thing that they are manifest. Otherwise from the
mere fact that I see one thing and you see one thing it would
be obvious that those things were not the same, whereas it
can only be a single thing that asserts their difference.
Sweetness, then, being a different thing from whiteness, it is
the same single thing that asserts them to be so, and as it
asserts so does it both think and perceive this. Clearly, then,
it cannot be by separate things that we discern what are
separate. Furthermore, the impossibility of such discernment
in separate time can be shown thus: just as it is the same
single thing that asserts that the good is different from the
bad, so that simultaneity is not incidental with which it
jointly asserts the mutual difference of each member of the
pair (incidentally simultaneous would be my now saying
that they are different but not *that* they are different now),
but the assertion is rather of the kind that both now (i.e.
simultaneously) asserts the difference *and* asserts that the
things are now, i.e. simultaneously different. The time of the
assertion is no less inseparate than the asserting thing.[85]

It is, however, surely impossible that the same thing, as an
indivisible, be moved simultaneously and in an indivisible
time through opposing motions.[86]

Now sweetness moves sensation and thought in the appropriate way and bitterness in the opposing way, while 427a
whiteness moves it in a *different* way. Is it then the case that
that which discerns is simultaneous in operation, numerically
indivisible and inseparate, but separable in what it is for it to
be this? Thus it remains in one way the case that the divisible
perceives divided objects, but in another way it does so, *as
something indivisible*. It is in *being* divisible, but spatially and
numerically indivisible. But can it really be so? It can, because the same single indivisible thing is both opposites in
potentiality but not in being, so that it is in actualization
that it is divided and cannot *be* white and black at the same
time, cannot then be affected at the same time by their
forms, if that is the sort of thing that sensation and thought
are. Consider the parallel with what some people call a

'point'. In the way that this is both one and two, it is both indivisible and divisible. That, then, which discerns is, as indivisible, single and simultaneous, but in its divisible presence it makes simultaneous use of the same symbol in two ways. It is then insofar as it makes double use of its boundary, that it discerns two things and has separate, and separately treated, objects, while it is in treating it as a single thing that it both discerns a single object and discerns simultaneously.[87]

After this fashion, then, let our account be of that first principle in virtue of which we say that an animal is capable of perception.

Imagination

Chapter Three: Imagination

In this chapter Aristotle moves on to a disjointed but highly original, indeed pioneering, treatment of the imagination. The concept that Aristotle is discussing in this chapter seems to be rather wider than our notion of imagination – indeed it might be suggested that there is no one concept that Aristotle is here discussing at all. Certainly the treatment branches away from what we consider non-standard cases of imagination to what Schofield[88] has labelled 'non-paradigmatic sense-perception' in general. The consequent incoherence is partly the effect of Aristotle's wish to form a bridge in the treatment of imagination between the discussion of sense-perception that has just ended and that of the intellect that is about to begin. Nor is Aristotle's general notion of imagination given any greater consistency by its use elsewhere in his works.[89] However, the incoherence of the treatment is surely a sign of its philosophical vitality and is certainly shared by modern discussions on the subject. It should also be noted that Aristotle's positive account of imagination as a motion arising in connection with sense-perception is firmly physiological in tone, even though the products of phantasia are to play an important part in explaining the operation of the intellect in the next chapter of the work. It is also of interest that Aristotle does not here say anything about the memory, though this is the

subject of one of the most interesting treatises of the Parva
Naturalia.[90]

Chapter Three

Now of the two features by which especially men define the
soul, locomotion, on the one hand, and thinking, understanding and perceiving on the other, both thinking and understanding are thought to be something like perceiving. In both
cases, after all, the soul discerns and has cognition of the
things that exist. Indeed the earlier thinkers assert the
identity of understanding and perceiving. Empedocles, for
instance, said:

'For human wisdom grows by what is present ...'

and elsewhere:

'Whence comes it ever
That thought of other things is put before them ...'[91]

And this is also the meaning of Homer's 'For such is mind
...'[92] For all these men suppose thinking to be, like perceiving, something bodily, and also make both perceiving
and understanding to be of like by like. This we set down in
our opening section. They should, however, also have spoken
at the same time about error as this is a more peculiar feature 427b
of animals, and the soul spends more time in this state. This
forces us either, with some, to accept that all appearances
are veridical or call illusion contact with the dissimilar, the
opposite, that is, of the knowledge of like by like. There
would not, however, seem to be a difference between the
illusion of one thing and true knowledge of its opposite.[93]

It is, however, clear that perceiving and understanding
are *not* the same. For while all animals have a share of the
former, only a few have a share of the latter. And as for
thinking, which can be both correct and incorrect, correct
thought being understanding, knowledge and true opinion,
incorrect thought their opposites, not even this is the same as
perceiving. For the perception of special sensibles is always
true and is enjoyed by all animals, while thinking admits of

being false and is enjoyed by no animal that does not also have rationality. For imagination is a different thing from both perceiving and thinking. Imagination cannot occur without perception, nor supposition without imagination.[94] Now the non-identity of imagination and supposition is obvious. For it lies in our power to be affected by imagination whenever we wish – one can produce something before the eyes, as do those who make images of things and arrange them in mnemonic systems – while holding beliefs is not up to us, these being of necessity either false or true. Furthermore, whenever we hold the *belief* that something is terrible or fearsome, we at once experience the corresponding emotion, as also with comforting beliefs. But in the case of imagination, we are in just the same state as if we were looking at the terrible or comforting things in a painting. (There are also varieties of supposition itself, knowledge, belief and understanding and their opposites. But let us discuss elsewhere the difference between these.)

Thinking, then, is something other than perceiving, and its two kinds are held to be imagination and supposition.[95] In our treatment of it, then, we should first give an account 428a of imagination and then speak of the other kind. Well then, if imagination is that in virtue of which we say that an image occurs to us, and we are not using the word in some metaphorical sense, is it one of those faculties or states in virtue of which we give judgement and arrive either at truth or falsity?[96] Now those of this kind are perception, belief, knowledge and intellect. That imagination is not the same as perception is clear from the following arguments. (i) Perception is either a potentiality or an activity, as, for instance, are sight and seeing, yet there are appearances in the absence of either of these, such as the appearances in sleep. (ii) Perception is, but imagination is not, always present. And if it were in *activity* that they were the same, it would be possible for all animals to have imagination; but it is held that while the ant and bee do, the grub does not, have imagination.[97] (iii) While perceivings are always veridical, imaginings are for the most part false. (iv) It is not when we are in a state of accurate activity in connection with the sense-object that we *say* 'This appears to me as a man', but rather whenever we do not clearly perceive whether it is a real or illusory man. (v) As we said above, visions appear even to those whose eyes are shut.

But then imagination will also not be one of those faculties that are always correct, such as knowledge or intellect; for imagination can also be false. It remains, then, to see if imagination is the same as belief, as there is both a true and a false variety of belief. Belief, however, is followed by conviction, as it is not possible for those that hold beliefs not to be convinced of the things in which they believe, and while none of the animals have conviction many of them have imagination. (In other words, the conviction that accompanies all belief is produced by persuasion, a task of reason, and while some of the beasts have imagination none has reason.) These points, then, show that imagination could not be belief with perception or belief through perception or a combination of belief and perception.

This conclusion is supported by another thought. If imagination is belief, the object of the belief will be none other than that, if any, of the perception. What I mean is that imagination will be a combination of belief in, and perception of, whiteness, say, and not, obviously, a combination of a belief in something good and a perception of something white. But then to be subject to an appearance will just be to believe 428b non-incidentally in what one perceives. There are, however, also false appearances, in connection with whose objects true supposition simultaneously occurs. For instance, the sun appears to be a foot across. Yet we are convinced that it is greater than the inhabited world. If then imagination is belief, there are two possibilities: either the subject has cast aside the true belief that he had, without any change in the facts and without his having either forgotten it or been persuaded to the contrary, or, if he retains the true belief, then the same belief must necessarily be both true and false. However, the belief would only really become false in circumstances in which the facts changed without his noticing. Imagination, then, is neither one of these things nor a combination of them.[98]

But it is possible that whenever anything has been set in motion there is something else that is moved by that thing. And imagination is held to be a kind of movement and not to occur without perception but in things that perceive and in connection with objects of which there is perception. Now it is possible that a movement might arise from the activity of sensation, and necessary that this would be similar to the sensation. This movement could not be without perception or be in those things that do not perceive, and whatever had this movement could act and be affected in many ways in virtue of it, and it could be both true and false.

This happens for the following reasons. The perception of special sensibles is veridical, or admits falsity to the smallest possible extent. Secondly there is the perception of the incidence to these of those things that are incidental to them, and this already admits of falsity – as to a thing's being white there is no falsity, but there is as to a white thing's being this or something else. Thirdly, there is the perception of the things that are common and attendant on the things incidental to the special sensibles (I mean such things as movement and size). And with these there is the greatest possibility of perceptual illusion. Now the movement that arises from the activity of sensation will differ in virtue of its arising from these three types. The first type of movement will, in the presence of the perception, be true; the others might be false in either its presence or its absence, and especially whenever the sense-object is remote.

429a If then there is no other thing but imagination that has the features mentioned – and this is what has been said – then imagination will be a movement coming about from the activity of sense-perception. And since sight is paradigmatically sense-perception, it is from light, without which seeing is impossible, that imagination takes its name.[99] And because of the duration of acts of imagination and their resemblance to sense-perceptions, it is in virtue of these that animals do many things, some, such as the beasts, through their not having intellect, some, such as men, through the occasional occlusion of their intellects by emotion, illness and sleep. Let this much suffice both as to what imagination is and as to how it comes about.[100]

Intellect

Chapter Four: Intellect (I)

This is the first of the three chapters devoted to the intellect. These have always been the most discussed chapters of the work, usually in connection with the light they may throw on the possibility of the separate survival by at least part of the soul of the death of the body.[101] Aristotle consistently maintained in this work and elsewhere[102] that the capacity for thought is the part of the soul most likely to survive the death of the body. In this discussion, however, the issue of whether the intellect is capable of separate existence is not expressly resolved. Rather, Aristotle seems to have felt that the question could only be answered by a division of the concept of intellect, such as is given in Chapter Five.

The fourth chapter itself treats the intellect in a manner strikingly parallel to the accounts of the senses. This involves two major difficulties that Aristotle does not fully confront. The first is that while all the senses are closely correlated to material sense-organs, the same cannot be said of thought, the second that whereas the objects of the special senses are relatively clear there is room for controversy as to what the objects of thought are on this theory.[103]

Chapter Four

Now as to that part of the soul by which it has both cognition and understanding, whether this be separate or not indeed spatially separate but conceptually so, we must consider what its characteristic features are and how thinking occurs at any time. If, then, thinking is like perceiving, it will either be some kind of affection by the thought-object or some such thing. It must then be something unaffected which yet receives the form and is potentially of the same kind as its object but not the same particular, and the intellect must stand in that relation to the objects of thought in which the

perceptive faculty stands to those of perception. It is necessary, then, since the intellect thinks all things, that the
intellect be unmixed, 'that it may rule', as Anaxagoras puts
it, which is a way of saying that it is thus so that it may have
cognition.[104] For an internal appearance would impede
and obstruct that from without – so that it cannot have any
nature of its own except just this, to be potential.[105]

That part of the soul then that is called intellect (by which
I mean that whereby the soul thinks and supposes) is before
it thinks in actuality none of the things that exist. This makes
it unreasonable that it be mixed with the body – for, if so, it
would have to have some quality, being either hot or cold, or
indeed have some organ like the perceptive faculty, whereas
it in fact has none. One must indeed applaud those who say
that the soul is the place of forms, adding only that it is not
the whole but the noetic soul and that this is the forms not in
actuality but in potentiality. Consideration of the sense-
organs and of sensation makes it clear that the unaffectedness
of the perceptive and of the noetic faculties are not alike. For
429b a sense loses the power to perceive after something excessively
perceptible; it cannot, for instance, perceive a sound after
very great sounds, nor can it see after strong colours nor smell
after strong smells, whereas when the intellect has thought
something extremely thinkable, it thinks lesser objects more
not less. For whereas the sense faculty is embodied, the
intellect is separate. But when the intellect becomes each
thing in the way that the actualized knower is said to be,
which happens whenever it is capable of being in activity
through itself, it is even then in a way potentiality, but not
indeed in the same way as before learning or finding out,
and it is then itself capable through itself of thinking.[106]

Now size and to be size are not the same, nor water and to
be water (and so with many other things, though not with
all, as in some cases they are the same), and so we discern the
being of flesh and flesh either by something else or by something in a different state. For flesh, far from being without
matter, is, like the snub, a this in a that. It is then with the
perceptive faculty that we discern warmth and coldness and
those things of which flesh is the formula, but with something

else that we discern being-flesh, and this is either separate or related to the perceptive faculty in the way that a bent line is related to itself when straightened. And again in the case of those things that exist in abstraction, the straight is like the snub in requiring extension, but what it is to be straight, if straightness and being straight are not the same, is different. Let us call this duality. And this we judge either with something else or with the faculty in a different state. In the way, then, that things are separable from matter in general, in that way are the things connected with the intellect.[107]

If, however, the intellect is something simple and un-affected and has nothing in common with anything, as Anaxagoras says, one might well ask how it is to think, if thinking is a kind of affection (for insofar as something common occurs to both things, one is held to be active, the other passive), and also whether it can itself be thought. There are two possibilities: either, if it is not in virtue of something else that the intellect can be thought, and if the object of thought is something single in form, then intellect will also be present in other things; or it will have something mixed with it which will render it an object of thought like other things. Now we distinguished above affection in virtue of something common, in saying that the intellect is in a way potentially the objects of thought, but nothing in actuality before it thinks, and the potentiality is like that of the tablet *430a* on which there is nothing actually written. Just the same happens in the case of the intellect. And it is itself thinkable just as the thought-objects are, for in the case of things without matter that which thinks is the same as that which is thought. For contemplative knowledge is the same as what is so known. (But we must further consider the cause of the intellect's not always thinking.) Each of the objects of thought is potentially present in the things that have matter, so that while they will not have intellect, which is a capacity for being such things without matter, the intellect will have within it the object of thought.[108]

Chapter Five: Intellect (II); Active and Passive

The structural similarity for Aristotle of sense-perception and thought in no sense requires what we are told in this chapter. Hamlyn is surely right to call the active intellect here introduced a mere metaphysical ground for the operation of the intellect.[109] Nothing in the chapter suggests for it a direct role in either the acquisition or the use of concepts. Aquinas gives the active intellect a quite unAristotelian role when he ascribes to it the abstraction of species from phantasms and the imposition of them on the passive intellect.[110] But if the active intellect has no functional role in thought-processes, neither is it explicitly connected with the first mover of Metaphysics *Lambda, though the temptation to make this connection may have been felt as early as Theophrastus.[111] Perhaps the most serious objection, however, to this chapter is that the distinction here being drawn is otiose within the general structure of the theory. It is not required by the previous chapter nor used in the following one. Given these facts and its brevity, there is a certain plausibility in the suggestion that the chapter is an afterthought or even a later interpolation designed to bring the doctrine of the* De Anima *in line with* Metaphysics *Lambda. In any case, the active intellect is clearly separable and thus presumably substantial, and since Aristotle does not distinguish it in this respect from the passive intellect it is reasonable to suppose that this too is in an Aristotelian sense substantial. This, of course, would corroborate the general substantialist interpretation of the doctrine of the soul as form.[112]*

Chapter Five

Now in all nature there is for each genus something that is its matter (and it is this that is all those things in potentiality), and something else that is their cause, productive of them in virtue of bringing them all about – as, for instance, a skill stands towards the matter it uses. No less in the soul, then, must these different features occur. And indeed there is an intellect characterized by the capacity to become all things, and an intellect characterized by that to bring all things about, and to bring them about in just the way that a state, like light, does. (For in a way, light also *makes* things that are potentially colours colours in actuality.) Now this latter intellect is separate, unaffected and unmixed, being in substance activity.

For in all cases that which acts is superior to that which is affected, and the principle to its matter. And while knowledge in the actualized state is identical with the fact known, knowledge in the state of potentiality, though temporally prior in the individual case, does not in general even have temporal priority.[113] Nor is it the case that the intellect is now thinking, now not. It is, further, in its separate state that the intellect is just that which it is, and it is this alone that is immortal and eternal, though we have no memory, as the separate intellect is unaffected, while the intellect that is affected is perishable, and in any case thinks nothing without the other.

Chapter Six: Intellect (III); Simple and Complex

This chapter, much of whose text like that of its successor is in a disputed state, deals with the connections between thought, propositional structure and veridicity. It asserts that only complex, propositional thoughts can be veridical. The general handling recalls the discussion of the proposition in the De Interpretatione. *Indeed, Aristotle does not here offer any purely psychological insights until, at the end of the chapter, he returns to the application to the intellect of the potential–actual distinction.*[114]

Chapter Six

The thinking, then, of indivisibles[115] is to be counted among those things with which falsity has no connection. In things, however, to which falsity and truth apply, there is already some synthesis of thoughts, which are treated as though they were one. Empedocles, after saying:

'And here there grew for many neckless heads . . .',

went on to say that these things were then put together by love. So, in our case, things are first separate and then conjoined – an example would be incommensurability and the diagonal. And if the conjunction is to be of things that have

430b been or will be, then the temporality is a further thought combined therewith. In all cases falsity occurs in a conjunction; even if white is asserted not to be white, there has been a conjunction, of whiteness and non-whiteness. (All these things could equally well be labelled division.) It is in any case not just to the claim that, say, Cleon *is* white that falsity or truth attaches, but also to those that he *was* or that he *will be*. And in all these cases it is intellect that effects the unity.

An undivided thing is so in two ways, either potentially or actually. This makes it perfectly possible for one to be thinking an undivided thing when one is thinking of a length. The length has *actual* undividedness. The thought of it can also be temporally undivided, time being divided or undivided in the same way as length. We thus cannot say what it is that we thought in either half of the time – unless the line has been divided, there are no such halves, except potentially. To think separately, on the other hand, of each half is to divide *au même coup* both line and time, which in these circumstances is to be treated as a length, and to think of the line *as composed* of two halves is also to think of it in the time appropriate to them both.[116]

Now divisibility is incidental to the content and time of the thought, as it is not to the objects, whereas indivisibility is not incidental to either. For even in the objects something undivided must be present, though perhaps not as something separate, to make them one time and one length, being present in the same way in all that is continuous, whether time or length.

That which is undivided not as to quantity but in its form is thought in an undivided time and with an undivided part of the soul. The point, however, and every instance of division, as well as that which is in this way divided are manifested in the same way as privation. And this account applies in the same way to other cases, such as the cognition of evil or of blackness, which are in a way known from their opposites. The cognitive must also be potentially its object, ‡which must be in it‡. But if there is something to which there is ‡amongst the causes‡[117] no opposite, then this has the properties of self-cognition, existence as actuality and separateness.

Assertion is also *of* something and *that* something is the case, as is also negation, and all cases admit of truth or falsity. But this is not the way with all thought; rather the thought of what a thing is will be veridical if it is in respect of what it is for the thing to be what it is, nor is this assertion of something that something is the case. There is a parallel with the way that the sight of a special sensible is veridical, whereas that of whether a white thing is or is not a man will not always be so. It is the same way with those things that are without matter.[118]

Chapter Seven: Appendix to Sense and Mind

This chapter is unfortunately in a fragmentary state but it goes again over some of the points previously discussed as well as introducing some new ground. No consistent line of argument can be extracted, however, from the resulting congeries. It has been plausibly suggested that the chapter was added by a later editor anxious to preserve all available scraps of Aristotle's writings on sense and thought.[119] Towards the end of the chapter the discussion concentrates on the differences and similarities between simultaneous perception of contrary, and simultaneous perception of merely different, sensations. Aristotle seeks to elucidate this with a schematic illustration that is one of the most vexed things in the entire work. In general, no substantial addition or modification is offered in this chapter to the doctrines of thought- or sense-perception. It forms in effect an appendix to the treatment of these topics.

Chapter Seven

Now while knowledge in the actualized state is identical *431a* with the fact known, knowledge in the state of potentiality, though temporally prior in the individual case, does not in general even have temporal priority. For all things that come to be do so from that which exists in actuality. It is clear, too, that it is the object of perception that converts the perceptive faculty from being it in potentiality to being it in actuality, without being itself affected or altered. This then is another species of movement, the activity of something incomplete as against that of a complete thing which is activity *tout simple*.[120]

Perceiving then is analogous to mere saying and thinking, but when it is of the pleasant or painful the soul engages in pursuit or avoidance and these are analogous to assertion and denial.

In fact, to experience pleasure and pain is to be active with the perceptive mean in relation to good or bad as such. Avoidance, what is more, and desire are, in their actualized state, the same thing, nor are their faculties different either from each other or from the perceptive faculty, but their way of being the same thing is different. For in the thinking soul, images play the part of percepts, and the assertion or negation of good or bad is invariably accompanied by avoidance or pursuit, which is the reason for the soul's never thinking without an image.[121]

Now it is the air that gives the eye-jelly the appropriate character, which the eye-jelly then gives to another part, and the same happens with the hearing. But there is a single terminus for these series and a single mean, though its ways of being this are many. Just so . . .[122]

We have indicated above with what it is that the soul discerns how sweet and hot differ, but let us also put the point in the following way. The part in question is something single, but single in the way that a boundary is. The sense-objects in question are one in analogy and number and their mutual relation is parallel to that of those things. How indeed can there be a difference between asking how the soul discerns things different in kind and asking how it discerns opposites, such as white and black? To see this, let C stand to D just as A, white, stands to B, black. (The relation produced by alternation will also hold.) If, then, A and B are present to some single subject, then they are one and the same thing, but the way in which each is this is different. Now the same will hold in these circumstances for C and D, and this will apply similarly to those things as well. And the argument is $_{431b}$ the same if we make A the sweet and B the white.[123]

The thinking faculty, then, thinks the forms in images, and, as what it should pursue or avoid is defined in the images, it is moved even in the absence of perception, whenever there are images before it. On the one hand, one perceives, say, that the beacon is alight, and it is in seeing it move that one reaches the cognition that it is, say, hostile, but, on the other, it is sometimes by the images and thoughts in the soul that, as though one were seeing, one calculates and deliberates about the future on the basis of the present, and in the latter case no less than the former the statement of pleasantness or painfulness involves avoidance or pursuit – in both cases these will be a single action.[124] An assertion that is non-practical, such as that of truth or of falsity, is in the same genus as that of good and bad – the difference is that the former are made absolutely the latter in relation to something.

One thinks those things that are spoken of as in abstraction in just the way that, were one to think in actuality of a snub, not as a snub, but after separation, as hollow, one would be thinking of the hollowness without the flesh. In the same way, when one thinks of mathematical objects, which are not separate, one thinks of them *as* separate.

In general, the intellect, in its actualized state, is the facts, and whether, insofar as it is not itself separate from size, it can or cannot think one of the things that are separate, we must consider later.[125]

Chapter Eight: Summary of Account of Sense-perception and Thought

This chapter marks the end of that part of the De Anima *which deals with the cognitive or quasi-cognitive functions of the soul. Only the soul's capacity of motivation remains to be discussed. Unfortunately, the chapter is a rather clumsy résumé and adds little substantial doctrine, apart from some clarification of the role of the imagination in providing the content of thought. Its untidy procedure catches nothing of the elegant structure of the discussion that has just occurred.*

Chapter Eight

But now by way of summing up what has been said about the soul, let us repeat that the soul is in a way all the things that exist. For all the things that exist are objects either of perception or of thought, and knowledge is in a way the things that are known, perception in a way the things that are perceived. But we must inquire how this is so. Knowledge, then, and perception are divided in relation to their objects, they in their potential state corresponding to the objects in their potential state, and the same correspondence obtaining between the actualized states. And the perceptive and cognitive faculties of the soul are also those of thought. Now it must either be the things themselves that the faculties potentially are or their forms, and, as it is obviously not the things themselves, since, clearly, stone, for instance, is not in 432a the soul, it must rather be the forms. There is thus an analogy between the soul and the hand – the hand is a tool of tools, the intellect a form of forms and the sense a form of sense-objects. And since there is, as it is thought, no separable thing apart from perceptible sizes, the objects of thought are in the forms that are perceived, both those that are spoken of as in abstraction and those that are conditions and affections of the objects of perception.

This is also the reason why if one perceived nothing one would learn and understand nothing, and also why it is necessary that, whenever one is contemplating, it is some image that one is contemplating; for the images are like sense-data but without matter. Imagination is also something different from assertion and negation – for it is the combination of thoughts that is true or false. What, then, distinguishes the *primary* thoughts from being images? Is it not better to say that neither they nor the others *are* images, but that they cannot occur without images?[126]

Motivation

Chapter Nine: Motivation (I) The Division of the Soul

In this and the subsequent two chapters, Aristotle discusses the soul's capacity to set in motion the ensouled body, the animal. This is the part of the traditional characterization of soul that is still to be explained. The motivating capacity is to be treated under the heading desire (orexis), which has a rather different meaning from its modern nearest equivalents. Above all, Aristotle never really makes clear whether the concept of desire belongs to psychology or physiology, so that he cannot show how the movement produced by the soul at least in the case of man can justly be called an action, the product of rational and conscious agency.[127]

In any case, before passing on to the subject of desire itself, Aristotle engages in a lengthy critique of the ways that the soul was in his time divided into faculties. It is interesting that, although his rejection of traditional principles of division involves him in a distinctly complex model of the soul himself, he remains reluctant to sacrifice the general principle of the faculty-division of soul. Needless to say, it is impossible to press the formal model here given too closely on the text of this work as we have it.

Chapter Nine

The soul, then, of animals is defined according to two capacities, that of discernment, which is the function of thinking and perceiving, and that of producing locomotion. On the subject of perception and intellect let the preceding account suffice, and let us turn to the investigation of what it is in the soul that is the producer of motion, whether it is some single part of it, separable either spatially or conceptually, or all the soul, and, if it is some part, whether it is some special one, other than those that are usually mentioned and have been mentioned by us, or some one of these.

Now we immediately encounter a problem as to the way in which we should say that the soul has parts and how many we should claim there to be.[128] For there seem in a way to be an infinity of such parts and not only those that some have given, distinguishing the reasoning, spirited and desiderative parts, or, with others, the rational and irrational. For by the differences in virtue of which they have separated out these parts, there would seem to be other parts too with a sharper distinction between them than these have. Indeed, we have in fact been discussing such parts. There is the nutritive part, which is present both in the plants and in all the animals, and the perceptive part, which could not 432b easily be given either as irrational or rational. Then there is the imaginative part. Though it is different from all the parts in its way of being what it is, it is very problematic, on the assumption of separate parts of the soul, with which it is to be identified and from which distinguished. In addition to these, there is the desiderative part, seemingly both conceptually and potentially distinct from all. The division of this part is a patent absurdity, as there is then wishing in the rational part, and appetite and passion in the irrational, and, on a tripartite division, desire in all three parts of the soul. And, indeed, à propos the topic just broached, what is the part that produces locomotion for the animal? (For that type of movement that is connected with growth and decay, being common to all, would seem to be produced by that part which is common to all, the reproductive and nutritive. And, since they are highly problematic, we shall have later to consider breathing in and out and sleep and waking.)

On the subject, then, of locomotion, let us consider what is the producer for the animal of the movement of travel. It is clearly not the capacity for nutrition, for it invariably has a purpose and is accompanied by imagination and desire. Nothing, in fact, that is not engaged in desire or avoidance is moved except by force. Such a circumstance would also make all the plants capable of movement and possessed of an organic part adjusted to this type of movement. No more can it be the perceptive faculty, and for similar reasons. There are many of the animals that have perception but are stationary and unmoved all their lives. If, then, nature neither does anything in vain [129] nor leaves out any of the things that are necessary, except in deformities and incomplete cases, while the sort of animals in question are complete and not deformities, as is indicated by their being reproductive and their both flourishing and declining, then they would also have the organic parts for travelling. But certainly it is not the calculative part and what is called the intellect that produces this movement. For the contemplative intellect contemplates nothing that is done, nor pronounces at all upon the objects of avoidance and pursuit, while the movement in question is invariably that of something in avoidance or pursuit of something. Not even when it contemplates something of the appropriate type does the intellect issue the order for avoidance or pursuit. Often, for instance, it thinks something fearful or pleasant, yet does not bid the animal be afraid; rather it is the heart that is moved or, in the pleasant case, some other part. But even if the $433a$ intellect does command us and our thinking does tell us to avoid or pursue something, we are not set in motion, but rather act, like the incontinent man, by appetite. And quite generally we observe that it is not the man just possessed of medical skill that cures, there being some other thing, not the knowledge, that is responsible for the production of the cure in accordance with the knowledge.[130] Finally not even desire is responsible for the movement we are investigating. For the self-controlled, though experiencing desire and appetite, yet do not do the things that they desire, but defer to the intellect.[131]

Chapter Ten: Motivation (II)

This chapter opens by summarizing the conclusions of its predecessor, that the two motivational faculties of the soul are desire and the intellect. The purpose of the first section of this chapter is to show how these two are in fact to be reduced to the single faculty, desire.

The second part of the chapter elaborates the operation of desire, by distinguishing a trichotomy of object–desire–animal. But the crucial question is not confronted, namely whether the desire that stands in this sequence between the two clearly physical items –object and animal – is itself a wholly physical item, or indeed a physical item at all.[132] However, the physiological character of the treatment, although not explicitly acknowledged, is strongly suggested by Aristotle's silence in the context. Certainly, if there is a suggestion here that desire is non-physical, there seems to be no awareness of the traditional difficulties of such a supposition. The close connection drawn at the end of the chapter between desire and the imagination is without prejudice to the question of desire's being or not being physical, as the status of imagination itself is quite unclear in Aristotle's theory.

Chapter Ten

There seem, then, to be these two producers of movement, either desire or intellect, if we take the imagination as a kind of thinking. For many men follow their imaginations as against their knowledge, and in the other animals, while there is neither thought nor rationality, there is imagination. Both these things, then, intellect and desire, are productive of locomotion, and the intellect in question is that which reasons for a purpose and has to do with action and which is distinct in its end from the contemplative intellect. All desire is also purpose directed. The object of desire is the point of departure for action.[133]

Thus it is no surprise that the two things that seem to be productive of movement are desire and practical thinking. It is because of the movement started by the object of desire that the thinking produces its movement, that which is desired being its point of departure. And even imagination, whenever it produces movement, does not do so without desire. Thus there is really one thing that produces movement, the faculty of desire. If there were two such things, intellect and desire, they would do so in accordance with some form in common, and in fact it is not clear that the intellect produces movement without desire, wishing being a type of desire, and the movement produced by reasoning being invariably accompanied by that produced by wishing, while desire even in the face of reasoning produces movement, a type of desire being appetite.[134]

And it is because, while intellect is always correct, desire and imagination are either correct or not, that movement always stems from the object of desire. This is either the good or what seems good, and not any such but only that which can be done, that is to say, that which admits of being other than it is.

We have shown, then, that it is the sort of capacity of the soul that is called desire that produces movement. Those, *433b* however, who divide the soul into parts, if capacities are the basis for the division and segregation, will find no small number – in addition to the nutritive, perceptive, ratiocinative and deliberative parts, there is also the part that desires. All these are markedly more mutually distinct than the appetitive and passionate parts. There arise, however, desires opposed one to another. The opposition of reason and the appetites invariably leads to this, and its occurrence is confined to those creatures enjoying resistance, while the appetite supports its case with the immediate facts. Inability to see into the future underwrites the appearance that what is immediately pleasant both is so absolutely and is absolutely good. In form, then, that which produces movement is a single thing, the faculty of desire as such. But first of all is the object of desire, which, by being thought or imagined, produces movement while not itself in motion. In number, however, there is more than one thing that produces movement.

There are three things here. One is that which produces the movement, a second is that whereby it does so, and a third that which is set in motion. Now the producer of the movement is double; on the one hand, unmoved, on the other, also being moved. The first is the good that can be done, the second the faculty of desire, which is moved insofar as it desires, desire in the actualized state being a kind of movement. The third thing is the animal, so that the organ whereby desire produces movement, it follows, is something bodily, whose investigation belongs with that of the common functions of body and soul.

For the moment, however, let us be summary. The organic producer of movement is located, like a hinge, at a point both of departure and arrival. (The point of arrival for the hinge is the convex part, the concave that of departure, whence the rest of the latter and the movement of the former, and these, while conceptually distinct, are spatially inseparable. Every movement being a push or a pull, there must be a still point as with the circle, and this will be the point of departure for the movement.) In general, then, to repeat, it is as being capable of desire that the animal is capable of self-movement. Nor can it have desires without imagination, of whose two exhaustive divisions, rational and perceptive imagination, the latter is enjoyed no less by the other animals than by man.[135]

Chapter Eleven: Appendix to Motivation

Here Aristotle extends the account already given of the motive faculty of the soul to include the treatment of abnormal specimens and elucidate further the concepts of desire, imagination and supposition.[136] As elsewhere, he is engaged in the task of conceptual analysis, and these remarks form a short appendix to the preceding discussion of desire, as Chapter Seven of this Book does to the discussions of sense-perception and the intellect. The only substantial addition to the doctrine of the work is the distinction between deliberative and perceptive imagination.[137]

Chapter Eleven

We must, however, extend to the incomplete cases our con-
434a sideration of what it is that produces movement. Can animals that have sensation only by touch have imagination or not? Can they have appetite? Well, there is no doubt that they have pain and pleasure, whose presence entails that of appetite. But how could they have imagination? Or perhaps they have these faculties but in an indeterminate way – after all, their movement is indeterminate. The presence even in non-human animals of perceptive imagination has already been noted. It is in those with reason that deliberative imagination occurs, it being a task for reasoning to decide whether to do one thing or another. It must be against a single thing that the options are measured and the better pursued, which implies the power to produce a single thing from many images.[138]

The apparent non-possession by these animals of belief is

explained by their non-possession of syllogistic belief – so that desire does not require the deliberative faculty.[139] Furthermore, between two desires, the prevalence will bounce from one to the other like a ball, in circumstances of incontinence, but by nature the loftier is at all times the more dominant and the producer of movement. Already, then, we count three types of movement. Supposition, thought, and reason are on the one hand of the general and on the other of the particular. The first prescribes a *kind* of action for a *kind* of agent, while the second says 'But this action is of the appropriate kind, and I such an agent.' We can either say, then, that it is the second and not the first that produces movement, or that it is both, though the first, unlike the second, remains more in a state of rest while doing so.[140]

Appendix: Animal Survival

Chapter Twelve: The Teleological Context (I)

Since the previous chapter has completed the explanation under the entelechist hypothesis of those things that tradition required to be explained by a theory of the soul, it remains for the last two chapters to set the whole study of the soul in its context within the study of life. Thus, the work ends on the same general note with which it has begun, a fact that would also facilitate transition from it to the subsequent parts of a continuous lecture course on biology.[141] The scientific approach is that of teleological physiology, and the first half of the chapter clears up a point that had been left until now, that the animal's body is necessarily composed of more than one element. Aristotle can, however, be accused of not satisfactorily showing that the body's capacity to touch requires that it be of elementarily plural composition.

Chapter Twelve

Everything, then, that lives and has a soul must have the nutritive soul, from birth to destruction. For whatever has come into existence must needs have growth, flourishing and decay, none of them possible without nourishment. The nutritive soul, then, must be present in all those things that grow and decay, but there is no need for perception in all living things. In fact, neither those animals whose body is simple nor those that do not receive the forms without matter can have touch. The animal, however, must have perception. Nothing can be an animal without this, if nature does nothing in vain. For all things in nature either exist for a purpose or are accidents of the things that so exist. If, then, any body that travels did not have perception, it would be destroyed and so not achieve nature's function by reaching 434b its purpose. After all, how is it to be nourished? For stationary things nourishment comes from that from which they have grown, but a body that is not stationary but rather has been born cannot, while having a soul and indeed a mind capable of discernment, fail to have perception – ‡ nor if it has not been born ‡.[142] What is to stop it having it? Either soul or body would have to benefit, but in fact neither would – the soul would not thereby think better, nor the body be in any way enhanced by the fact. No non-stationary body has a soul without perception.

If, then, it is to have perception, the body must be either simple or mixed. Simple it cannot be, as it would then lack touch, which it must have – as is made clear by the following argument from the animal's being an ensouled *body*. All body being tangible, that is, perceptible by touch, the preservation of the animal requires its body's being capable of touch. While the other senses, smell, sight and hearing, perceive through other things, but anything that makes contact will, if it have no perception, be unable to avoid some things and acquire others. In which case, it will be impossible for the animal to be preserved. This is also why taste is a kind of touch. For it has to do with what nourishes, and this is a tangible body. On the other hand, sound, colour and smell are non-nutritive and non-productive of either growth or decay. The reason, then, for taste's being necessarily a kind of touch is its being a sense of what is tangible and nutritive. And while these senses are necessary to the animal, which we have shown to be incapable of existence without touch, the others are for its living well and are not for any chance genus of animal, though some, such as those that travel, must have them. The survival of these depends upon their having perception not just by contact but also at a remove. This condition would be satisfied if the animal were to have perception through a medium which on being affected and set in motion by the object in turn acted on the animal.

Whatever produces locomotion produces a change to a certain degree, and whatever has pushed something else produces in that thing an act of pushing, the movement occurring through a middle item, with the first item pushing without being pushed, the last only being pushed without pushing, and that in the middle, or rather the many in the 435ᵃ middle, doing both. With the exception that it occurs for things spatially at rest, the situation is identical for alteration. Wax, for instance, into which something is dipped, is moved to a degree correlative with the dipping, while stone in the same circumstances is not moved at all, and water to a greater degree. It is, however, air that is moved most and acts and is affected the most if it stays together as a single amount. This is why rather than say that reflection is sight issuing from the eye and being reflected we should say that the air is affected by shape and colour to the degree that it remains a single amount, as above a smooth surface, and so again produces movement in the sight, just as if an imprint had permeated right through a lump of wax.

Chapter Thirteen: The Teleological Context (II)

The theme of the final chapter is the supreme importance of touch as the sense without which the animal's survival cannot be prolonged. This point has been mooted elsewhere in the work [143] and most clearly in the preceding chapter. A corollary of it is that it is the excesses of touch alone that are destructive not merely of their proper sense-organ but of the animal as a whole.

Chapter Thirteen

It is clear that the animal's body cannot be simple, that is to say fiery or airy, for instance. For without touch it can have no other sense, every ensouled thing being, as we said, a tactile body, and, while the other elements apart from earth might be sense-organs, they would all produce sensation by indirect and mediate perception, whereas touch consists, as its name suggests, in *contact* with objects. The other sense-organs seem to perceive *by* touch, but *through* something else, touch alone being thought to do so through itself. Thus none of such elements could compose the body of an animal. But neither indeed could earth. For it is between all tangible things that the sense of touch is as it were a mean and its organ is receptive not only of the characteristics of earth but of hot and cold as well and all other tangible things. This is why we have no perception with the bones and hair and

435b such parts, as they are of earth, which same feature accounts for the lack of any perception by plants. The sense-organ, then, of touch, without which there can be no other sense, is neither of earth nor of any one other of the elements.[144]

This makes it clear that it is the deprivation of this sense alone that leads to death in animals. Just as it is impossible for anything that is not an animal to have this sense, so there is no other sense that something must have to be an animal except this one. Accordingly, the objects of the other senses do not, by their excesses, destroy the animal but only the organ – colour, sound and smell are examples – unless, that is, they do so incidentally, for instance if an impetus or blow accompanies the sound. Indeed, other things, whose contact is destructive, are set in motion by sights and smells, and it is only by its incidental property of being simultaneously tactile that flavour is destructive. But the excess of objects of touch, whether hot, cold, hard or whatever, eliminates the animal. The elimination of the sense of touch by an excess of its object is indeed a special case of the general elimination of sense-organs by the excess of their objects. But *this* sense is definitive of the animal, as it has been shown that nothing can be an animal without it. For this reason, excess of the touch-objects destroys not only the sense-organ but the animal as well, as this is the only sense that it must have. It is, on the other hand, as has been said, not for being that the animal has the other senses but for well-being. Sight, for instance, if the animal dwells in air or water, or in general in something transparent, it has so that it may see, taste because of the pleasant and painful, to perceive them in its nourishment and so have appetite and be set in motion, and hearing that it may receive a sign †and the tongue that it may give such to another†.[145]

NOTES TO *DE ANIMA*:
INTRODUCTION

1. Hegel, *Phenomenology of Spirit*, Oxford, 1977, p. 67.
2. Barnes, *Aristotle* p. 1.
3. Ross, *Fragmenta*, pp. 64 ff.
4. See McGinn, *The Character of Mind*, p. 30.
5. Barnes, *The Presocratic Philosophers*, p. 4.
6. Mentioned at *In De An*, 405a19.
7. Aristophanes, *Clouds*, 11. 227 ff.
8. Plato, *Phaedo*, 97b8 ff. This is a clear reference to the substantialist theory of the soul ascribed to Diogenes of Apollonia and discussed by Aristotle at 405a21.
9. Plato, *Timaeus*, 28c3.
10. Aristotle, *Metaphysics*, 1072a20 ff.
11. Nussbaum, *De Motu*, p. 243. The point of calling a description 'low-level' is that it is thereby indicated that what is to be described can be fully captured by a descriptive framework wholly reducible to the lowest level of descriptive adequacy of which the overall system of scientific explanation admits.
12. See pp. 106–11.
13. 406b15 f.
14. See pp. 48 ff.
15. Barnes, for instance, in his treatment of Pythagoras in *The Presocratic Philosophers*, imputes to him a purely formal doctrine of psychic immortality, based on the notion of Eternal Recurrence, which is on any account a prominent feature of Pythagorean thought. He acknowledges, of course, that no such idea can admit of that continuity of consciousness between the formally identical souls that induces us to ascribe to them a personal identity.
16. *The Presocratic Philosophers*, pp. 490–91.
17. See Barnes, 'Aristotle's Concept of Mind', in *Articles on Aristotle*, Vol. 4, pp. 32–41.
18. Philoponus, pp. 23–6, 146, Themistius, pp. 24, 324, 45, 250. The argument of the whole passage in the *De Anima* rather gives the

impression of being composed to some extent against the background of the *Eudemus*.

19. The problem of the dating of the *Timaeus* nicely focuses disagreement between two schools of thought on the intellectual relationship between Plato and Aristotle. Those who see the two philosophers collaborating closely after the arrival of Aristotle at the Academy tend to point to those features of the work that seem to anticipate the later Aristotelian position, while those who imagine Plato to have held aloof from the discussions of his neophytes point to certain riddles, such as the treatment of flux, that seem to be treated as resolved in the first dialogues of the late period. The internal evidence, both that of content and that yielded by the findings of stylometrists, is inconclusive as to dating, so that we are left to date the work so as best to fit in with the general theory of the evolution of the Academy in Plato's later decades.

20. A great deal has been written on the theoretical implications of Homer's psychological terms. The best summary is offered by Furlie (London University Bulletin of Classical Studies, 1959). The general tendency is currently to stress the Physicalism even of the Homeric treatment of the gods. In any case there is no evidence to suggest that the advancers of physicalist substantialist theories of the soul in the Ionian age and the fifth century thought that they were in serious breach with the traditional and thus Homeric view in this respect.

21. This is a point that Hamlyn has stressed, notably in the Introduction to his *De Anima* edition: 'Aristotle has little interest in attempts to justify the claim of the senses to provide Knowledge, and his account contains practically nothing of the paraphernalia of such attempts – the appeal to sense-data and the like. His account is elucidatory rather than justificatory.'

22. Simplicius, *In De An*, 221.20–33, Ross frg. 8.

23. The entire treatment of the *Eudemus* given here is essentially Lloyd's. He has set out his view clearly in *Aristotle: The Growth and Structure of his Thought*, pp. 28 f.

24. Jaeger, *Aristotle*, pp. 15 f.

25. First published in Flemish in 1939.

26. The most important objectors to Nuyens have been Block, 'The order of Aristotle's psychological writings', Kahn, 'Sensation and consciousness in Aristotle's psychology', and Hardie, 'Aristotle's treatment of the relation between the soul and the body'. So far, no really impressive attempt has been made to

explain the Instrumentist features of the *De Anima* to which Nuyens drew attention without the resort to the apparatus of Nuyens' own theory or some revised form of it. Even if we wish to conclude that the whole notion of the Heart Theory is merely an illusion born out of untypically careless use by Aristotle of terms of art, yet there is surely an onus to explain the untypical carelessness.

27. I. Block, 'The order of Aristotle's psychological writings', pp. 50–77.

28. D. W. Thompson, *Historia Animalium*, Oxford, 1910.

29. Perhaps the most convincing presentation of the growth of the Biologist Aristotle out of the Platonist is to be found in M. Grene's *A Portrait of Aristotle*, though this is unashamedly Jaegerian in a way that is now rather out of date.

30. Barnes, 'Aristotle's Concept of Mind', in *Articles on Aristotle*, Vol. 4, p. 33.

31. Ibid., p. 33.

32. 412a1.

33. Grayeff, *Aristotle and his School*, pp. 89 ff.

34. 'Aristotle's Definitions of *psyche*', in *Articles on Aristotle*, Vol. 4, pp. 65–75.

35. Aristotelian biology divides the component parts of all living things into the homoeomerous and the anhomoeomerous groups. The former comprises all those components of which a part (*meros*) is of the same kind (*homoios*) with the whole, as is the case with flesh, for instance, or bone. The other group comprises all those parts of which this is not true.

36. 1049a1–16.

37. Hylomorphism is a term derived from the two Greek words *hule* (matter) and *morphe* (shape). It is used to denote the view that the soul provides the form for the body's matter, and, while it has a wider range of reference, it embraces the Entelechist view that is advanced in the *De Anima*.

38. From many Greek verbs a noun can be formed which ends in the termination '-*ikon*' and which denotes a thing capable of performing or disposed to perform the action or capable of undergoing or disposed to undergo the affection of the parent verb.

39. The theoretical need for the doctrine of the Active Intellect has led Hamlyn in 'Aristotle's Cartesianism' to ascribe to Aristotle a similarity with Descartes not, of course, as regards an interest in subjectivity but in point of their both drawing a

large distinction between men and other living things. This thesis has been further developed by Robinson in a way that involves a rejection of Nussbaum's claim that Aristotelian theology is ultimately compatible with Democritean reductionism.

40. Esp. 'Aristotle's account of Aesthesis in the *De Anima*', *Classical Quarterly* (1959), pp. 6 ff.

41. Hamlyn's edition of the *De Anima*, p. xvii.

42. See note 27.

43. Sorabji's article 'Body and Soul in Aristotle' (in *Articles on Aristotle*, Vol. 4) is particularly useful in drawing out the distinctions between the position of Aristotle and that of all those philosophers for whom the central issue in the philosophy of mind is that of consciousness.

44. The importance of Descartes' legacy to philosophy justifies the remark of Kenny that: 'Those who accept a Cartesian view of the mind, I suppose, can admire Descartes for being the first to state truths with cogency and elegance and precision. But only one who is cured of Cartesianism can fully be awed by the breathtaking power of an intellect which could propagate, almost unaided, a myth which to this day has such a comprehensive grasp on the imagination of a large part of the human race.' (C. Diamond and J. Teichman (eds), *Intention and Intentionality*, p. 3).

45. *Art and Imagination*, p. 97.

46. 'Aristotle on the Imagination', *Articles on Aristotle*, Vol. 4, p. 106. Amongst the jejune literature on the imagination in the *De Anima*, Schofield's article stands out as an exception. I have tried to present here his close assimilation of the areas covered by the absolute verb *phainetai* and the abstract noun *phantasia*, but his own article is essential reading for anyone seeking a true entrée into this difficult subject.

47. 'Imagination and Perception', in *Experience and Theory*, eds Foster and Swanson, p. 54.

48. *Articles on Aristotle*, Vol. 4, p. 56.

49. The whole question of motivation as presented in the *De Motu Animalium* has been expertly analysed by M. Nussbaum in her recent edition. What does not seem to be possible on her or any other account is the building of an absolutely clear bridge between the view set out in that work and that of the *Nicomachean Ethics*. Indeed, it is not even clear to what extent Aristotle would have felt the need of such a bridge.

50. Teleologists, whether or not they believe that in the end all

explanation *can* 'boil down' to the lowest-level account, must develop a conceptual framework to capture the essentially functional aspects of their subject-matter to which they wish to assign a central role. Modern interpreters of Aristotle construe him as locating this conceptual framework in the metaphysical apparatus of Form, Matter and the composite. It must be said, however, that Aristotle is never very explicit on the way in which this is to operate as a functional concept-set, and, insofar as he is interested in the distinction dear to modern Functionalists and Teleologists between scientific explanation and ontological hypothesis, he consistently stresses that the metaphysical scaffolding comes in the latter area. Thus it is not clear what further explanation of the *function* of desire might be hoped for or even read into the position offered in the *De Anima*. See, however, Sorabji, in *Articles on Aristotle*, Vol. 4, p. 56. (This is not necessarily to agree with Robinson as against Nussbaum that the elaboration of the metaphysical apparatus in itself excludes the possibility of Compatibilism, the view that Aristotle's teleology and Democritus' physics are ultimately not at odds.)

51. Ibid., pp. 56–9.
52. Hamlyn draws out, in his edition (pp. 140–42), the contrast between the roles assigned by Aristotle and Aquinas to the Active Intellect, perhaps the most conspicuous area of difference between the two thinkers in the area of psychology. For a lively contemporary assessment of Aquinas, see Kenny, *Aquinas*, in the OUP Modern Masters series.
53. It is not that the general Entelechist thesis has been neglected, of course, but rather that it has been looked on too much from the distorting perspective of the bearing that it has on the possible role of the Aristotelian Intellect as the vehicle of personal survival.
54. Hicks (pp. 498 ff.) gives a very full discussion of the notorious interpretative problems, though without fully accounting for the incongruity of the chapter as it stands with the surrounding theory.
55. See note in the translation, p. 110.
56. The standard history of medieval Christian thought is still Gilson's *A History of Medieval Thought*, which also gives a fairly comprehensive survey of the Arab background. Knowles, *A History of Medieval Philosophy*, is also useful. My own discussion is heavily indebted to P. Moraux's 'Le *De Anima* dans la tradition grecque', in *Aristotle on Mind and the Senses*.

57. *De Generatione Animalium* 716a4–7.
58. 1074b15.
59. It is noteworthy that Aristotle does not use the expression *noesis noeseos* at 429b26 f, and this perhaps calls into question the extent to which we should treat the discussion in *Metaphysics* Lambda as relevant here. (I owe this point to Professor Hamlyn. The interpretation of *neosis noeseos* as amounting in the *Metaphysics* to the self-creation of thought is presented and defended by Norman in *Articles on Aristotle*, Vol. 4, pp. 93–103.)
60. The importance of Andronicus' edition is well brought out by Grayeff, who also discusses what can be made of the background to the edition, though here his treatment must be said to be speculative in some respects.
61. The Aristotelian Commentators are scholars who, from the second to the tenth centuries, produced exegetic material on the most important Aristotelian texts for the educated world of the Roman and Byzantine Empires. Though their perspectives are often affected by the dogmata of neo-Platonism, Stoicism and Christianity, at least two of them, Alexander in the second century and Philoponus in the sixth, can be accorded the status of original thinker, and the others, especially Simplicius and Themistius, often preserve useful material and make acute suggestions.
62. See P. Moraux, 'Le *De Anima* dans la tradition grecque', in *Aristotle on Mind and the Senses*, pp. 296–9.
63. Ibid., p. 309 f.
64. See F. Rahman, *Avicenna's Psychology* and G. M. Wickens (ed.), *Avicenna: Scientist and Philosopher*.
65. William of Moerbeke was a thirteenth-century Flemish Scholar who made translations of most of the Aristotelian corpus into Latin, thereby rendering them accessible to the Schoolmen, and indeed helping to forge the conceptual language that the modern vernaculars have inherited from them.
66. See W. I. Matson, 'Why isn't the Mind–Body Problem Ancient?' in P. K. Feyerabend and J. C. Maxwell (eds), *Mind, Matter and Method*, p. 101. The non-antiquity of the problem does not, of course, require that the ancients and specifically Aristotle were denied even a non-theoretic psychological vocabulary that implied consciousness. See Hamlyn, 'Aristotle's Cartesianism', p. 253; the distinction there drawn between everyday and theoretical talk is echoed by Wilkes in Chapter 3 of *Physicalism*.

67. L. Wittgenstein, *Philosophical Investigations* and G. Ryle, *The Concept of Mind.*

68. The first of these is available in the English translation of R. George as *The Psychology of Aristotle.*

69. Loc. cit., pp. 51–3.

70. Ibid., p. 53.

71. *Physicalism*, p. 115.

72. Ibid., p. 116.

73. Op. cit., p. 118.

74. Op. cit., p. 66.

75. 424b14–18.

76. Op. cit., pp. 121–2.

77. The distinction between *sapience* and *sentience* is roughly that between the capacity to react in a skilful manner to the stimuli of the environment and the capacity to receive the stimuli in the first place.

78. *Articles on Aristotle*, Vol. 4, p. 5.

79. Any link which Aristotle is to be construed as making between sense-perception and purposive activity must involve the concept of *phantasia* in an intermediary role. Apart from the general difficulties this involves, it is not easy to see just how it corresponds to Wilkes' model of purposive activity.

80. One move that might make her case more persuasive would be to show how her brand of Functionalism could be integrated into a general biological theory of the same scope as Aristotle's. She indeed alludes to the desirability of this at p. 118.

81. It is no doubt the case that the detailed theories of Jaeger and his immediate followers are now somewhat outmoded, especially as regards the postulation of an early Platonizing period, but this does not of course mean that there is any danger of a return to the static conception of the traditional view of the corpus. Jaeger remains a watershed.

82. *Aporetic* is the label which, derived from the Greek word for a puzzle or difficulty, is used to denote those aspects of a philosopher's thought which arise in relation to specific problems to whose solution system is in no way integral.

83. Indeed, it could be argued that in the treatment of the higher faculties of desire, intellect and imagination the affinities with the central model for the treatment of psychic states are outweighed by the differences. This, however, is never acknowledged by Aristotle. If one seeks a metaphor for the theory as a whole, perhaps that of a flower growing unpredictably from

a root is more apt than the regular construction of a building on its underlying plan. Aristotle is often accused of tidy-mindedness but there is little evidence for this in the *De Anima*.

84. Barnes, *Aristotle*, p. 87.

85. *De Anima*, Introduction, p. xv.

86. Professor Hamlyn adopts the convention of flagging key terms with subscript letters, connecting any translation to the original Greek word, so that any translation of Aristotle's *logos*, for instance, will be marked by a subscript L (Hamlyn, p. xvii). This has the very considerable advantage that a certain minimum of elegance and indeed clarity can be introduced without the risk of tendentiousness. Its obvious disadvantage, however, is that it may prove disruptive to fluent reading of the text, and for this translation that consideration has seemed decisive.

87. Knowles, *A History of Medieval Philosophy*, p. 186.

NOTES TO *DE ANIMA*: THE TRANSLATION

1. For those unfamiliar with the Aristotelian taxonomic hierarchy, it should be said that a species is a sub-division of the larger classificatory unit of the genus. If soul is to be construed, as Aristotle consistently maintains, as an entity, then it will as a whole constitute a genus, of which its instantiations at particular biological levels will be the species.

2. The variations in meaning of the term *pathe* are further explored in the Glossary. It forms in general in the psychological and biological texts of Aristotle the complementary term to *energeia*. It is introduced here, however, in a still wider sense, so as to be a catch-all for any natural functions that may present themselves for special consideration.

3. The business of First Philosophy, we are told at *Metaphysics* Book 3, is the study of things that exist insofar only as they exist. For Aristotle the notion of independent existence is closely linked with that of *chorismos* or separation, and, as this passage suggests, it is their quality of separatedness that marks off the objects of First Philosophy from those of mathematics.

4. Characteristic or not, this survey is very far from being wholly in order as an exercise in intellectual history. The philosophers whom Aristotle has in mind are, in his order, Leucippus and Democritus, the late fifth-century atomists from Abdera on the Thracian coast of the Aegean, that school of Pythagoreans that asserted the soul to be the motes in the air, and all those who take the soul to be that which moves itself, amongst whom are Anaxagoras of Clazomenae in Asia Minor, as well as Plato and Empedocles, the followers in contemporary Athens of the Academic Xenocrates, Thales of Miletus, father of Ionian natural speculation, Diogenes of Appollonia, Heraclitus of Ephesus, Alcmaeon of Croton, Hippo of Elis, and Critias of Athens. No attempt is made, however, to group these into either historically or dogmatically illuminative arrangements. For the most part, however, the passage does serve its purpose, which is to illustrate

the consensus of authoritative opinion behind each of the two property ascriptions that he is taking to be cardinal to his construal of the plain man's conception of the soul.

5. This association of course long pre-dates Aristotle and indeed is an example of the kind of simplistic conception that Aristotle hopes that his freshly minted metaphysical distinctions will enable him to handle in a uniquely illuminating way.

6. It seems likely that, as suggested in the Introduction, Xenocrates had by the time of composition of this work been preferred to Aristotle on political grounds as the successor to Speusippus and third Scholarch of the Academy and that under his influence the school had progressed still further than under the ageing Plato down the road of number mysticism and other suchlike puerilities. This fact might help to account for the animus that Aristotle brings to his dismissal of Xenocrates' view later in this book.

7. *Timaeus* 64a.

8. The Harmony Theory is not introduced until 407b27.

9. The notion that the hallmark of the soul is a capacity for self-movement enjoyed wide popularity in Ancient Greece. Aristotle's most detailed discussion of self-movement in connection with animal life is in the eighth Book of the *Physics*. See D. J. Furley, 'Self Movers', in *Aristotle on Mind and the Senses*.

10. This line is not found as such in the *Iliad*.

11. It is important to bear in mind that in this passage as elsewhere *arche* is a much wider term than *stoicheion*. To the question 'What are the *archai*?' one possible answer would be 'The *stoicheia*'.

12. In the *Timaeus*, Plato represents both the world and the soul as being constituted by fundamental numerical relations. Thus, in his Pythagorean way he maintains the notion that perception is of like by like that is so marked in its simpler form in the materialists.

13. Barnes (*The Presocratic Philosophers*, pp. 473–4), after noting that Aristotle's account of Heraclitean psychology is markedly more sophisticated than the simple ascription to him by later sources of the view that the soul is fire, suggests that the notion of *anathumiasis*, here translated 'emanation', may be designed to present with the rudimentary sophistication of Ionian physics the Homeric and pre-Homeric idea of the 'breath-soul', breath being a substance that well lends itself to construal as any one of the early thinkers' favoured elements. However, given Heraclitus' apparent belief in the constitution of all matter

from condensed or rarefied fire, it is not clear that we should press on his psychology, such as it is, even so mildly naturalistic an interpretation as Barnes'.

14. The exception is Anaxagoras.

15. The pair of 'puns' here are, as usual, untranslatable. In the first, it is suggested that the infinitive of the Greek verb 'to live', *zen*, is derived from or connected with the infinitive of the verb 'to boil', *zein*. In the second, an affinity is seen between *psyche*, soul, and *katapsuxis*, a process of cooling. Needless to say, there is little in favour of either of these etymological speculations. Etymology was indeed a science to which the Greek mind seems to have been peculiarly speculatively disposed at all times, as is illustrated by even Aristotle's taking seriously flights of fancy in this area.

16. 406b18.

17. Sorabji (*Philosophy*, 49, pp. 79–83) has suggestively developed the idea that Aristotle circumvents the problem of the causation of the physical by the mental by simultaneously describing desire materially as a physiological process and formally as a cause of action. It is, of course, one of the strikingly unCartesian aspects of Aristotle's psychology that the very expression 'mental state' cannot be translated into his Greek. In any case, whatever is to be made of the role that he assigns to *prohaeresis* in this chapter, it is surely more promising than the justly satirized Democritean account.

18. Aristotle's critique of the psychology of the *Timaeus* is certainly opaque, but it surely serves at least to remind us how retrograde the earlier work is in its treatment of the soul. For in his mythical presentation of the demiurge ladling out soul like a kind of soup from his mixing bowl and distributing it in varying degrees of purity among sundry recipients, Plato is reverting to the naive materialist conception of the soul that renders so much Presocratic psychology so jejune.

19. It is in such passages as this that the temptation to translate Aristotle's word *kinesis* as 'process' is especially strong. Randall, in his stimulating account of the corpus from a broadly Functionalist point of view, is not alone in seeing *kinesis* in its widest sense as being the central Aristotelian problem not just in the life sciences but in the whole study of nature. (The chief reason for not translating *kinesis* as process is its derivation from the transitive verb *kinein*, to move, a connection which Aristotle constantly exploits and which cannot be preserved except

by translating *kinesis* cumbrously as 'movement' or 'motion'.)

20. This passage is evidently unintelligible without some knowledge of the psychological theory of the *Timaeus*, of which I shall here attempt a concise summary. Timaeus, having described the construction of the world body by the demiurge, passes to the description of his construction of the world soul with the caveat that the narration has reversed the actual order of creation. The world soul, we learn, began as a long and broad strip itself compounded from intermediate compounds of the divisible and indivisible forms of Existence, Sameness and Difference. This strip is elaborately divided into sections whose lengths form harmonic intervals and then cut down its middle into two strips. These are now placed across each other so as to form an X and then bent into circles, one inside the other, with rectangular axes. The outer circle, which is responsible for the motion of the fixed stars, is left undivided, but the inner one is further sub-divided into seven circles, each corresponding to a Platonic planet. It is the complex but harmonious motions of these circles that accounts for the essential rationality of the heavens and thus ultimately of the soul of man.

21. All that Aristotle seems to be meaning in this passage – though it must be admitted that he expresses the point rather obscurely – is that there are on both theoretical and practical trains of thought certain structural constraints, logical in the former and intentional in the latter case, which are incompatible with these processes being thought of as even in an extended sense circular. In all this passage it is tempting to see Aristotle rather missing the mythic aspects of the *Timaeus*, an interesting reflection on how seriously that work was initially taken and how well received simple substantialist psychologies still were.

22. 408b13–15.

23. 408b32–5.

24. There are comparably inappropriate chapter breaks elsewhere in the corpus, though none elsewhere in this treatise. There is, however, something unsatisfactory about the present division between Books II and III, though this has been defended by Kahn (*Articles on Aristotle*, Vol. 4, p. 6). It must, of course, always be remembered that both Book and chapter divisions are post-Aristotelian and thus have little authority in throwing light on the contents of the work.

25. In discussing the Harmony Theory, which he seems to have considered hardly more than a *jeu d'esprit*, for all the similarities

that have been seen by some between it and the mature entel-echist view, Aristotle often has recourse to a kind of laboured levity. Here he captures the inadequacy of the Harmony Theory to fit the facts of psychic life by saying that it would be hard to *epharmozein* them to the theory. Fortunately, this pun, for what it is worth, translates well into English.

26. There is some controversy as to the sophistication of Empe-docles' conception of the soul, and Aristotle's evidence can be used by both parties. One possibility is that Empedocles simply believed, in the words of a famous fragment (frg. 105), that 'thought is the blood around men's hearts' and that this is also soul; the other, to which the present passage lends colour, is that he conceived the soul as a mixture of elements, at its finest in the blood about the heart, whose corre-spondence to the elemental mixture of the external world constitutes perception. It is not easy to see how this latter view would differ in substance from the Harmony Theory. All this is readably discussed by Barnes (*The Presocratic Philos-ophers*, pp. 480 ff).

27. The general obscurity which surrounds Xenocrates' doctrine that the soul is a moving number is little brightened by Aris-totle's refutation. 'We rub our eyes,' says Gomperz (*Greek Thinkers*, Vol. IV, p. 7), 'on reading this marvellous definition for the first time. Well might Aristotle call it "the summit of absurdity".' However, as he himself points out, it is possible to see a clear ontogenesis for the theory. To the Academic commonplace that the soul is a self-mover is added the thought that its cognitive nature requires, traditionally enough, an affinity between it and the objects of its knowledge. Xenocrates' only real innovation is to suggest that affinity indicates that the soul will be not as for the naive physicists a material substance, however primary, but the most abstract and thus primary object of all knowledge, namely number. It seems to me very reasonable to suggest that the Number Theory, the Logos Theory and the Harmony Theory are in fact correlated species of a genus of Ratio Theories of the soul, and that in Xenocrates' version the former has built into it, albeit in a rather crude way, an attempt to obviate the main objection to the latter, namely its inability to account properly for the soul's motive role.

If it is legitimate to gloss Xenocrates' 'number' as 'ratio', then it is not really clear why Aristotle's attempt to assimilate the view to Democritean atomic psychology need not be equally valid or invalid against the congener Harmony or Logos Theories. At the root of the whole critique, however, we surely see a central Aristotelian insight, namely that all Presocratic and Academic concepts of Order and Arrangement, of which Number, Harmony and Logos are but a few examples, are essentially static and thus cannot be introduced to explain the essentially dynamic character of soul. The views that seek to do this balance the views of such thinkers as Democritus who capture the dynamic or more precisely still *kinetic* character of the soul but not its rationality and intentionality. Entelechism is to provide the necessary synthesis.

28. As mentioned above, Aristotle provides ammunition for both sides in the controversy as to Empedocles' psychology. It is curious, however, that he should seem himself to be so indifferent to the apparent clash of interpretations. (He is not of course here ascribing to Empedocles a panstoicheic account of the soul, but it is interesting that the Empedoclean example that he takes to illustrate the necessity of structure in the objects of knowledge should itself be part of a subject of knowledge.)

29. *Asomatotaton* is an interesting example of an adjective's superlative being weaker than its positive, meaning, of course, 'most nearly bodiless'. *Leptomeres* and its synonyms enjoyed a long and mostly undistinguished part in the history of ancient psychology.

30. The Tales of Orpheus were a corpus of legendary narratives recording the exploits and teachings of Orpheus. Clement of Alexandria and the Byzantine Dictionary *The Suda* have independently preserved for us Epicles of Alexandria's list of these writings.

31. Homoeomereity is the property of having parts of the same kind as one's whole. It is possessed by flesh, cement and ice, but not by a plant or a man. It plays, together with its converse, anhomoeomereity, a large part in Greek physiology both before and after Aristotle.

32. It seems fairly clear that the *De Anima* formed the first part in a General Biology lecture course delivered by Aristotle at the Lyceum in the last ten years of his life, of which the other components will have been the *Parva Naturalia*, the *Historia Animalium*, the *De Partibus Animalium* and the *De Generatione*

with the inclusion of the *De Motu Animalium*, if, as now seems certain, that intriguing text is genuine. For all this, see the extensive introduction to A. L. Peck's Loeb edition of the *De Generatione*.

33. See Introduction, section IV.

34. The precise distinction that Aristotle is drawing between the first and second Entelechies of a body is a matter of some obscurity. It is, of course, clear that the first Entelechy is a potentiality and the second an actuality, but the difficulty is that Aristotle countenances in his jargon a certain superfluity of terms for potentiality, and it is not entirely clear how the first Entelechy is to be fitted into this scheme. On the one hand, there is the concept of a *dunamis*, mere potentiality, and on the other that of a *hexis*, settled dispositional state or, in our modern derivation, habit. We could seek to assimilate the first Entelechy to one or other of these or see it as having an intermediary position. However, it is not easy to see what room there is here for an intermediary position and, if we seek to assimilate, we are drawn in the direction of the *hexis* by the thought of the first Entelechy being the soul of a man or higher animal but equally strongly in the direction of the *dunamis* by the thought of its being the 'soul' of a plant or lower animal. Aristotle certainly does not do much to enlighten us in his discussion of the *hexis* in the fourth chapter of this Book.

35. As Hamlyn clearly explains, neither the parallel between the soul and the essence of an axe nor that between the soul and the essence of an eye is totally satisfactory, the first because an axe is an artefact and therefore has only the purpose that we give it, and the second because the eye clearly has a specific single physiological function, while this is not the case with the body as a whole of which the first Entelechy is, loosely, the essence.

36. Barnes enters a cautionary note (*Articles on Aristotle*, Vol. 4, p. 34) which is apposite here, to the effect that 'separation' in Aristotle's psychology may mean the separation or supposed separation of a psychic from a physical element or it may mean the separation of one psychic, or for that matter, bodily, element from another. He gives the end of II.1 as an illustration of the former and the end of II.2 as an illustration of the latter.

37. Aristotle's illustration of correct method in definition is slightly complicated but, if properly understood, serves his purpose

well. Suppose we have a rectangle of a certain size and wish to know the length of sides of the square of the same area. How do we determine this? We, as it were, flatten the rectangle so that its two sides form a straight line. This we now make the diameter of a semi-circle. If we drop a perpendicular from the point on the circumference which marks the join of the two sides of the original rectangle to the circumference of the semi-circle, then the length of this perpendicular will be the length that we seek. However, we still do not know why this should be so. We have merely constructed the required square, not proven that it has the same area as the original rectangle. Since the whole operation is known as 'squaring', to define squaring simply as the finding of a square equal in volume to a given rectangle is in a sense like giving only the conclusion of a syllogism without the middle premise that justifies it. Anyone who understands no more than that cannot be said to understand a syllogistic explanation. (For instance, the fact that all men are mortal is not explained by the fact that all animals are mortal without the additional premise that all men are animals.) In the case of squaring, the full definition is given only when it is added that the procedure yields the square sought by virtue of the fact that the perpendicular is the mean proportional of the diameter, i.e. that it so dissects the diameter that it is the same fraction of the larger section as the smaller section is of itself.

38. See 435a11 ff.

39. The Greek word here translated 'conceptually' is *logoi*, the dative of *logos*. It is peculiarly difficult to feel entirely free from a certain anachronism of interpretation in translating this word into almost any feasible English equivalent in such uses as this. From this point of view the introduction of the notion of a concept is far from ideal but considerations of economy must at some point prevail over those of an elusive exactitude.

40. The presentation here of the hierarchy of soul has led some fastidious scholars to eschew altogether talk of an Aristotelian 'definition of soul'. I, however, find the reasons advanced by Barnes (*Articles on Aristotle*, Vol. 4, p. 33) sufficient grounds for retaining the locution.

41. *De Anima*, p. 94.

42. See the discussion of the special senses in Book II, Chapters 7–11.

43. 427a17 ff.

44. Book III, Chapters 4–6.

45. In his eminently readable survey of information theory, *Grammatical Man*, Jeremy Campbell concludes with an Afterword entitled 'Aristotle and DNA'. In the course of explaining the regard for Aristotle that is common among contemporary molecular biologists, he cites the remark of Max Delbrueck, a professor at the California Institute of Technology, that 'if the Nobel committee were able to award the prize for biology posthumously, they should consider giving it to Aristotle for the discovery of the principle of DNA'.

46. This somewhat vestigial work is also referred to, apparently, at *De Somno* 456b6.

47. The distinction being drawn here is that between an objective and a beneficiary, but, presumably, eternity (*to aei*) is only supposed to be the objective, not the beneficiary of the nutritive soul.

48. The Greek word here translated 'formal substance' is *ousia*, a key notion in Aristotle's general conceptual scheme, whose ramifications are explored at various points in the *Metaphysics*. The standard exposition of the doctrine of the four *aitiai* is given in *Physics*, II 3.

49. It is interesting to see here a certain embarrassment on Aristotle's part over the inherent tendencies of the elements that are part of his intellectual legacy from Empedocles. This is in fact only one aspect of the difficulties he faces in connection with the idea of the formless body that is required by his theory as a counterpart to the informing soul. It must be said that he never directly confronts these difficulties and that his talk here of the natural motions being in some sense ancillary causes of growth has an air of fudge about it.

50. I owe to Hamlyn two possible glosses of this at first sight puzzling remark, that Aristotle has in mind the advantages of using not totally dry fire wood (p. 101) or that he is thinking of oil or some other more readily combustible liquid. Perhaps the thought is really only the more simple one, here a little dressed up by Aristotle, that things are more easily converted from a damp to a burning condition than vice versa.

51. See note to Introduction, p. 110.

52. *De Anima*, Introduction, p. xiv.

53. In Chapter 3 passim.

54. Aristotle's scheme of sense-objects has been the subject of con-

siderable exegetic controversy but it is not clear that this has been wholly in order. Aristotle distinguishes three species of sense-object (*aistheton*), the special, the common and the incidental. The first two are essentially perceived, in that they are the objects of faculties into whose definitions they enter, while the last is not so perceived. The special sense-objects are each definitive of one of the five special senses of sight, hearing, smell, taste and touch, to whose discussion Aristotle is about to proceed, and the common sense-objects will turn out to be definitive of the common sense, though this is admittedly not made as clear as it might have been here. Incidental sense-objects are on the other hand not definitive of any sense faculty, not, as Hamlyn is at pains to point out (p. 105), because they are in any way indirectly perceived, but because we are not affected by them *as such*. They are features of an object not in virtue of which it is essentially perceptible.

55. Hamlyn objects to the notion of a sight-object's being definitive of sight, on the grounds that there is a difference between actual and perceived colour, but it is not at all clear that this distinction, if indeed it is to be accepted on Aristotle's behalf, is not encompassed in the distinction between actual and possible sight to be drawn later. However, the principal objection to the scheme of special sense-objects as here presented would seem to be that it does not really explain why we say only that there is one, not that there are many faculties of touch. Aristotle may be being over-generous to the disproportionate variousness of the tactile as against the visual and auditory.

56. This passage is well discussed by Sorabji (*Articles on Aristotle*, Vol. 4, p. 47). The possibility that in using *aisthanesthai* Aristotle may have some kind of Cartesian mental act in view is discounted both because a mental act would have to be a further component in an act of perception, for which Aristotle's terminology of formal causation does not allow, and because the mental act could not be other than a *pathos* and Aristotle nowhere admits non-physiological *pathe*.

57. The eternal upper body is the *aither* or upper air, which pervades the supralunary world.

58. In logic an intentional context is one such that the complex sentence can be true when the constituent sentence within the context is false, e.g. 'I believe that Napoleon was the king of Prussia.' The possibility of such contexts illustrates the extent to which language is autonomous from the environment, a

semantic feature that notoriously renders language non-amenable to biological Functionalism.

59. It is interesting to compare the immobility of the air in the sounding box of the ear with the formlessness of the Passive Intellect. Just as the ear must be able to detect all the disturbances of the outer air and so in some sense take them into itself, so must the recipient Intellect be able to take into itself the form of any and every external object.

60. In this curious passage, Nuyens, with some plausibility, detected one of the clearest traces of the Instrumentist Theory, which, in his view, came in Aristotle's development as a psychologist between primitive Platonism and mature Entelechism.

61. This matter is never directly taken up in the biological works.

62. Op. cit., p. 110.

63. This remark seems only too clear evidence of Aristotle's occasional willingness to sacrifice common sense to theory.

64. It is very doubtful that he here achieves a genuine conceptual discrimination between these two senses, rather than merely offering certain physiological observations on the apparatus of taste.

65. This whole conception of the primacy of touch, which is indeed emphasized at the very end of the work, makes peculiarly clear the standpoint of general biological Functionalism from which the work is composed.

66. This radical conservation of the unity of the faculty of touch by supposing its organ not to be the flesh is discussed and debunked by Sorabji (*Articles on Aristotle*, Vol. 4, pp. 85 f).

67. Hamlyn, in a series of articles, has established that the account of sensation offered in the *De Anima* can appropriately be called transitional, away, that is, from the crude notion of affection by the like towards the more subtle one of the reception of Form without Matter.

68. But see note 56 for a deterrence against seeing this too much as a sign of latent Cartesianism.

69. Perhaps a more satisfactory rendering here of *logos* would be 'ratio' or even 'proportion'. (I have retained the translation that stands on the ground of consistency.)

70. For discussion see Introduction, p. 75 f.

71. Hicks, *De Anima*, p. 422.

72. See Introduction, notes 27 and 49.

73. This extraordinary piece of argumentation, a worthy start to the vexed third Book, is well analysed by Hamlyn (pp. 115–

16). He is surely right to diagnose the source of the trouble as being that Aristotle is seeking to show the *necessity* of what is in fact only an empirical fact, that we have only five senses. He therefore has to take as necessary certain premises that are, at best, only contingent, viz. that there can be no elements other than fire, air, water and earth through which perception might occur, that for perception to be possible the sense-organ must be akin to its medium (in those senses, of course, in which a medium is involved), and that all sense-organs are in fact composed of air or water. As Hamlyn point out, it is clearly the case that even if we grant Aristotle the second of these premises, the first and third could turn out on experimental evidence to be wrong (even, of course, in terms of his physiology), thus denying any necessity to the conclusion of the argument. But, in any case, given that sight and hearing, two different senses, both perceive through the two media (in fact the only possible ones) of air and water, not, say, sight through air and hearing through water, then what is there to stop there being many similarly constituted distance senses equally capable of perception through these two media. In other words, Aristotle has not shown why the physical constitution of the sense-organ is the definitive hallmark of the sense. In these circumstances, the main interest of the passage becomes its virtuosity as a *tour de force* of syntactic and logical agility.

74. Aristotle is throughout this passage seeking to distinguish the incidental relation of the common sensibles to the special sensibles from two other types of incidental relation, that between special sensible and special sensible, and that between incidental sensible and special sensible. The argument as it stands is confusing because of its heavy reliance on somewhat opaque jargon and its paucity of illustrations. The latter, a characteristic Aristotelian trait nowhere more present than in this treatise, can perhaps be remedied by the following: I see before me a honey cake. What I actually see (the sight object, *to horaton*) is merely a patch of colour (*chroma*), but to this it is incidental (a) that it is a honey cake (the incidental sense-object proper), (b) that it is sweet (this sweetness is the special object of another sense, taste, but it is also incidentally *seen*), and (c) that it is at rest (its rest-state being a common sense-object which I also incidentally see but in a different way from that in which I incidentally see its sweetness).

75. It is noteworthy that Aristotle describes as an illusion (*he aisthesis*

apatatai) a situation in which on seeing a yellow patch we mistakenly assume it to be bile.

76. Aristotle's argument here is again puzzling and it is not clear that he has a valid point. His answer to the question why we have many senses, namely that it is to improve our awareness of the common sensibles, seems neither necessary nor sufficient. For it is not at all clear that with only one special sense, say sight, we would be unable to perceive the common sensibles. As Hamlyn says, 'what the plurality of senses makes clear is that the common objects are *common*, not that they exist'. On the other hand, even if the argument were valid, what need would there be of five and not just two senses?

77. See Introduction, note 27.

78. Kahn's important article 'Sensation and consciousness in Aristotle's psychology' (*Articles on Aristotle*, Vol. 4, pp. 1–31) is essential reading for this demanding but fertile chapter.

79. *De Anima*, p. 122.

80. Aristotle is confronting the question how it is that we see or in some other way perceive that we see. It is a commonplace of post-Cartesian philosophical psychology that an act of seeing is constituted by a physiological component (currently the operation of rods and cones) and a phenomenal element (an awareness of colour). Aristotle has given his account of the physiological component in some detail, but he still feels that sight has not been exhaustively dealt with. Yet he by no means introduces here a purely phenomenal component or anything very like it, and this is a most telling indication of the difference between his view and that of Descartes. In effect he merely continues the physiological account a stage further, asking by what sense it is that we detect the sense-organ of sight in the act of seeing. It cannot be by any other sense than sight, but, given that perception of colour is definitive of sight, then surely the sense-organ of sight must, at least in actually seeing, be coloured. This, however, is paradoxical, and Aristotle, rather superfluously, deals with the problem in two ways. He suggests that perception by sight might be more complex than mere seeing, of which the perception of colour remains definitive, but he also asserts that in any case the sense is 'as though coloured'.

81. I introduce 'harking' here, perhaps rather awkwardly, to denote actualized hearing, for which there is no natural English term. It should be clear that 'listening' would be inappropriate

here as Aristotle is not speaking of an act of will, such as listening is.

82. Aristotle means that if, for instance, a bell rings in my earshot, then the potential hearing faculty in my ear is actualized into 'harking' and the potential noise-giving character of the bell is actualized into 'sounding', and it is in my ear that both actualizations take place. A bell that gives unheard noise will not 'sound', for what is happening to the bell itself will not amount to 'sounding', which is more than merely being rung – it is being apprehended in being rung.

83. Here, as elsewhere, there is a strong temptation to translate *logos* not as 'formula' but as 'ratio'.

84. In this passage Aristotle is introducing his second general puzzle about sensory perception. How do we perceive that a black colour is a sight-object and a sweet flavour a taste-object? His answer will be that we do so in virtue of the fact that there is a unity of the sense faculty as a whole (once again the concept of consciousness is conspicuously absent). But first the idea that flesh itself is the ultimate sense-organ in virtue of which we make this distinction is disposed of by the consideration that, as Hamlyn puts it, 'flesh cannot be the ultimate sense-organ for all perception including the perception that what we are feeling is not an object of vision'. (A simpler construal along the lines of Ross's account would be that flesh is not the ultimate sense-organ for its special sense of touch any more than the eye is the ultimate sense-organ of sight, for in both cases there must be some anterior principle which distinguishes between their operations and this will be the unified faculty of sense-perception.)

85. It is evidently at the same time that we notice of a co-incidence of sensations that they co-incide.

86. It has been established that the unified sense faculty must be single, but here Aristotle reminds us that its functions must be diverse. Given that its being affected is constituted by its being moved in a certain way, this appears to raise the logical difficulty that it must be moved simultaneously in contrary motions. Aristotle does not consider the possibility of obviating this difficulty by supposing that the motions involved in the unified sense faculty's being moved both by whiteness, say, and by sweetness are not so much contrary as merely different.

87. The logical difficulty is resolved by an analogy between the unified sense and a point. A point is paradigmatically a single thing, and yet the same point can be the start of two different

lines. Just so the sense-perception faculty as a unified whole is both single in essence and multiple in activity, which makes possible its *simultaneous* affection by a number of movements. This whole passage should be compared with the parallel discussion in the last chapter of the *De Sensu*.

88. In his article 'Aristotle on the Imagination', Schofield puts forward a unifying principle for what otherwise seems an inconsistent concept of *phantasia* in this chapter. It is that the abstract term should be taken to denote all and only occasions on which the verb from which it derives would naturally be deployed in ordinary speech. This he seeks to extend to cover both cases of seeing-as, which Aristotle certainly seems to be considering, and even the production of mental imagery, though here he acknowledges that the conceptual unity may be over-strained.

89. The principle role of *phantasia* elsewhere in the *De Anima* is in connection with thinking. In the *Parva Naturalia* it is used to throw light on dreaming and remembering, and in the *De Motu Animalium* it is connected with animal motivation. It is connected with the discussion of action in Book VI of the *Ethics*, but plays a surprisingly small part in the *Poetics* and *Rhetoric*.

90. See Sorabji, *Aristotle on Memory*.

91. Empedocles frg. 106 (Diehls).

92. *Odyssey* 18. 136.

93. Aristotle's point, though obscurely phrased, is in essence simply that while in perceptory error we become acquainted with the opposite of the standard percept, if knowledge were similar to perception, then in being illuded as to a subject of knowledge we would still have knowledge but of a contrary subject, but no belief can be both an illusion and a piece of knowledge.

94. It is possible that this sense should be taken merely to be saying that neither imagination nor supposition is possible without perception.

95. This sentence requires our taking 'thinking' (*dianoia*) at 427b15 to be synonymous with supposing rather than with thought as a whole.

96. Aristotle here seems to be specifying *phantasia* as 'that in virtue of which we say that an image (*phantasma*) appears to us'. This has an encouragingly modern ring to it, but it is possible that we should rather take *phantasma*, as Schofield favours, to mean here at least 'appearance', in which case the concept has a wider and less recognizable look.

97. The manuscript tradition here favours the ascription to Aris-

totle of the view that neither ants nor bees nor grubs have imagination, but the text can be amended without excessive strain to avoid this unAristotelian conclusion.

98. The second argument that Aristotle brings to show that imagination cannot be, as Plato thought, a combination of perception and belief is interesting. It seems to be eminently possible simultaneously to believe truly that the sun is larger than the earth and imagine that it is a foot across. But if this is so, and if imagination is a species of belief or involves belief, then we are confronted by the dilemma that a person in this position has either cast aside his true belief for no evident reason or is simultaneously maintaining contradictory beliefs about an object immediately present to him, both of which possibilities are clearly counter-intuitive. Hamlyn, in agreement with Lycos (*Mind* (1964), pp. 496 ff.) accepts this as a valid dilemma, refuting 'any theory which attempts to analyse all cases of appearance or seeing as in terms of beliefs or judgements'. Nonetheless, he feels that cases like that of the sun's appearing a foot across can only be understood *against the background* of cases of appearing which do seem to involve belief.

99. Aristotle sees an etymological link between *phos* (light) and *phantasia*, which itself seems a little phantastic.

100. It is notable that there is no special treatise on the imagination in the *Parva Naturalia*, although, as remarked, it plays an important role in the explanation of dreams and of remembering.

101. See Introduction, pp. 91 ff.

102. What he does not make clear is how exactly this capacity is related to the rest of the soul in the case of man. This question is certainly not conclusively answered in the ensuing chapters.

103. In any case, as Hamlyn points out, there is a certain tension between the repudiation of the over-assimilation of perception and thought in early philosophers to be found in Chapter 3 and the close isomorphism of treatment that the two faculties actually receive. The two problems of the organ and of the objects of thought both stem from the transfer of an essentially physiological approach from perception to thought, which Aristotle is much less disposed to regard as a purely physiological process (as, indeed, were most, but by no means all, of the Greek thinkers).

104. The reference to Anaxagoras reminds how powerfully in-

fluential his one book with its famous slogan that mind rules all things was over the Academy and the Lyceum, though this influence might be said to be rather architectonic than dogmatic. Certainly the theory here being developed owes little to any view we might plausibly ascribe to Anaxagoras.

105. Another important asymmetry between sense and thought is that there is with thought nothing corresponding to the five special senses. It is for this reason that Aristotle requires the faculty of thought to be 'unmixed', i.e. to have no intrinsic character which might diminish its receptivity to the thoughts of some objects. This both renders still more difficult the notion of an organ of thought and prepares the way for the introduction of the problematic Active Intellect in Chapter 5.

106. The move from potentiality to actualization in the intellect is tripartite rather than bipartite. To acquire, for instance, a skill, the intellect is in one way actualized from pure potentiality, and in actually applying that skill it is actualized in another.

107. By the obscure phrase 'a this in a that', Aristotle means a thing that cannot exist on its own but only in a certain context. His favourite example is the one given here of the snub, which can only exist as a nose.

108. Just as the realization of sensibles is in the sense faculty so is the realization of intelligibles in the intellectual faculty. Thus the objects of the world are intelligible without themselves being intelligent as they are sensible without being sensitive. (Aristotle has already explained how the objects of the intellect are separably connected with matter.)

109. Op. cit., p. 140.

110. It is also hard to accept the conclusion of Brentano, however impressive one may find his reasoning and his general exegesis of Aristotle's psychology, that it is the Active Intellect that is responsible for the intentional character of intellectual states. Rather, the Active Intellect seems to be introduced to balance the otherwise wholly passive character of the intellect in a way that is not necessary for the sensitive soul, and, of course, to acknowledge the originative capacity that distinguishes intellectual from perceptive states.

111. To what extent it forms a link with the Divine Intellect of *Metaphysics* Lambda is one of the central traditional problems

in interpreting Aristotle's psychology. An attempt has been made to outline the history of the controversy in the Introduction.

112. This does not, of course, involve Aristotle in the belief in non-physical substances *per se*. Substance (*ousia*) is not a category that can subsist in actuality wholly denuded of the concomitant material cause for whatever it is that it composes. It is open for Aristotle to hold that the body is the material cause as much at least of the Passive Intellect as of the Nutritive Soul.

113. This sentence recurs at 431a1–3, and there is considerable reason to think that it belongs, as Hamlyn and others suggest, in the later place, being here interpolated in place of some more relevant but perhaps more obscure comment on the relation of Active and Passive Intellects.

114. It is also very noticeable that he makes no real use of the Active Intellect in his account of propositional thought. Indeed, there is no really organic connection between the three chapters on the intellect as a whole, though at the same time they are not in flagrant disagreement.

115. Just as the ultimate 'atomic' building blocks of a sensory state are the essential objects of the special senses about which there can be no error, so the ultimate components of intellectual states are indivisible thoughts, to which truth and falsity do not pertain. These, however, are composed by the intellect into combinations which are characterized by truth and falsity. We might say that truth is a molecular not an atomic property of the Aristotelian intellectual state.

116. A line of any length can be divided and it can be thought of both before and after it is divided. In the thought of the divided line there are the thoughts of each of the divisions, but it does not follow that in the thought of the whole undivided line, although the divisions are potentially present in the line, the divisions are also even potentially present in the *thought*.

117. Ross obelizes the words marked. Their inclusion, though it contributes little enough, hardly mars the sense.

118. Again, it is noticeable how carefully Aristotle stresses the close isomorphism of his accounts of perception and intellection. He clearly sees this as a strength of his view, an opinion not shared by all his commentators.

119. Hamlyn, *ad loc.*, following Torstrik.

120. The contrast between a *kinesis* (movement or process) and an

energeia (activity) is that the latter but not the former is complete at any given time. For instance, I can be in the process of building a house but I will not have completed the process until the house is built. This then is a *kinesis*. On the other hand, if I am walking then I am completely walking at any time during my walk, so that walking is an *energeia*.

121. It is interesting that the word translated here as 'image' is not *phantasma* but *aisthema*, a rare word only used once elsewhere in the *De Anima*. As Hamlyn suggests, its use there seems to remind us of the close dependence that Aristotle sees in the intellectual soul on the sensitive soul immediately below it in the hierarchy. It is unclear, in any case, why Aristotle sees the connection between assertion and negation of good and bad and avoidance and pursuit as the *reason* for the soul's never thinking with an *aisthema*.

122. The single terminus is presumably to be identified with the unified sense faculty of Chapter 2, which, like the point, is both single and double. The abrupt transition from the previous paragraph to this one certainly seems to bear out the view of Torstrik and other editors that the chapter is a mere scrapbook. However, there is at least some connection between the single terminus of this paragraph and the further discussion of the unified sense faculty in the next one, difficult as that may be in itself.

123. This passage is notoriously obscure and the difficulties may well stem in part from the state of the text in which there seems to be the strong possibility of a lacuna. However, the sense may be conjecturally reconstructed in an interpretation proposed by Neuhaeuser. The passage begins clearly enough with a reference back to the discussion of the unified sense faculty, which is here compared to a boundary in a way eminently consistent with the original analogy between it and a point. The difficulties begin in the next sentence, which is scarcely comprehensible as it stands. The word translated 'the sense-objects in question' is *tauta*, a demonstrative pronoun meaning 'these things', whose reference unless it is as the translation has it to the sweet and hot is extremely obscure. If this is so, then 'those things' (*ekeina*) at the end of the sentence might refer either (a) to the white and the black, as suggested by the subsequent question, or (b) to the opposites of sweet and hot, or (c) to the senses of taste and touch whereby the sweet and hot are perceived, which can be supposed to have

been mentioned in the lacuna that obviously divides the paragraphs. The point of the symbolic passage which follows is that the unity of the sense faculty is required equally by contrary and by different movements. This is the interpretation favoured by Hamlyn, but it seems at least as attractive to take option (a) for the reference of *ekeina*, so that the consistent theme of the paragraph is that the sense faculty acts as a boundary in just the same way between the percepts of different senses and the opposing percepts of the same sense. The difficulty then is to see how Aristotle thinks that the present discussion of the point is in any way an improvement on its predecessor. The passage is, of course, fully discussed by both Hicks and Ross.

124. Ross's emendation of *en* to *hen* is here adopted. On the manuscript reading the point seems to be no more than the rather platitudinous one that pursuit and avoidance are active states. On the emended reading we are at least given the further information that the connection between image and thought is as close in the case of anticipatory thought as it is in that of present-directed thought. However, this consideration is hardly overwhelmingly decisive. It is noteworthy that Aristotle has reverted in this passage to the use of *phantasma* rather than *aisthema* to denote the images with which the intellect thinks.

125. These dark words provide a worthy conclusion to the three difficult chapters on thought, among the hardest in the whole corpus. Aristotle's question is how it can be possible that the intellect can both (a) be not wholly separable from the body, and (b) think by a constitutive affinity with its object, and (c) think 'the things that are separate', the immaterial entities. It is a question which he neither answers himself nor provides us with the materials for answering.

126. Aristotle is here making quite clear a point that had not been made precisely enough in the preceding discussion of the relation of intellect and the senses, namely that the most basic forms of thought remain thoughts close as is their connection with the images without which they are impossible.

127. Perhaps it would be more accurate to say that Aristotle has no notion of the modern concept of psychology in its clear distinction from physiology, neurology and phrenology. This might well be found compatible with the criticism in the first Book of the Democritean account of motivation. Of course,

Aristotle's most complete discussion of *prohaeresis* comes in the sixth Book of the *Nicomachean Ethics*, where the standpoint of modern psychology is more nearly approached than anywhere in the *De Anima*.

128. This subtle digression on the partitions of the soul heralds the end of the 'faculty psychology' bequeathed to the Academy by Plato, and suggests the growing interest in psychological realism that is so strongly to characterize the Hellenistic Age. To what extent, however, it is compatible with the theory and structure of the *De Anima* is another matter.

129. This famous or notorious doctrine has perhaps here no more alarming import than that we do not find in nature incomplete sets of apparatus for life-processes. Just as no animal will have a mouth but no stomach, so if the urge to move in place is connected with the faculty of perception then no animal will have the means for the latter but not the former. Since there clearly are animals that can perceive but not move about, there cannot be such a connection.

130. This connects with the discussions of action in the *Ethics* (Book VI) and *Metaphysics* (Book IX). On this see Sorabji, *Articles on Aristotle*, Vol. 4, pp. 56-8.

131. This is fully discussed in Book 7 of the *Nicomachean Ethics*.

132. Once again, it is not even clear how Aristotle would have formulated this problem, so that his perspective on the central problem of motivation transpires as being radically different from our modern one.

133. The words translated 'purpose-directed' are *heneka tou*, literally meaning either (a) for the sake of something, or (b) on behalf of something. It seems clear that (a) is more appropriate here, and this is Hamlyn's view, but there is perhaps something to be said for a vaguer translation which catches some of the ambiguity of the expression, on which Aristotle himself twice comments.

134. Much the same ground is covered by the discussion of the practical syllogism and *akrasia* (weakness of the will) in the seventh Book of the *Ethics*. Aristotle is certainly consistently clear that mere thought in itself cannot be productive of movement.

135. There persists a certain confusion about the classification of imagination among the mental faculties. It is sometimes looked on as a species of thought collateral with supposition, and sometimes is itself divided into a rational and irrational

part. We are never told whether even the irrational part of imagination is part of a species of thought.

136. The need to include even malformed specimens within the general theory is an indication of the work's being intended to serve as the presentation of the central notion that will unify the discussion of an immense range of evidence in the lecture course on the life sciences.

137. It cannot be said that this distinction is wholly reconciled with the general treatment of the Imagination in Chapter 3 of this Book.

138. The thought in these rather laboured words seems to be that any process that merits the name 'choice' must involve the extraction of a standard from however wide a range of evidence, and this will be part of the discriminative power of the intellect so that choice will be the exclusive prerogative of the intellect.

139. Animals desire but they do not deliberate, as deliberation involves a capacity for syllogistic reasoning that they do not possess. Therefore desire cannot be inherently deliberative.

140. A much fuller account of practical reasoning is given in Books Six and Seven of the *Ethics*.

141. One might compare the transition from the *Ethics* to the *Politics*.

142. The obelized passage appears to contradict the first part of the preceding sentence. All bodies are either stationary or have been born; in the former case nourishment comes from their roots, but in the latter case nourishment must be sought and so a perceptive faculty is necessary. This point is made explicitly at the end of the paragraph.

143. Especially Book III, Chapter 2.

144. This connects clearly with the discussion of touch in the second Book. The present passage stresses rather more than was appropriate in the original discussion exactly why touch is the primary sense in that it is possible for the animals to go without any of the others by nature but not touch.

145. The obelized words, which hardly fit the scheme of explanation for the senses other than touch with which the work is ending, looked very much like a ham-fisted later addition.

BIBLIOGRAPHY

A vast amount of scholarship has been, and continues to be, produced on the *De Anima*. I list here only works that offer a reliable introduction to the work and its background or that I have made extensive use of myself. A good place to begin further investigations would be the Bibliography to the fourth volume of J. Barnes, M. Schofield and R. Sorabji's *Articles on Aristotle* (London, 1979).

Editions and Translations

HAMLYN, D. W., *Aristotle's De Anima Books II and III* (Oxford, 1968).
HETT, W. S., Volume VIII of Loeb Aristotle edition (London, 1936).
HICKS, R. D., *Aristotle, De Anima* (Cambridge, 1907).
ROSS, W. D., *Aristotle's De Anima* (Oxford, 1961).

General Background

BARNES, J., *The Presocratic Philosophers* (London, 1979).
CROMBIE, I. M., *An Examination of Plato's Doctrines* (London, 1962–3).
DODDS, E. R., *The Greeks and the Irrational* (Berkeley and Los Angeles, 1963).
GOSLING, J. C. B., *Plato* (London, 1973).
GRUBE, G. M. A., *Plato's Thought* (London, 1935).
HUSSEY, E., *The Presocratics* (London, 1972).
KIRK, G. S., RAVEN, J. E. and SCHOFIELD, M., *The Presocratic Philosophers* (Cambridge, 1983).

Aristotle

ACKRILL, J. L., *Aristotle the Philosopher* (Oxford, 1981).
BARNES, J., *Aristotle* (Oxford, 1982).
LLOYD, G. E. R., *Aristotle: The Growth and Structure of His Thought* (Cambridge, 1968).

RANDALL, J. H., *Aristotle* (New York, 1960).
ROSS, W. D., *Aristotle* (London, 1923).

Aristotle's Biology and Psychology

Books

BRENTANO, F., *The Psychology of Aristotle*, translated by R. George (Berkeley, 1977).
NUSSBAUM, M., *Aristotle's De Motu Animalium* (Princeton, 1978).
NUYENS, F. J., *L'Evolution de la psychologie d'Aristote* (Louvain, 1948).

Collections of Articles

BARNES, J., SCHOFIELD, M., and SORABJI, R., *Articles on Aristotle*, Vol. 4 (London, 1979).
LLOYD, G. E. R., and OWEN, G. E. L., *Aristotle on Mind and the Senses* (Cambridge, 1978).

Individual Articles

BLOCK, I., 'Truth and error in Aristotle's theory of sense perception', *Philosophical Quarterly* (1961), pp. 1–9.
BLOCK, I., 'The order of Aristotle's psychological writings', *American Journal of Philology* (1961), pp. 50–77.
BLOCK, I., 'On the commonness of the common sensibles', *Australasian Journal of Philosophy* (1965), pp. 189–95.
CASHDOLLAR, S., 'Aristotle's account of incidental perception', *Phronesis* (1973), pp. 156–75.
GOTTSCHALK, H. B., 'Soul as Harmonia', *Phronesis* (1971), pp. 179–98.
HAMLYN, D. W., 'Aristotle's account of Aesthesis in the *De Anima*', *Classical Quarterly* (1959), pp. 6–16.
HARDIE, W. F. R., 'Aristotle's treatment of the relation between the soul and the body', *Philosophical Quarterly* (1964), pp. 53–72.
HARDIE, W. F. R., 'Concepts of consciousness in Aristotle', *Mind* (1976), pp. 388–411.
LYCOS, K., 'Aristotle and Plato on appearing', *Mind* (1964), pp. 496–514.
SLAKEY, T., 'Aristotle on sense-perception', *The Philosophical Review* (1961), pp. 470–84.

Other Works Mentioned

CAMPBELL, J., *Grammatical Man* (Harmondsworth, 1983).

DIAMOND, C., and TEICHMAN, J. (eds), *Intention and Intentionality* (Brighton, 1979).

FEYERABEND, P. K., and MAXWELL, J. C., *Mind, Matter and Method* (Minnesota, 1966).

FOSTER, F., and SWANSON, E. (eds), *Experience and Theory* (Amherst and London, 1971).

GILSON, E., *A History of Medieval Thought* (London, 1965).

GRAYEFF, F., *Aristotle and His School* (London, 1974).

GRENE, M., *A Portrait of Aristotle* (London, 1963).

JAEGER, W., *Aristotle* (Oxford, 1948).

KENNY, A., *Aquinas* (Oxford, 1982).

KNOWLES, D., *A History of Medieval Philosophy* (London, 1969).

MCGINN, C., *The Character of Mind* (Oxford, 1982).

PECK, A. L., *De Generatione Animalium* (Harvard, 1953).

RAHMAN, F., *Avicenna's Psychology* (London, 1951).

RYLE, G., *The Concept of Mind* (London, 1949).

SCRUTON, R., *Art and Imagination* (London, 1972).

SORABJI, R., *Aristotle on Memory* (London, 1972).

WICKENS, G. M., *Avicenna: Scientist and Philosopher* (London, 1952).

WILKES, K., *Physicalism* (London, 1978).

WITTGENSTEIN, L., *Philosophical Investigations* (Oxford, 1958).